Joseph Ritson, Edmund Goldsmid

Ancient English Metrical Romances

Vol. 1

Joseph Ritson, Edmund Guldsmid

Ancient English Metrical Romances
Vol. 1

ISBN/EAN: 9783744776349

Printed in Europe, USA, Canada, Australia, Japan

Cover: Foto ©Thomas Meinert / pixelio.de

More available books at **www.hansebooks.com**

Ancient English Metrical Romances.

Selected and Published

By JOSEPH RITSON,

AND REVISED BY

EDMUND GOLDSMID, F.R.H.S.

VOL. I.

"*Quæ priscis memorata Calonibus atque Cethegis*
Nunc situs informis premit ac deserta vetustas."
                                        —HORATIUS.

EDINBURGH:
E. & G. GOLDSMID.
1881.

Printed by Hazell, Watson, & Viney, Limited, London and Aylesbury.

TABLE OF CONTENTS.

ORIGINAL ADVERTISEMENT.

THE nature, importance, and utility of such a publication as the present have been displayed to so much advantage by a writer of the highest eminence for his acquaintance with the subject, and for his ingenuity and taste, that it would be almost an act of injustice to the undertaking not to make use of such a powerful and elegant recommendation, to which no attempt of the present editor could possibly be equal.

"As many of these METRICAL HISTORIES and ROMANCES contain a considerable portion of poetic merit, and throw a great light on the manners and opinions of former times, it were to be wished that some of the best of them were rescued from oblivion. A judicious collection of them, accurately published, with proper illustrations, would be an important accession to our stock of ancient English literature. Many of them exhibit no mean attempts at epic poetry, and though full of the exploded fictions of chivalry, frequently display great and inventive powers in the bards who composed them. They are at least generally equal to any other poetry of the same age. They cannot indeed be put in competition with the nervous productions of so universal and commanding a genius as Chaucer; but they have a simplicity that makes them be read with less interruption, and be more easily understood; and they are far more spirited and entertaining than the tedious allegories of Gower, or the dull and prolix legends of Lydgate; yet, while so much stress is laid upon the writings of these last, by such as treat of English poetry, the old metrical romances, though far more popular in their time, are hardly known to exist. . . . . Should the public encourage the revival of some of those ancient epic songs of chivalry, they would frequently see the rich ore of an Ariosto or Tasso, though buried, it may be, among the rubbish and dross of barbarous times.

"Such a publication would answer many important uses : it would throw new light on the rise and progress of English poetry, the history of which can be but imperfectly understood, if these are neglected : it would also serve to illustrate innumerable passages in our ancient classic poets, which, without their help, must be for ever obscure."

The publication so much desired, and so eloquently recommended by this learned and ingenious writer, has been at length undertaken and to what he has said in its favour nothing remains to be added but some little information as to the mode in which it makes its appearance.

This collection, then, of ANCIENT ENGLISH METRICAL ROMANCES, consists of such pieces as, from a pretty general acquaintance, have been selected for the best. Every article is derived from some ancient manuscript, or old printed copy, of the authenticity of which the reader has all possible satisfaction ; and is printed with an accuracy, and adherence to the original, of which the public has had very few examples. The utmost care has been observed in the GLOSSARY, and every necessary or useful information (to the best of the editor's judgment) is given in the NOTES.

Brought to an end with much industry, and more attention, in a continued state of ill-health and low spirits, the editor abandons it to general censure, with cold indifference, expecting little favour, and less profit; but certain, at any rate, to be insulted by the malignant and calumnious personalities of a base and prostitute gang of lurking assassins, who stab in the dark, and whose poisoned daggers he has already experienced.

DISSERTATION

ON

ROMANCE AND MINSTRELSY.

§ I. ORIGIN OF ROMANCE.

IF what is called a metrical romance, in its most extensive
acceptation, be properly defined a fabulous narrative, or fictitious
recital in verse, more or less marvellous or probable, it may be
fairly concluded that this species of composition was known at a
very early period to the Greeks, and in process of time adopted
from them by the Romans. The *Iliad* of Homer in short, the
Odyssey ascribed to the same poet,* the *Argonauticks* of Onoma-
critus, or *Orpheus* of Crotona, those likewise of Apollonius
Rhodius† and the *Hero and Leander* of Musæus, among the

---

* It seems highly probable that both these poems were not written by the same
person. In the latter, the goddess Venus is the wife of Vulcan, who surprises her
in the act of adultery with Mars (B. 8) :
> " Mean time the bard, alternate to the strings,
> The loves of *Mars* and Cytherea sings."

In the former they have no sort of connection. Venus has no husband and Vulcan
has a different wife (B. 13) :
> " *Charis,* his spouse, a grace divinely fair,
> With purple fillets round her braided hair."

Such an inconsistency, it is believed, cannot be easily detected in any other poet.
It has been, moreover, a very generally received opinion that he was likewise the
author of a mock-epic, entitled *Batrachomuomachia,* or *The Battle of the Frogs and
Mice.* It is by no means probable that the oldest manuscript copies of Homer's
poems should exhibit his name in the title, or colophon ; and as it never occurs
in the book, it must have been retained, if at all, by tradition. It should be
remembered at the same time, that he is mentioned by no writer till between 400
and 500 years after his death.

† This poem, according to Quadrio, was treated by many as a Grecian romance
of chivalry (*Storia d'ogni Poesia,* iv., 453). It is the original of the northern
romances of *Jason and Medea.* "*Il faut remarquer,*" observes Huet, "*pour
l'honneur des troubadours qu'* Homère *l'a esté devant eux*" (*De l'Origine des
Romans,* 1678, p. 123). Virgil makes Dido to reign at Carthage in the time of

former, and the *Æneid* of Virgil, the *Metamorphosis* of Ovid,* the *Argonauticks* of Valerius Flaccus, and the *Thebaid* of Statius† among the latter, however distinguished by superior art and merit, or the more illustrious appellation of epic poems, are, in reality, as perfect metrical romances as the stories of King Arthur and Charlemagne, all those venerable monuments of ancient genius being no less the work of imagination and invention than the more modern effusions, upon similar subjects, of the French and Norman *trouvères*, or Italian *romanzieri*. The Trojan story is no more fabulous and unfounded in the oldest French romance on that subject in point of historical fact, than it is in the *Iliad* or *Æneid;* nor is the siege of Troy, as related by Homer, at all more certain or more credible than that of Albracca as asserted by Boiardo ; nor are Hector and Achilles of more identity than Roland and Oliver. It seems, therefore, a very hasty assertion of the historian of English poetry, that the "peculiar and arbitrary species of fiction, which we commonly call romance, was entirely unknown to the writers of Greece and Rome."‡ Was this voluminous author unacquainted with the romances of Antonius Diogenes, of which Photius has given an account, the love tales of Longus, Heliodorus, and Xenophon of Ephesus ? He himself even cites an old English version of the *Clitophon and Leucippe* of Achilles Tatius (though actually in plain prose), "as a POETICAL NOVEL of GREECE;" and at any rate a novel is a species of romance.

The Milesian tales of Aristides, likewise, so famous in their day, though none of them now remain, must have been some kind of romances, whether in prose or verse. A copy of these tales—or at least the Latin version of Sisenna—according to Plutarch, was, after the defeat of Crassus, in Parthia, found in the baggage of Roscius, a Roman officer.

Homer, in fact, is much more extravagant and hyperbolical—or sublime, if it must be so—than Ariosto himself, the very prince of

Æneas, though in reality she did not arrive in Africa till three hundred years after the supposed destruction of Troy. Such a violent anachronism is only admissible in a romance.

* Chaucer, in his *Dreme*, to pass the night away, rather than play at chess, calls for a *romance*, in which "were writtin fables of quenis livis, and of kings and many other thingis small." This proves to be Ovid. See V., 52, etc., or Warton's *History of English Poetry*, i., 388.

† The ingenious doctor, or Bishop Percy, who has great weight in matters of this sort, says of *Lybeus disconus*, of which he has given an excellent analysis, "If an epic poem may be defined ' A fable related by a poet to' excite admiration and inspire virtue, by representing the action of some one hero, favoured by heaven, who executes a great design in spite of all the obstacles that oppose him ;' I know not why we should withhold the name of EPIC POEM from the piece which I am about to analyse (or that of ROMANCE to the epic poem above defined)." (*Reliques of Ancient English Poetry*, III., xxviii.; citing *Discours sur la poésie épique* prefixed to *Telemachus*.)

‡ *History of English Poetry*, i., sig. a.

romance. His poetical machinery is composed of the Grecian deities (worshipped and adored by himself and his countrymen), who take a decided part on each side, fight, and are wounded or victorious, like the ordinary mortals with whom they engage. Many of his heroes, at the same time, are the offspring of these identical and illusory divinities ; as Helen, for instance, the fatal authoress of this sanguinary ten years' war, was the daughter of Jupiter, the supreme god of the Greeks, by Leda, whose embraces he experienced in the form of a swan; the issue, of course, was an egg, out of which proceeded this female firebrand, who must, however, have been pretty far advanced in years long before her elopement with the juvenile and gallant Paris, having been ravished by Theseus forty years before, and being now, of course, like our Queen Elizabeth, a matchless beauty in her grand climacterick. The two demigods—Castor and Pollux, her brethren—came into the world in the same miraculous way. Achilles, likewise, the celebrated champion of the Greeks, was the son of Thetis, a sea-goddess ; as Æneas, the pretended founder of the Roman empire, was of Venus, the Goddess of love ; and all these fancies of a poetical imagination are to be firmly believed, though nothing more than mere romance. With respect to the famous city of Troy, which stood so long a siege, and was laid " at last in ashes," there is not the slightest evidence that such a place even existed, in or before, that is, the æra fixed upon by this immortal rhapsodist ; and the antagonists of Mister Bryant, the only modern author who has attempted to demolish this magnificent but ideal fabric,* have reasoned, like the advocates of Geoffrey of Monmouth, by arguments and authorities—that is, deduced from Homer himself, or writers who lived many centuries after him. Herodotus, however, the father of Grecian history, who flourished (according to his own account) about four hundred years after Homer, whose works he must needs have been familiar with, since he wrote his life, and cites them in his history, is a decisive evidence that no such expedition ever took place.

Being a professed antiquary, he must necessarily, from his assiduous researches into the remotest periods of Grecian history, or at least from the traditions which would be naturally preserved of so important and celebrated an event in the very country from which these heroic kings and princes, with their ships and forces, had proceeded, have known if such an expedition had taken place. He appears, on the contrary, to have known or heard, at least amongst his own countrymen, nothing at all of the matter, except what he himself and everyone else had read in Homer, and certain spurious

---

* The existence of the Trojan war was disputed by Dio Chrysostom more than a thousand years ago. Even Homer himself has been proved by his last editor, the learned Wolf, incapable to write or read ; nor does either writing or reading appear, from his elaborate Prologomena, to have been known till many centuries after the æra of Homer.

Cyprian verses, falsely ascribed to that same illustrious bard; for,
going into Ægypt, peradventure for this express purpose: "When
inquiring," says he, "whether the Greeks have related falsehoods
concerning the deeds performed at Ilium, or not, the priests an-
swered me thus—that they knew, from Menelaus himself, that,
Helen being carried off, great forces of the Greeks had come to the
assistance of Menelaus into Teucris; which, having landed and
fortified a place, sent messengers to Ilium, with whom, also, Mene-
laus went himself; that these, after they had entered the walls, not
only demanded Helen and the treasures which Alexander by robbery
had carried away, but also required the atonements of injuries;
that the Teucrians, however, both then and afterward, either sworn
or unsworn, had related the same things; that they themselves had
neither Helen nor the treasures whereof they were accused, but that
all those things were in Ægypt; that neither could they suffer them-
selves to be arraigned with justice of those goods which Proteus, the
King of Ægypt, withheld; that the Greeks, thinking themselves de-
rided, had so besieged Ilium, till at length they took it by storm;
that the city being taken, when Helen did not appear, and they
heard the same defence as before, at last, faith being given to the
former words, the Greeks sent Menelaus himself to Proteus. When
this man arrived in Ægypt, and ascended to Memphis in a ship, the
truth of the matter being explained, and himself welcomed with
hospitality, in a most honourable manner, he received Helen full of
injuries, and all his treasures."*

And such was the fable of the Ægyptian priests, which the
inquisitive historian appears to have swallowed as perfectly rational,
though in diametrical opposition to the infallible Homer.

The *Odyssey*, whether by that same poet or not, is devoid of truth
from beginning to end, and abounds with adventures as hyperbolical
or extravagant as those of any French romance. The historian of
English poetry justly observes that "all the romances have an
enchantress, who detains the knight from his quest by objects of
pleasure; and who is nothing more than the *Calypso* of Homer, and
the *Armida* of Tasso (or the *Alcina* of Ariosto)."

Huet, who imagined it of the essence of a romance to be in prose,
professes not to treat of those in verse, much less of epic poems;
which beside that they are in verse have, moreover, different essen-
tials which distinguish them from romances, though otherwise he
admits there is a very great relation; and following the maxim of
Aristotle (who teaches that a poet is more a poet by the fictions he
invents than by the verse he composes), makers of romances may be
ranked among the poets.

After Statius there is no metrical romance writer or epic poet, in
the Latin tongue, known to have existed before Joseph of Exeter,

---

* *Euterpe*, § 118.

called by some *Cornelius Nepos*, who wrote, in six books, *Of the Trojan War*, and, in one book, *The War of Antioch*, and flourished, according to Bale, about the year 1210; or Philip Gualtier, a Frenchman, author of *The Alexandreid*, or actions of Alexander the Great, about the same period; all three in imitation of Lucan or Statius.

It appears, however, difficult to demonstrate that the comparatively modern romances of the French owe their immediate origin to the epic poetry, or fabulous tales, of the Greeks or Romans; but it may be fairly admitted, as by no means improbable, that these remains of ancient literature had some degree of influence, though the connection is too remote and obscure to admit of elucidation.

The Latin language continued, after the dissolution of the Roman empire, to be in use with the common people of France and Italy; but ceasing, it may be, to be studied grammatically, and becoming gradually intermixed with the barbarous jargons of the different northern nations which had subjugated or expelled the Romans, and occupied their seats till about the ninth century, an entirely new speech or dialect gained a complete ascendency in both.

At one period, it is said, there were not less than three distinct languages spoken in France: the old Celtic or Gaulish, the Latin; and this new dialect, called the *Roman*, or Romance,—a mixture, it would seem, of Latin, Frankish, and Celtic, the last of which, it is supposed, was speedily exterminated.* The term Roman ought, in fact, to have been the distinguishing characteristic of the Latin tongue, which the French appear to have understood at the beginning of the seventh century;† but this was by no means the case, as will appear from a passage quoted by Fauchet from the *Roman d' Alexandre*, composed, he says, by persons living in the year 1150:

> " *La verté de l'histoir' si com' li roix la fit,*
> *Un clers de Chasteaudun*, Lambert li Cors *l' escrit,*
> *Qui de* Latin *la trest, et* en Roman *la mit.*"

It is plain, therefore, that *Latin* and *Roman* were different languages; since this poet drew a history out of the latter to put it into the former. It is true, he observes, that these verses are made more than three hundred years after Charlemagne,‡ and although it were not so, that one understood five hundred years ago that to

---

* See a good account of the conversion, or perversion, of the Latin tongue into Italian, from authentic documents, in Muratori's *Antiquitates Italiæ*, ii., 990.

† See Le Beuf's *Recherches*, etc., *Mémoires de l'Aca. des inscrip.*, xvii., 712.

‡ It is said of this emperor, by Eginhart, his chaplain or secretary, that "he wrote down and committed to memory the barbarous and most ancient songs, in which the acts and wars of the old kings were sung" (c. xxix.). These in all likelihood were in the Theotisc or Teutonic language, mentioned in the text. In Schilter's *Thesaurus* are two very ancient poems in this dialect, on the expeditions of that emperor.

speak the rustic *Roman* was the common language of the inhabi-
tants on this side of the Meuse, it only behoves to read that which
Nitard hath written in his history of the discord of the children of
the emperor Lewis, the *debonnair*, happening in the year 841. For,
making mention of Lewis, King of Germany, and of Charles the
Bald, King of Western France (that is to say, between the Meuse
and the Loire), he says that the two kings, willing to assure those
who had followed them that this alliance should be perpetual, they
spoke each to the people of his *pair* (the word of which Nitard
makes use), to wit, Lewis, King of Germany, to the Western French,
who followed Charles, in the *Roman* tongue (that is to say, the
rustic), and Charles, to those of Lewis, who were Austrasians,
Germans, Saxons, and other inhabitants beyond the Rhine, in the
Teutonic tongue. The words of the oath which Lewis took, in the
Roman tongue, were such as, saith our author, I have taken from
a book written more than five hundred years ago : "*Pro don amur
& pro christian poblo & nostro commun salvament, dist di en
avant in quant deus Savir & potir me dunat, si salvarai eo cest
meon fradre karlo, &, in adjudta & in cadhuna cosa, si cum
hom per dreit son fradre salvar dist, ino quid il imi altre si
faret, et ab Ludher nul plaid nunquam prindrai, qui meon
vol cest meon fradre Karle in damno sit.*" * The people of
Westria answered in the same language : "*Si Lodhwigs sacra-
ment que son fradre karlo jurat conservat & Karlus, meos
sendra, de fuo part non los tanit; si io returnar non lint pois
in ne io, ne neuls, cui eo returnar nit pois in nulla adjudha
contra Lodhuwig nun li iver.*" † He elsewhere says (from a very
ancient copy of Nitard,‡ extant in the library of Magloire at Paris),
that Lewis, as the elder, swore first in the *Roman* tongue, as before.
This oath being made, Charles said the same words in Teutonic or
Theotisc : "*In godes minna, ind durhtes Xristianes folches ind
infer bedhero gehaltnissi fonthesemo dage frammordes, so fram
so mir got gewizeindi mahd furgibit, so halt ih tesan minan
bruodher so so man mit rehtu sinan bruodher scal, inthi ut
hazer mig so so maduo, maduo, indi mit Lutherem inno thein-*

---

* Corrected from *Bouquet*, vii, 36. In English thus : "For the love of God
and of the Christian people, and for our common safety, from this day forward,
insomuch as God will give me knowledge and power, I shall save my brother
Charles, and I will aid him in everything, as a man by right ought to serve his
brothers, in this that he will do as much of it for me ; and I shall not make with
Lothair any treaty with my will, which may be prejudicial to my brother Charles."

† Corrected as above. In English thus : "If Lewis keep the oath which he
has sworn to his brother Charles, and Charles, my lord, on his part, do not hold
it ; if I cannot divert him from it, nor myself or others can divert him from it, we
shall not go with any aid against Lewis."

‡ *De la Langue & Poësie Françoise*, ch. iv. La Combe only gives the oath of
Lewis, and the answers ; and La Ravailliere but one of the answers.

nithing ne gegango zhe minan willon imo ce scadhen werhen."
The most learned Germans of our author's day thought that this
language held more of the Frison than of any other dialect of
Germany. After this, the people swore each in his own tongue,
to wit, those of Charles these words: "Si Luduwigs," etc., as
before; and the people of King Lewis these words in Theotisc, or
Teutonic: *" Oba karl then eid, then er sinemo bruodher Lud-
huwig gesuor geleistit, inde Ludhuwig min herro then er imo
gesuor forbrichit, ob ih ina nes arwenden nemag, noh ih, noh
thero thein his inewenden mag, imo ce follusti widhar karle ne
wirdhit."* Our author himself found that the *Roman* language
approached to the Provençal, or Lyonnois, more than to his own,
on the north of the Loire.*

The present Swiss have the Bible *en Rumansch*, that is, in their
vulgar tongue, and use the same expression for that of the French.†
The Spaniards still call their native language *romancé Castellano;*
and *hablar en romancé* is to speak Spanish.

In the library of Berne is a MS. of the thirteenth or fourteenth
century (Num. 646), entitled *" Le livre du tresor lequel maistre
Brunes . . . translata de* Latin *en* Romans." ‡

In about a couple of centuries afterwards the word *Roman* was
used by the French, not only as designative of their language, but
also of any book written therein, though in process of time it was
confined to books of chivalry,§ as *romance* was to a ballad or
narrative song.

" Toutesfois," says the old prose *Roman de Paris et Vienne,*
"le frère ne pensoit pas parler Romain" (*i.e.,* François). In
Spanish, to this day, *romancé* means both the vernacular language
and a vulgar ballad; while *romanzi,* in Italian, is appropriated
solely to books of chivalry in rhyme.

An ancient topographer (supposed to be Girald Barry, Bishop of
St. David's, commonly called *Giraldus Cambrensis*) even uses the
word *Romanè* for the English, or vulgar language of his own time:
"Ab illa aquâ optima," says he, *"quæ* Scotticè (*sub.* Hibernicè)
vocata est Froth. Britannicè (Wallicè, sci.) Verid, Romane (*i.e.,*
Anglicè) vero Scotte-wattre, i aqua Scottorum."‖ He means the
Firth of Forth.

---

* *Des Antiquités Françoises,* 1610, 4to, Book IX., ch. vi., fo. 330, 331. Cor-
rected from *Bouquet,* vii. 35, etc.

† *Ibid.,* 1610, 4to, Book IX., ch. vi., fo. 34.

‡ Sinner's *Catalogue,* iii., 20.

§   " All is calde *geste Inglis,*
                That on this language spoken is,
                Franke's spech is cald *romance,*
                So says clerkes and men of France."
                                   ROBERT OF BRUNNE, p. cvi.

‖ Innes's *Critical Essay,* 770.

The learned Tyrwhitt, with obvious plausibility, thinks it evident that poets in the vulgar languages, who first appeared about the ninth century, borrowed their rhymes from the hymns of St. Ambrose and St. Damasus as early as the fourth, and from the Christian poets Sedulius and Fortunatus in the fifth and sixth, and the other Latin poetry of that age. There is even a Latin song in rhyme extant in print, which was made upon a great victory, obtained by King Clothair the Second, over the Saxons, in the year 622, and serves to support the above opinion that the vulgar poets of that period had already adopted the art of rhyming from the hymns of the Church. It proves, also, that the Latin tongue was still in use even among the common soldiers in the seventh century. The following stanza is offered as a specimen :

" *De Clotario est camere rege Francorum,*
Qui ivit pugnare cum gente Saxonum,
Quam graviter provenisset missis Saxonum,
Si non fuisset inclitus Faro de gente Burgundionum."*

There is likewise an elegy, composed by Gotescalc in his exile, which has both rhyme and poetry :

" Ut quid jubes, pusiole,
Quare mandas, filiole,
Carmen dulce me cantare,
Cum sim longè exul valde,
Intra mare,
O cur jubes canere ? "

Many of the church hymns, about that period, are in the same metre. The most numerous, however, and decisive proofs, are to be found in the *Antiquitates Italiæ* of Muratori.†

There is an instance, in Usher's *Primordia*, of a couplet in Irish rhyme, made by St. Patrick in the fifth century.‡

Different authors have attributed the origin of romance to three sources, altogether remote from each other:—1. The Arabians; 2. The Scandinavians; 3. The Provençals. It appears, from an observation of the historian of English poetry, "to have been imported into Europe by a people whose modes of thinking and habits of invention are not natural to that country. . . It is generally supposed to have been borrowed from the Arabians. . . It is

---

* L'Evêque de la Ravilliere, *Poësies du Roi de Navarre*, i., 193.
   " 'Tis time to sing of Clothair, King of French,
   With Saxon people he who went to fight,
   Their messengers he grievously had treated,
   Had it not been for Pharaoh, the Burgundian."
Le Beuf has published another upon the Battle of Fontenay, in 841 (see *Divers écrits*, i., 165).
† Dissertation XL.
‡ P. 450.

an established maxim," he proceeds, "of modern criticism,* that
the fictions of Arabian imagination were communicated to the
western world by means of the crusades. . . But it is evident that
these fancies were introduced at a much earlier period ; the Saracens
or Arabians having entered Spain about the beginning of the eighth
century.† It is obvious to conclude, he continues, that at the same
time they disseminated those extravagant inventions which were so
peculiar to their romantic and creative genius. . . The ideal tales
of these eastern invaders, recommended by a brilliancy of descrip-
tion, a variety of imagery, and an exuberance of invention, were
eagerly caught up and universally diffused. From Spain, he asserts,
they soon passed into France and Italy.‡ It is for this reason, he
pretends, the elder Spanish romances have professedly more Arabian
allusions than any other.§ There is, in fact, not one single French
romance now extant, and but one mentioned by any ancient writer,
which existed before the first crusade, under Godfrey, Earl of
Bologne, afterwards King of Jerusalem, in 1097. Neither is anything
known concerning the literature of the Moors, who came over from
Barbary and settled in Spain in 711; nor is it at all probable, or
capable of proof, that even the Spaniards, much less any of the
other nations of Europe, had an opportunity of adopting any literary
information, or did so, in fact, from a people with whom they had
no connection but as enemies, whose language they never under-
stood, and whose manners they detested, or would even have con-
descended, or permitted themselves, to make such an adoption from
a set of infidel barbarians who had invaded, ravaged, and possessed
themselves of some of the best and richest provinces of Spain, with
whom they had continual wars, till they at last drove them out of
the country; whom, in fact, they always avoided, abhorred, and
despised. There is, doubtless, a prodigious number of Arabic
poems in the library of the Escurial, which has been plundered from
the Moors, but which no Spanish poet ever made use of, or, in
short, had ever access to. It was not in the historian's power to
cite one single old Spanish romance that has the slightest Arabian
allusion, except, indeed, that of the *Cid Ruy Dias*, where, as in
those of *Charlemagne*, the Moors or Saracens are introduced as
enemies, and in two modern books, the *Historia verdadera del rey
don Rodrigo*, printed in 1592, and the *Historia de los vandos de los
Zegries y Abencerrages*, printed at Seville in 1598, and under the
title of *Historia de las guerras civiles de Granada*, at Paris, in
1600; both falsely pretended to have been translated from the
Arabic, and ridiculed, on that account, by Cervantes, who makes

---

* That he means, of Warburton and the Warburtonian school, of which the
distinguishing characteristics are want of knowledge, extreme confidence, and
habitual mendacity.

   † I., sig. *a.*   ‡ I., *a, b.*   § I., iii.

use of the same pretence in his *Quixote*. The Spaniards are so far
from having any ancient *historias de cavallerias*, which we call
romances, that they have not a single ballad (which they call
romance) upon the subject of the Moors, except it may be a few
composed after, or about, the time of their expulsion, and extant in
the *Romancero general*, or other compilations of the like kind.

With respect to the Oriental literature for which we are indebted
to the Crusades, besides the *Clericalis disciplina* of Peter Alfonsus,
a converted Jew, baptized in 1106,* in which are many eastern tales,
there is but one single French romance in rhyme or prose of the
thirteenth or fourteenth century, which appears to have been taken
from an Arabian or Oriental source; it is that of *Cleomedes*, by
King Adenes (a minstrel-monarch or herald), after "The story of
the enchanted horse," in *The Thousand and One Nights*. As to
the rest, this eloquent and flowery historian, whose duty it was to
ascertain truth from the evidence of facts and ancient documents,
and not to indulge his imagination in reverie and romance without
the least support or even colour of veracity or probability, has not
the slightest authority for this visionary system, but assumes with
confidence that which he knew himself unable to establish by
proof.

There are no limits, at the same time, to the extravagance of his
imagination or invention in thus wildly labouring to account for a
subject of which he had no adequate or rational conception nor
any authentic information. In France, he says, "no Province or
District seems to have given these fictions of the Arabians a more
welcome or a more early reception than the inhabitants of Armorica
or Basse-Bretagne, now Brittany, for no part of France can boast of
so great a number of ancient romances. Many poems of high
antiquity composed by the Armorican bards still remain, and are
frequently cited by Father Lobinean in his learned history of
Basse-Bretagne."† "On the whole," he adds, "we may venture to
affirm that the chronicle of Geoffrey of Monmouth, supposed to
contain the ideas of the *Welsh* bards, entirely consists of *Arabian*
inventions."‡ It must be confessed that this poetical historian is
very ready, at a venture, to affirm anything, however imaginary and
absurd. In another place he says: "*Gormund*, king of the
Africans, occurs;" and to prove how well he understood Geoffrey
of Monmouth, and how accurately this impostor was acquainted with
Arabian allusions, this *Gormund*, in authentic history, was a king
of the Danes, who infested England in the ninth century, and was
defeated and baptized by Alfred.§

---

* See Tyrwhitt's *Chaucer*, iv., 325.   † I., *a*. 2.   ‡ I., *b*. 3.

§ "That Stonehenge," he says, "is a British monument erected in memory of
Hengist's massacre, rests, I believe, on the sole evidence of Geoffrey of Monmouth,
who had it from the British bards. But why should not the testimony of the British
bards be allowed on this occasion? For they did not invent facts so much as

In all this high-flown panegyric there is not a word of truth, nor a particle of common-sense. There is no vestige or shadow of any ancient authority that this pitiful nation, a small colony from South Wales, or Cornwall in Britain, had any other fictions than such as they had carried over with them ; nor is it true, excepting three poems, if they deserve such an appellation, of so low a period as the fifteenth century (a book of predictions, that is, of a pretended prophet named Gwinglaff, the MS. whereof was of the year 1450; the life of Cwenolo, abbot of Landevenec, one of their fabulous saints, and a little dramatic piece on the taking of Jerusalem), that they have a single fragment of poetry in their vernacular language. The learned priest who published the dictionary of Pelletier* after his death, candidly admits "that the Armorican Britons have not cultivated poetry, and the language, such as they speak it, does not appear able to ply to the measure, or to the sweetness, or to the harmony of verse."† That they might or may have *chanters* or *musicians*, which the French call *minstrels*, we *fiddlers*, and themselves *barz* or *bards*, is sufficiently probable or certain, but if by *bard* be meant a composer of possibly epic or lyric poetry in his vernacular idiom, no proof can be adduced of such a character. At any rate, that Father Lobineau "frequently," or even in one single instance, cites "many poems of high antiquity," or any poem whatever, ancient or modern, in the Armorican language, is a most monstrous falsehood. The editor of this book has a right to be thus positive, having repeatedly and unsuccessfully examined the *Histoire de Bretagne* (a work, by the way, of no veracity or authority, though in two ponderous folios), with a view to discover these pretended citations, and has received an assurance to the like effect from Francis Douce, Esq., whose intimate acquaintance with every branch of French literature cannot possibly be disputed.

The pretended *Breton Lais* of a certain *Marie de France*, a Norman poetess of the thirteenth century, will be considered elsewhere.

In the circumstance just mentioned he says about Wales, of its connection with Armorica, "We perceive the solution of a difficulty which, at first sight, appears extremely problematical ; I mean," says he, "not only that Wales should have been so constantly made the theatre of the old British chivalry, but that so many of the

---

fables. In the present case, Hengist's massacre is an allowed event. Even to this day, the massacre of Hengist is an undisputed piece of history " (i. 53). In the first place, Geoffrey does not say that he had this intelligence "from the British bards," and, secondly, there is not a word of truth in this massacre by Hengist, which Geoffrey borrowed from Nennius (c. 47). A similar story is related by Witikind.

* *Dictionnaire de la langue Bretonne par dom Louis de Pelletier.* Paris, 1752, *fo.*

† Preface, viii., ix.

favourite fictions which occur in the early French romances, should also be literally found in the tales and chronicles of the elder Welsh bards."*   In this passage also is scarcely a word of sense or truth. The Welsh have no "tales" or "chronicles" to produce of the "elder Welsh bards," nor by any other writer more early, at least, than Geoffrey of Monmouth, whose fabulous *British History*, it must be confessed, was seized with great avidity by the French or Norman poets. If the Welsh have any such stories, they are doubtless from the French or English, and, by way of further proof of their recency, are all in PROSE, as, for instance, *Lhyvyr y Greal* from the *Roman de S*ᵗ *Graal*, *Ystori Boun o Hamtun*, from that of *Beuves* or *Bevis of Southampton*, *Ystori Owen ab Yrien*, from the *Roman d' Ivain*, the *Cavalier au Lion* or "Ywain" and "Gawin"†; and as to the idea of Warton, "that the Welsh bards might have been acquainted with the Scandinavian scalds," nothing was ever more extravagant or absurd.‡

That the inhabitants of Sweden, Denmark, and Norway, being the latest converts to Christianity, retained their original manners and opinions longer than the other nations of Gothic race,§ may certainly be true, though such sort of conversion usually makes some difference in those matters ; but it by no means follows that, therefore, they have preserved "more of the genuine compositions of their ancient poets than their southern neighbours." This is a fact to be proved, not by affirmative assertions, but by the production of ancient manuscripts, or the testimony of contemporaneous or veracious historians, neither of which is possessed by all or any one of these three northern nations. "Hence," however, it is maintained that "the progress among them, from poetical history to poetical fiction, is very discernible,"—meaning, it is presumed, that they are equally fabulous. They have some old pieces, it is said, that are in effect complete romances of chivalry,‖ and a specimen is referred to in the second volume of *Northern Antiquities*, etc., p. 148, etc., the age whereof is not ascertained, nor do its contents perfectly resemble any French or English romance that we are at all acquainted with. In another part of the same work (page 321) are, apparently, introduced the Ovidian tales of *Perseus and Andromeda*, under the no less fictitious names of *Regner Lodbrog*, or hairy breeches, afterwards King of Denmark, and *Thora*, the beautiful daughter of a Swedish prince, who was "guarded," as the poets

---

* I., *a*, 3, *b*.

† See Lhuyd's *Archæologia*, 265.

‡ Some such unauthorised opinion had already induced the elegant Gray to pollute his sublime Pindaric on the bards with the Scandic mythology, of which the Britons had not a particle, and, for anything that appears, were totally ignorant.

§ *Reliques*, etc., III., xi., xii., xiii. The eloquent passages of the original were at first intended to be given at length, but retrenchment was found necessary.

‖ *Reliques*, etc., III., xviii.

took occasion to say, "by a furious dragon;" and this, it seems, upon the authority of *Regnara Lodbrog's saga*, which appears to be in print, and has been also translated by the above learned and ingenious prelate, who gives the passage thus: "We fought with swords: when in Gothland I slew an enormous *serpent:* my reward was the beauteous *Thora*. Thence I was deemed a man; they called me Lodbrog from that slaughter. I thrust the monster through with my spear, with the steel productive of splendid rewards." *

That they may likewise "have a multitude of sagas or histories on romantic subjects, some of them written SINCE the time of the Crusades," will be readily admitted; but there is not the slightest proof or pretext for asserting that "others" were so "LONG BEFORE." These *sagas*, in fact, are, for the most part, if not totally, translated, or imitated, from the French, and at the same time of very recent date. The *Saga of Ivent England Kappe*, in the royal library of Stockholm, is clearly the French romance of *Yvain*, or *Le Chevalier au Lion*, both of the twelfth or thirteenth century, accommodated apparently to the Scandic traditions.† A large collection of such things is in the British Museum, transcribed chiefly between the years 1660 and 1700, among which are the *Saga af Likle Peturs og Magelona*, *Saga af Virgilio*, *Saga af Parcevals*, *Melusina og Remunds saga*, *Remundar Keissara Saga*, *Apollonius Saga*, etc.,‡ all or most of which are well known French romances. The Danes have no historian whatever before the eleventh century.§

It is not at all more probable, or at least there is no sort of authority for supposing, that Rollo "doubtless carried many scalds with him (into France or Neustria) from the north, who transmitted their skill to their children and successors." It is, in fact, a mere *gratis dictum, a petetio principii*, an unfounded conjecture, an assertion without a proof. After the Normans had acquired the Christian religion, adopted the French language, and French manners, and in a word become perfect Frenchmen, they unquestionably displayed equal, if not superior, talent and invention in the manufacture of romantic poems in that tongue; all which, however, are on French or British subjects; and none of them can be asserted, without a flagrant violation of truth and fact, to contain one single allusion to the Iceland scalds, or Scandinavian poetry, none of whose puerile and extravagant fictions can be proved of so early an age.

There is not, in short, the weakest possible authority, the slightest possible proof, that the minstrels were "the genuine successors of

---

* See *Five Pieces of Runic Poetry*, p. 27. Even Warton suspects that the romantic amour between *Regner* and *Aslauga* is the forgery of a much later age (l., i., 2, *b*). This scabby sheep, indeed, infects the whole flock.

† See Wanley's *Antiquæ Literaturæ Septen. Catalogus*, 325.

‡ See Mr. Ayscough's *Catalogue*, No. 4857, etc.

§ Stephens' *Notæ in Saxonem*, ii.

the ancient BARDS, who, under different names, were admired and
revered, from the earliest ages, among the people of Gaul, Britain,
Ireland, and the North." It is a mere hypothesis, without the least
support from fact or history, or anything, in a word, but a visionary
or fanciful imagination. There is no connection, no resemblance,
between the scalds of Scandinavia and the minstrels of France ; nor
can any ancient historian be produced to countenance the extrava-
gant and absurd fables with which the introduction to the *Histoire
de Dannemarck*, by Mallet, translated into English under the title
of *Northern Antiquities*, is stuffed from beginning to end. The
original author was so ignorant as to confound the *Cimbri* with the
Cimmerii,* and the *Germans* or *Goths* with the *Celts* or *Gauls*,
in defiance of ancient history and of common sense, without a word
of truth. The *Edda* itself, if not a rank forgery, is at least a com-
paratively modern book of the thirteenth or fourteenth century,
manifestly compiled long after Christianity was introduced into the
north,† nor was such a system of Paganism brought hither by either
Saxons or Danes, or ever entertained by any people in the world ;
nor are these scalds or poets ever mentioned by any old English
historian, though we have several of the Saxon times. Saxo, a very
ancient historian, knew nothing of any *Odin* but a magician, whom
the stupidity of the inhabitants of Upsal adored as a god, and sent
to him from Constantinople a golden image, out of which his wife
Frigga drew the gold, which being consumed he hung up the
statue on the brink of a precipice, and by the wonderful industry
of art, rendered it vocal at the human touch ; but, nevertheless,
Frigga, preferring the splendour of finery to divine honours, sub-
ected herself in adultery to one of her familiars, by whose cunning,
the image being demolished, the gold, consecrated to public super-
stition, she converted to the instrument of private luxury. Odin
then flies, but afterwards returns, and disperses the magicians who
had risen up in his absence. He attempts to kiss Rinda, daughter
to the king of the *Ruthes*, and receives a slap on the face. Accord-
ing to Torfæus, he even ravished this young lady ; but the passage,
on looking into Saxo, to whom he seems to refer, could not be found.
See, however, *Series regum Daniæ*, 149, where he supposes him
contemporary with Hading, King of Denmark, in the year 816 before
Christ. He is blind of an eye, etc.‡ There cannot be a more

---

* He calls the latter " Cimmerian Scythians," utterly ignorant that the *Scythians*
were the bitterest enemies of the *Cimmerians*, and actually drove them out of
Europe into Asia.

† The pretended author *Snorro* (no bad name for a *dreamer*) brings down this
chronology thirty years after his death. See *Northern Antiquities*, II. xxii. This
outdoes Geoffrey of Monmouth. " Huet," according to Warton, " is of opinion
that the *Edda* is entirely the production of Snorro's fancy " ; and cites *Origin of
Romance*, 116 (1. *h* 4, *b*, *n*, 2).

‡ He died in 1204 ; but has not one single date throughout his whole history.

ridiculous story of a Pagan deity! The forged and fabulous *Edda*, indeed, speaks of another Odin, surnamed the Persian, the father of the gods, to whom the origin of the art of the scalds was attributed, and who, according to the lying coxcomb already noticed, was defeated and put to flight by Pompey.* This groundless and absurd falsehood is, likewise, adopted by the learned and ingenious translator. †

After all, it seems highly probable that the origin of romance in every age or country is to be sought in the different systems of superstition which have from time to time prevailed, whether pagan or Christian. The gods of the ancient heathens, and the saints of the more modern Christians, are the same sort of imaginary beings, who alternately give existence to romances, and receive it from them. The legends of the one, and the fables of the other, have been constantly fabricated for the same purpose, and with the same view—the promotion of fanaticism, which, being mere illusion, can only be excited or supported by romance; and, therefore, whether Homer made the gods, or the gods made Homer, is of no sort of consequence, as the same effect was produced by either cause. There is this distinction, indeed, between the heathen deities and the Christian saints, that the fables of the former were indebted for their existence to the flowery imagination of the sublime poet, and the legends of the latter to the gloomy fanaticism of a lazy monk or stinking priest.

If the hero of a romance be occasionally borrowed from heaven, he is as often sent thither in return. John of Damascus, who fabricated a pious romance of *Barlaam* and *Josaphat*, in the eighth century, was the cause of these creations of his fanciful bigotry and interested superstition being placed in the empyreal galaxy, and worshipped as saints. Even Roland and Oliver, the forged and fabulous existences of the pseudo Turpin, or some other monkish or priestly impostor, have attained the same honour.‡ This idea is rendered the more plausible, if not positive, by the most ancient romances of chivalry, those of Charlemagne, for instance, and his Paladins, Arthur and his knights of the round table, Guy, Bevis, and so forth; all of whom are the strenuous and successful champions of Christianity, and mortal enemies of the Saracens, whom they voluntarily and wantonly invade, attack, persecute, slaughter, and destroy. It was not, therefore, without reason, said by whomsoever, that the first romances were composed to

---

* P. 59.
† *Reliques*, III. xvi.
‡ See Quadrio, *Storia d'ogni Poesia*, ii. 594, where, from the annals of Pighi, he gives the following extract: "*In* Roncisvalle *i* santi Orlando, *conte e paladino cenomanense nepote di Carlo magno, e* Oliviero, *duca di Ginevra* martir; *e sono celebrati da altri a* 21 *di Maggio e i altri a* 17 del *medesimo mese.*" It is, indeed, somewhat difficult to fix the precise era of a saint that never existed.

promote the Crusades, during which period, it is certain, they
were the most numerous; and to prove how radically these mis-
chievous and sanguinary legends were impressed upon the minds
of a bigoted and idiotic people for a series of no less than five
centuries, about the year 1600 appeared "the famous history of
the seven champions of Christendom," in which the Roland,
Oliver, Guy, Bevis, etc., the fabulous heroes of old romance, are
metamorphosed into Saint George, Saint Denis, Saint James, Saint
Anthony, Saint Andrew, Saint Patrick, and St. David, the no less
fabulous heroes of legend and religious imposture, most of whom
receive a certain amount of adoration, like the pagan deities of
old, by the dedication of churches, devotional days, and the like;
which celebrated work being a compound of superstition and,
as it were, all the lies of Christendom in one lie, is in many
parts of the country believed at this day to be "as true as the
Gospel."

The first metrical romance, properly and strictly so-called, that is
known to have existed, and may possibly be still extant in the dark
recess of some national or monkish library, is the famous *Chanson
de Roland*, which was sung by a minstrel, or juggler, named
Taillefer, riding on horseback, at the head of the Norman army,
when marching under Duke William to the Battle of Hastings.
The earliest mention of this celebrated song appears to be made
by William Somerset, a monk of Malmesbury, who finished his
history and, as it is presumed, his life, in the year 1142. "*Tunc*,"
says he, in his description of the above engagement, "CANTILENA
ROLLANDI *inchoata, ut Martium viri exemplum pugnaturos
accenderet*," * etc. *Maistre* Wase, or Gace, who completed his
metrical romance of *Le Brut*, a free but excellent translation of
Geoffrey of Monmouth's *British History*, in the year 1155, is the
only writer to whom we are indebted for a knowledge of the subject
of this ancient poem. His words are these:

> " Taillefer, *qi mlt bien chantout*,
> *Sor un cheval qi tost alout*,
> *Devant le duc alout chantant*,
> *De* Karlemaigne, *et de Rollant*,

---

* *De Gestis Regum*, Book III., p. 101. All our old historians, as Matthew Paris
and Matthew of Westminster, as well as the *Chronicle* of Albericus, nearly follow
the words of this oldest author. Henry of Huntingdon, Ralph de Diceto, Robert
of Gloucester, and Abbot Bromton, though they notice the pranks of this juggler,
say nothing of his song. Fabyan, on whatever authority, mentions a still earlier
instance of the military use of this favourite performance. In describing the battle
of Fountanet, between Charles the Bald and his two brothers, in 941, he says:
"When the shote was spente, and the speres to shateryd, then both hostes ranne
togyther WYTH ROLANDS SONGE, so that, in short whyle, the grene felde was
dyed into a perfyte redde " (*Chronicle*, 1533, fo. 93).

> *Ed*, Oliver, *et des vassals,*
> *Qi morurent en* Rencevals."*

Geoffrey Gaimar, an earlier poet than Wace, though he only appears as his continuator, speaks likewise of this gallant minstrel ; and gives a curious relation of the behaviour of his horse, the tricks he played with his spear and sword, and his exploits in the action, which are likewise mentioned by some of our old historians.†

Doctor Burney, in his *History of Music* (ii. 276), has inserted a pretendedly genuine copy of the *Chanson de Roland,* by the Marquis de Paulmy, with a spirited translation ; but the Marquis, in this *jeu d'esprit,* apparently mistook the nature of the ancient *Chanson,* confounding it with that of a more recent period. The Chevalier de Tressan, in his *Corps d'extraits de Romans* (i. 356), gives a stanza, in modern French, of a different song said to be chanted by the peasants of the Pyrenees ; but most probably of his own invention. The real *Chanson de Roland* was, unquestionably, a metrical romance of great length upon the fatal battle of Ron-cevaux, of which Taillefer only chanted a part.

Le Grand d'Aussy pretends that the *Chanson de Roland* sub-sisted down to the third race, as, he says, it appears by that reply so bold, known to everybody, of a soldier to King John, who re-proached him with singing it at a time when there were no longer any Rolands. This assertion, however, so far as respects the above, or any other song, is an absolute falsehood. The story alluded to, which has no better authority than that of Hector Bois, a fabulous writer of the sixteenth century, is, literally, as follows : "When King John was come to Paris, calling the parliament to-gether, he complained, with a pitiful tone, of his misfortunes and the calamities of the realm, and amongst the rest, lamented that he could now find no Rolands or Gawins ; to which one of the peers, whose valour had been famous in his youth, and, therefore, an enemy to the king's sloth, answered there would be no want of Rolands if there were Charleses." ‡ The anecdote, no doubt, supposing it true, has some merit ; but no sort of connection with, or allusion to, the *Chanson de Roland,* unless as confounded among the number of metrical romances on the same subject. This, however, or some other song or romance of Roland, appears to have been popular

---

* *Histoire ou Roman des ducs de Normandie* (R. MSS. 4 c. XI.) ; and by no means *Le Roman de Rou,* as hath been completely proved by *abbé* de la Rue.
      " Telfair, who well could sing a strain,
      Upon a horse that went amain,
      Before the duke rode singing loud,
      Of Charlemagne and Roland good,
      Of Oliver, and those vassals,
      Who lost their lives at Roncevals."
† Le Brut, R. MSS. 13, A. XXI.
‡ *Scotorum Historiæ,* B. 15, fo. 339.

in Italy in the fourteenth or fifteenth century, as we learn from a story of Poggius (speaking of one who deplored to the bystanders the fall and subversion of the Roman empire) : *hic par similis est, inquit* (Antonius Luscus) *viro Mediolanensi, qui die festo cum audisset unum ex grege* cantorum, qui gesta heroum ad plebem decantant, recitantem MORTEM ROLANDI, *qui septingentis jam ferme annis in prœlio occubuit* CŒPIT ACRITER FLERE, etc. The wit, however, of Signor Lusco seems to have, for this once at least, been rather misplaced.*

Despairing of the existence of the *Chanson de Roland* among the number of ancient French poems which remain upon the subject of Charlemagne, Roland, Oliver, and Roncesvalles,† the most ancient romance in that language, still preserved, has been thought to be one upon the achievements of Charlemagne respecting the destruction of the monastery of Carcassonne and Narbonne, and the construction of that of *De la Grace.* This history is said to have been written, at the command of the above monarch, by a certain writer named *Philomena,* and to have been afterward, at the instance of St. Bernard, abbot, and the convent of the said monastery, turned into Latin by one Paduan, or Vital, between the years 1015 and 1019; but as it mentions the twelve peers of France, *Le Comte de Flandres,* a title which did not exist till fifty years after the death of Charlemagne, and the city of Montauban, which was not built till 1144, it cannot possibly be of such high antiquity. It is extant, though apparently in prose, in the National Library (Num. 27).‡

Another, nearly of the same age, is the *Roman de Guillaume d'Orange, surnommé au Court nes* (or short nose), which contains the history of *St. Guillaume de Guillone,* and is conjectured to be of the tenth century, but is more probably of the following. Many copies of it are extant in different libraries ; and a full account of it may be seen in Catel's *Memoires de Languedoc.*§ The author calls himself *Guillaumes de Bapaume.*|| It appears, from a passage of *Ordericus Vitalis,* who flourished in 1140, to have been sung, in his time, by the minstrels, though not so worthy of attention as a more authentic narrative. His words are : " *Canitur Vulgo à* joculatoribus, de illo (Sci. S. Gulielmo) cantilena, *sed jure prœ-*

* *Faceie,* Basil, 1488, 4to. See more concerning Roland and Oliver being sung upon the stage in the *Antiquitates Italiæ* of Muratori, ii. 844.

† This romance, the authors of the *Histoire Littéraire* seem positive, was no other than that which bears the name of *Roland et Olivier,* and is marked among the MSS. of Charles V., VI., and VII. ; and refer to the *Histoire de L'aca, des inscrip.,* t. I., part I., p. 317.

‡ See Montfaucon Bib. Lit. II. 1283 ; *Histoire Lit. de la France,* IV. 211, 212; VI. 13, VII. lxxi. ; and Catel, *Memoires de Languedoc,* 404, 409, 517, 566.

§ 549, 569, etc. See also *Histoire Lit. de la France,* VII. lxxi.

|| Sinner's *Catalogue,* tome 3, page 333.

ferenda est relatio authentica, quæ à religiosis doctoribus, solerter est edita, et à studiosis lectoribus reverenter lecta est in communi fratrum audientia." *

Dom Calmet maintains that the *Roman de Garin le Loheran*, the author whereof lived in 1050, is the most ancient romance which the French have;† and to prove the age of *Ogier le Danois* (not that of Adenez), the authors of the *Histoire Litteraire* quote the authority of Metellus, a monk of Tegornsée, in Bavaria, who wrote about 1060; and having occasion to speak of the hero of that romance, adds, "whom that people (the Burgundians), singing old songs, call Osiger" (VII. lxxvi.).

The next, in point of age, that is yet known, is probably a chronicle-history of the Britons and English, from Jason and the achievement of the golden fleece to the death of Henry I., which appears to have been composed at the instance of Dame Constance FitzGilbert before the year 1147; in which year died Robert, Earl of Gloucester, natural son of King Henry I., who had sent the book he had caused to be translated, according to those of the Welsh kings, to Walter Espec, who died in or before 1140, ‡ of whom Lady Constance borrowed it (this seems, from the mention of Walter the Archdeacon, to be Geoffrey of Monmouth's *British History*, which is addressed to Earl Robert), a fragment of which is annexed, by way of continuation, to the *Brut* of *Maistre* Wace, in the king's MSS., 13 A XXI., no other copy being known to exist.

Alexandre Bernay, surnamed Paris, and Lambert li Cors, are the joint authors of a romance of *Alexander* in French verse, beginning "Qui vers de riche histoir veut scavoir," in 1051, or, according to others, in 1193, which may only be the date of the MS.

The next is *Maistre Wace, Gace*, or *Gasse*, a native of the isle of Jersey, and canon of Caën in Normandy, an excellent poet, who composed the romance of *Le Brut*, as he tells us, in 1155, the *Roman de Rou*, the romance of William Longsword, the romance of Duke Richard I. his son, the history of the Dukes of Normandy, a compendium or abridgment of the same history, the life of St. Nicholas, and the *Roman du Chevalier au Lion* in 1155, all performances of considerable merit. § Benoit or Benedict de Saint-

---

* L. 6.
† *Histoire Lit.*, vi. 13.
‡ This date is ascertained by the death, in that year, of Archbishop Thurstan, a witness to his foundation-charter of Rievaux Abbey.
§ The Christian name of *Maistre Wace* is said by Huet (who cites no authority), to have been *Robert* (*Origines de Caen*, Rouen, 1702, p. 607). In *La Vie de S. Nicholas*, cited by Hickes, *Gr. A.S.P.*, pp. 146, 147, he is called " *mestre Guace* " (Tyrwhitt's *Chaucer*, iv., 59); and in the MS. of *Le Chevalier au Lion* his name is written Gasse. Tyrwhitt suspects that *Le Martyre de St. George en vers François par Robert* Guaco, mentioned by M. Lebeuf as extant in the Bibl. Colbert, Cod. 3745 (Mem. de l'acad., D.I., & B.L.V., xvii., 6., 731), is by this Wace or Gace,

More, contemporary with Wace, wrote *Lestoire des Duc de Normendie*, and the *Roman de Troie*, both which are among the Harleian MSS.

Le Roman de Florimon is of the year 1180, the author being unknown.

Christian or Chrestien de Troyes wrote in 1191 *Les Romans de Chevalier à l'Epée (ou L'Histoire de Lancelot du Lac), du Chevalier à la Charrette ou De la Carette* (perhaps the same with the preceding), *du Chevalier à Lion, du Prince Alexandre*, etc., *de Graal, de Perseval, d'Erec*, with others which are now lost.[*]

There are numerous MS. romances in verse, in different libraries, some of which, no doubt, are as ancient as any here noticed. The rest are too numerous to specify, as the two subsequent centuries were still more prolific.

The authors of the earliest French *romans* in rhyme generally declare their names in the course of their own works, "*Meistre* Wace *ki fist cest livere*," and are occasionally noticed by a brother poet, as, for instance, Geoffrey Gaimar, the author of a British chronicle, already mentioned, who not only names himself, but David, his contemporary, of whom nothing more is known ; Lambert li Cors, one of the authors of the *Roman d'Alexandre, Maistre* Wace, the author of *Le Brut, Le Roman de Rou, L'Histoire de Normandie, Le Chevalier au Lion, Le Geste de Alisandre*, and several other poems, name themselves, and the last, in some, repeatedly, all of whom, or of which, are of the twelfth century

"Almost every one of the (numberless) tales called *fabliaux*,"

whose name, by the way, is frequently corrupted into *Eustace, Wistace*, or Huistace, Vacces, and Vaches, particularly by Warton, who believes them to be two distinct persons, and confounds the *Brut* with the *Roman de Rou* (i., 62). *Wace* or *Gace*, however, was certainly a baptismal name, there being two other French poets who bore it, *Gasse Brulés* and Gasse de Vigne.

The title of master, or *maistre*, also is constantly prefixed to the *Christian* and never to the *surname*, instances of the latter, of the twelfth century, being, at the same time, exceedingly rare. Had the name of *Wace* been *Robert*, he would have called himself *Maistre Robert* and not *Maistre Wace*.

The passage in Lebeuf (*Recherches sur les plus anciennes Traductions en Langue Françoise*) is as follows : "*Un manuscrit de la bibliothèque Colbert* (Cod. 3745) *nous fournit le* martyre de St. George *en vers François par* Robert Guaco, *une vie* de St. Thomas de Canterberi *en vers François, Alexandrins, par* frere Benet, & *une* histoire du martyre de Hugues de Lincoln, *enfant tué par un Juif, l'an* 1206." *Guaco*, however, is not *Guace*.

[*] In the *Roman de Perceval* he says :—

> "*Cil qui fit d'Enée & d'Enide,*
> *Et les commandemens d'Ovide,*
> *Et l'art d'aimer en roman mist,*
> *Del roy 'Marc' & d'Uselt la blonde,*
> *Et de la Hupe, & de l'Eronde,*
> *Et del Rossignol la muance,*
> *Un autre conte, commence,*" etc.

says M. Le Grand, " are known to be by some poet or other whose name is mentioned." Of the authenticity of these names there can be no suspicion; but those whose names appear now and then in the old prose romances, printed or manuscript, are mostly, if not constantly, men of straw, such, for instance, as *Robert de Borran*, the pretended author or translator of *Lancelot du Lac, mise en Francois du Commandement d'Henri, Roi de Angleterre* * ; *Lucas* (or *Luces*), *chevalier sieur du chastel du Gast pres de Salisberi, Anglois*, the pretended translator, "*de Latin en François*," of *Le Roman de Tristan et Iseult* † ; *Maistre Gualtier Map* (ad adviz au roy Henry son seigneur), of the *Histoire de Roy Artus et des Chevaliers de la Table Ronde* (*avec le Saint Graal*),‡ and *Rusticien de Pise* or *Pisa*, otherwise *Rusticiens de Puise*, who translated *Gyron le Courtois*, from the book of the lord Edward, King of England, when he went beyond sea to conquer the Holy Sepulchre.§ No French romance of chivalry, it is believed, or should, at least, be believed without seeing it in ancient MS., is in the Latin language (except those of the pseudo-Turpin and Geoffrey of Monmouth maybe so called, or, it maybe, a translation or imitation), though the pretence is common. *Perceforest* was first "*ecrit en grec, puis traduit en* latin," etc., and *Berynus* "*de langaige incongneu.*" It was a weak and unfounded observation of Menage that whenever these faggots pretend to translate from the *Latin*, they mean the Italian. ‖

" The professed romances of chivalry," in the opinion of Dr. Percy, " seem to have been first composed in France, where also they had their name," though he elsewhere, with little consistency, thinks " the stories of King Arthur and his round table" (the most

---

* Warton, i., 114.

† *Idem*, i., 115.

‡ *Idem*, ii., fig. ch. 3. It is not meant to assert that there was no such person, as he was, in reality, archdeacon of Oxford, and a very excellent and humorous Latin poet. He was merely drawn into this scrape by the French romancers (and after them, by the Welsh writers), who confounded him with another of the same name, also archdeacon of Oxford, who is the man said by Geoffrey of Monmouth to have presented him with the original Welsh of the *British History*. Warton, as is usual with him, prefers Walter de Mapes (ii., ch. 2, *b*) because the chronology proves absurd and impossible, he not being archdeacon of Oxford before 1197, about forty-four years after the death of Geoffrey ; but this, it must be confessed, is a very temperate anachronism for " honest Tom."

§ This and two other *romans, du Bruth* and *de Meliadus de Leonnois*, are in the Duke of Valliere's catalogue, attributed to this " *maistre Rusticiens de Pise* " ; and in *Bib. du Roi*, 6796 *à* 6983, are *plusieurs volumes de Giron de Courtois*, mis en François par Huc (Luc), seigneur du chateau du Gat."

‖ *Dans la Bibl. Nation.* No. 3713 (*est*) *un MS. de la fin du* XII. *siecle qui renferme le roman de Turpin et celui D'Amis et Amillon en vers* Latins. The former, at least, was in Latin prose, of the preceding age, and the latter of that in which they were, in all probability, both versified by the same hand.

fruitful and popular subjects of the French and Norman poets) "may be reasonably supposed of the growth of this island, both the French and the Armoricans," he adds, "probably having them from Britain." The former indisputably made great use of Geoffrey of Monmouth's fabulous history, but what they had before it does not appear; neither, in fact, does this impostor ever mention *the round table*, though Master Wase does, not many years after; and with respect to the Armoricans, who are not known on any ancient or respectable authority to have ever possessed a single story on this subject, however confidently the fact may be asserted, or plausibly presumed, it is ridiculous to account for their mode of getting what it cannot be proved they ever had.

Before the year 1122,* and even, according to the French antiquaries, in the eleventh century, had appeared a book entitled, in the printed copies, *Joannis Turpini Historia de Vita Caroli Magni et Rolandi.* This Turpin is pretended to be the Archbishop of Rheims, whose true name, however, was Tilpin,† and who died before Charlemagne, though Robert Gaguin, in his licentious translation of this work, 1527, makes him, like some one else, relate his own death. Another pretended version of this pseudo-Turpin, which is said to have been made by one Mickius (or Michel) le Harnes, who lived in the time of Philip the August, or 1206,‡ has little or nothing in common with its false original, being, in fact, the romance of *Regnaut*, or Reynald, and not that of *Roland*, who is never once mentioned in the head chapters, and very rarely in the book. Mr. Ellis, who took it, without inspection, to be a fair translation of the false Turpin, in 1207, says: "The real author was perhaps a Spaniard"; but this is without authority; and, in fact, the Spaniards have no romance of any such antiquity.§ Mr. Warton calls this fabulous history "the groundwork of all the chimerical legends which have been related concerning the conquests of Charlemagne and his twelve peers"; but this, at least, requires it to have been composed before the year 1066, when the adventures or exploits of Charlemagne, Roland, and Oliver, were chanted at the battle of Hastings. As a strong internal proof, however, that this romance was written long after the time of Charlemagne, he says that the historian, speaking of the numerous chiefs and kings who came with their armies to assist his hero, among the rest mentions Earl Oell, and adds, "Of this man there

* Warton, i., ch. 2, who cites *Magn. Chron. Belgic*, p. 153, *sub anno*, and refers to Long's *Bibl. Hist. Gal.*, No. 6671, and *Lambac.*, ii. 333.
† See Flodoardus' *Historia Ecclesiæ Remensis*, l. 2, ch. 17.
‡ See *Memoires de l'Academie des inscript.*, iv., 208.
§ The original Latin was never printed separately, and first of all inserted in a collection, entitled, *Germanicarum rerum quatuor Chronographi*, etc., Francofurti, 1566, fo.

is a song commonly sung among the minstrels even *to this day*." *
In another place he says that "Turpin's history was artfully forged
under the name of that archbishop about the year 1110, with a
design of giving countenance to the Crusades from the example
of so high an authority as that of Charlemagne," whose pretended
visit to the Holy Sepulchre is described in the twentieth chapter, †
which seems highly probable.

In the year 1138, Geoffrey of Monmouth, afterwards bishop of
St. Asaph, set forth a certain work, which, in his epistle dedicatory
to Robert, Earl of Gloucester, he says he had translated from a
very ancient book in the British tongue, which had been brought
to him by Walter, archdeacon of Oxford, a man of great eloquence,
and learned in foreign histories, containing, in a regular story and
elegant style, the actions of them all, from Brutus, the first king of
the Britons, down to Cadwallader, the son of Cadwallo. Whether
Geoffrey's Latin book, which has certainly made its way in the
world, and infected or influenced, more or less, national history in
almost every part of the globe, was an actual translation, or entirely
or partly of his own manufacture, is not a question here intended to
be discussed; but all allow that the British original has never been
found, unless in the shape of a translation from the Latin. Mr.
Warton, indeed, modestly enough, inclines to think "that the work
consists of fables thrown out by different rhapsodists at different
times," which afterward "were collected and digested into an
entire history," and perhaps with new decorations of fancy added
by the compiler, who most probably was one of the professed bards,
or rather a poetical historian, of Armorica or *Basse Bretagne.* In
this state, and under this form, he supposes "it to have fallen into
the hands of Geoffrey of Monmouth." ‡ However this may be, as
there is little or no evidence, though much improbability, upon the
subject, the readers of the learned historian may be permitted, for
the present, to retain his opinion; but "amid the gloom of super-
stition, in an age of the grossest ignorance and credulity," he says,
"a taste for the wonders of Oriental fiction was introduced by the
Arabians into Europe." These fictions coinciding with the reigning
manners, and perpetually kept up and improved in the tales of
troubadours and minstrels, seem to have centred about the eleventh
century in the ideal histories of Turpin and Geoffrey of Monmouth,
where they formed the groundwork of that species of fabulous narra-
tive called romance.§ Whatever became of the inducing causes, the
conclusion is, unquestionably, very plausible, if not perfectly true,

---

* I., ch. ii.
† I., 124. In the national library, No. 3718 is a MS. of the end of the twelfth
century, which contains the romance of Turpin, and that of *Amis* and Amillion in
Latin verses.
‡ I., *b.*
§ I., i., 4.

for whether there were anything upon the subject of Charlemagne
and Arthur before the appearance of these two books, it is very
certain there was a prodigious number after it.

The *fabliaux* of the twelfth and thirteenth centuries (a name for
which the English language affords no appropriate term, nor the
French any synonym), extant in MS. in several libraries, are almost
innumerable. Three volumes have been published by M. Brabazan,
under the title of *Fabliaux et Contes des Poetes François des XII.,
XIII., XIV., and XV. siecles* (Paris, 1756, 1776, 3 vols. 12mo),
which afford a sufficient specimen of this species of French poetry;
while several, as well of these as others, have been epitomised and
transposed by Le Grand d'Aussy, who has accompanied them with
ingenious and interesting dissertations and notes, at first in two
volumes 8vo, and secondly in five 12mo.

It has been imagined, as Warton thinks, that the first romances
were composed in metre, and sung to the harp by the poets of
Provence at festival solemnities *; but, according to more authentic
writers, these poets borrowed their art from the French or Normans.
He likewise asserts that the troubadours were the first writers of
metrical romances.† The Provençal poetry, in fact, was for the
most part of a different description, and abounded chiefly in allegory
and satire. There is but one single romance existing that can be
imputed to a troubadour, that of *Gerard de Roussillon* ‡; nor is it
certain that if they had composed ever so many, they would have
rivalled the French in point of either merit or precedency.

Warton, indeed, misled, apparently, by that *ignis fatuus* War-
burton, Bishop of Gloucester, and even wishing, it would seem, to
emulate and outdo that confident and mendacious prelate,§ has been
induced to assert that "before these expeditions into the East
became fashionable, the principal and leading subjects of the old
fables were the achievements of King Arthur, with his knights of
the round table, and of Charlemagne with his twelve peers. But, in

---

* I., 112. He elsewhere affirms that "the troubadours of Provence, an idle
and unsettled race of men, took up arms and followed their barons in prodigious
multitudes to the conquest of Jerusalem" (110). An absurd falsehood.

† I., 147.

‡ The Provençal poets had got an extravagantly high character, which this
ingenious writer has entirely deprived them of. M. de Sainte-Palaye, who had
made large and interesting collections upon the history and poetry of the trouba-
dours, which he perfectly understood, suffered, unfortunately, his papers to fall
into the hands of one Milot, a perfect blockhead, who neither knew the Provençal
nor anything else.

§ See his pretended hypothesis of the origin of romance, first printed in the
supplement to Jarvis's *Don Quixote*, and afterward in his own and several subse-
quent editions of *Shakespeare*, a complete specimen of ignorance, impudence, and
falsehood, which has been so ably and decisively confuted and exposed by the
learned and judicious Tyrwhitt, and deserves only to be treated with indignation
and contempt.

the romances written after the Holy War, a new set of champions, of conquests, and of countries, were introduced. Trebizonde took the place of Rouncevalles, and Godfrey of Bulloigne, Solyman, Nou-raddin, the caliphs, and the cities of Ægypt and Syria, became the favourite topics.''

In all this rhapsody there is scarcely a single word of truth. It is sufficiently notorious that before the first Crusade, or for more than half a century after it, there was not one single romance on the achievements of Arthur or his knights. Neither is it more true that any such change took place with regard to the subjects of romance, as he here pretends. That there was a romance on *Godfrey of Bologne* is certain; but that it ever obtained the popularity of those of *Charlemagne, Roland, Oliver*, and *Roncevalles*, which are almost innumerable, or that *Solyman, Nouraddin*, the *caliphs*, and the cities of *Egypt* and *Syria*, were ever "the favourite topics,'' is nothing but random assertion, falsehood, and imposition, there not being a single romance on any one of these subjects.*

A curious passage in the ancient chronicle of *Bertrand Guesclin*, as cited by Du Cange, under the word MINISTRELLI, preserves the names of several ancient French *romans*, some of which are not otherwise known to have existed, and expressly says they were composed by the minstrels :

" *Qui veut avoir renom des bons & de vaillans,*
Il doit aler souvent a la pluie et au champs,
Et estre en la bataille, ainsy que fu Rollans,
Les quatre fils Haimon, *et* Charlon li plus grans,
Li dus Lions de Bourges, *et* Gulon de Connaus,
Perceval li Galois, Lancelot, *et* Tristans,
Alixandres, Artus, Godfroi li sachans,
De quoy cils menestriers *font les* nobles romans.''

None of these rhyming romances have been ever printed, unless a comparatively modern one, entitled *Le Roman de la Rose*, which is well known, and as is somewhere said, *Tristan & la Belle Yseult, Richard sans peur*, at Paris, without date, and at Lyons, in 1597, *Duc Guillaume, Roy d'Angleterre, Guisgardus & Sigismund*, 1493, etc., *Le Roman de Troye*, by Jean de Meun, one of the authors of the *Roman de la Rose;* but if really so, the copies (of all but the last) are as scarce as manuscripts.

In the course, it is thought, of the fourteenth and fifteenth centuries, and possibly even in the latter part of the thirteenth, many of the old metrical French romances were turned into prose, and afterward printed. A numerous and invaluable collection of the former were in the Chateau d'Anet, the residence of Diane de

---

* *History of English Poetry*, i., 110.

Poitiers, the favourite mistress of Henry III., in 1724, but now everywhere dispersed.

Nicholas de Herberay, *sieur des Essars*, who published, in 1574, a French version of the first eight books of the celebrated Spanish romance of *Amadis de Gaule*,* asserts that this far-famed and exquisite story made its first appearance in France, affirming that he had, moreover, found some remnant of an old manuscript in the Picard language from which he thought that the Spaniards had made their translation, and which is possibly still extant.† This, it is presumed, was in verse, in the manner of all or most other ancient romances, which is the most probable, as the printed history of *Theseus de Cologne*, by Anthony Bonnemere, at Paris, in or about 1534, professes to be translated "*de vielle rime* Picarde." There was likewise, in the collection of M. Lancelot, a MS. about the year 1330, entitled *Autre Roman du Renard*, in verse, *en langue* Picarde.

The progress of the Italian and Spanish was much like that of the French, but possibly less corrupted, as it is said that there are specimens of the Spanish and Italian poets which are at once Latin and the vernacular idiom. Romance did not make its appearance in Italy before the time of Dante or Boccace, nor, perhaps, in a stricter sense, previous to the *Morgante Maggiore* of Pulci, from which time, down to the seventeenth century, the number of their *romanzi*, or *rimi cavalareschi*, all in the same kind of metre, is prodigious, some of which are sufficiently known to be of great and sterling merit. Voltaire, who was in one part of his life so disgusted with a translation of Ariosto, in French prose, after having become acquainted with the original, preferred it to the poetry of Homer and Virgil.‡

It arrived still later in Spain, which can boast of nothing in the shape of a metrical romance but an epic poem or two of the thirteenth century, their *historias de cavallerias*, or what we call *romances of chivalry*, being, though sufficiently numerous and occasionally of great merit, uniformly in prose. That which we term a *ballad*, or lyrical narrative, is called in Spain *uno romancé*. Among the prodigious quantity of these compositions there are few or none older than the close, at most, of the fifteenth century. Some, it is true, are upon Moorish subjects; but it is false that

---

* Warton calls this "a romance written in Spain, by Vasco de Lobeyra, before the year 1300," but the author or translator, in fact, is totally unknown ; neither was Vasco de Lobeyra a Spaniard, but a Portuguese ; nor could it be written before 1450, or, as Mr. Tyrwhitt thinks, before the invention of "the art of printing."

† See Tressan, *Corps d'Extraits de Romans*, iii., 4 ; also Fontenelle, *Theatre*, tome 3.

‡ See, as to the progress of the Italian dialect, *Muratoris Antiquitates*, a book of prodigious learning and authenticity.

any one is a translation from Arabian poetry, not even among the curious and beautiful specimens in the *Guerras Civiles de Grenada*, published originally under such a pretence.

II. SAXON AND ENGLISH LANGUAGE.

WITH respect to the original letters or characters of the Saxons, we are able to obtain no satisfactory information. It is highly improbable that they had a written language when, in a state of paganism, they arrived, as the allies of the Britons, in 449.

The Britons, who had already professed Christianity, though not popery, for two or three centuries, appear to have had books and writings, and, consequently, letters and characters, long before the time of Gildas, who wrote about 560, and expressly mentions that all such had been destroyed in hostile convulsions, or carried abroad. The Saxons were much fonder of exterminating them, than of learning their language.

St. Augustine arrived in 597, and made considerable progress in the conversion of the Saxons from pagan to popish superstition ; but neither Bede, nor any other ancient writer, relates that he taught them their letters : in process of time, however, they certainly had the art of writing, both in Latin and Saxon, and, in the following age, abounded with men of learning, if not of sense, of whom Bede, who died in 731, is a sufficient instance. According to Nennius, St. Patrick, who came to Ireland in 434, wrote three hundred and sixty-five alphabets (one for every day in the year) and upward (in order, it is presumed, to teach the Irish to read).*

Neither the Britons, nor the Irish, nor the Saxons, had a K or a Q, an X or a Z, in their language.†

The Britons, according to Lhuyd, " had letters before the time of Juvenal and Tacitus," for, says he, " I have lately seen a coin of *Berach* (or *Bericus*), with his name upon it, in the time of the Emperor Claudius ; and there are others also that bear the name of Caswallon, prince of the Britains (Britons) who fought against Julius Cæsar, beside several others, the times of which cannot be determined."‡

Cæsar, however, has given his positive testimony that the Britons had no coined money, making use of brass rings, etc.,§ and Gildas asserts that whatever they had of brass, silver, or gold, was marked with the image of Cæsar.‖

Many Irish clerks came over to England, and, being esteemed for

---

* Ch. 58.
† See Lhuyd, *apud* Lewis, 61.
‡ See Lhuyd, *apud* Lewis, 62.
§ *Gallic War*, B. 6.
‖ Ch. 5.

their learning (which consisted, it is presumed, chiefly in a knowledge
of the Scriptures, the expositors thereof, and the ancient fathers),
were preferred to bishoprics and abbeys. King Oswald, in 635, as
we learn from Bede, who had, in banishment, received the sacrament
of baptism among the Scots (*i.e.*, Irish), sent to the elders of that nation,
desiring they would send him a bishop, which they did. This was
Aidan, a man of singular meekness, piety, and moderation, to whom
the king appointed his episcopal see in the isle of Lindisfarn ; and,
being unskilful in the English tongue, the king, when he preached
to the people, used to interpret for him. From that time, he says,
many of the Scots began daily to come to Britain, and, with great
devotion, to teach the word of faith to those provinces over which
Oswald reigned. Churches were erected in several places ; posses-
sions were given, of the king's bounty, to build monasteries ; the
English, great and small, were by their Scottish masters instructed
in the rules and observance of regular discipline, for most of them
that came to preach were monks.* Maildulfus, the founder of
Malmesbury, in 675, was likewise a Scot of Ireland. It is therefore
sufficiently probable that these Irish priests taught the Saxons their
letters, between which and the Saxon there is a considerable affinity,
whereas, admitting the Britons capable of doing this themselves, it
cannot be proved that their characters at all resembled the Saxon, as
if they be able to produce a manuscript or inscription of the sixth
century, as they pretend they are, it will, indubitably, turn out to be
in the Roman letters of that time.

When Coinvalch (or Cenwalch), king of the West Saxons, was, in
650, reinstated into the kingdom, there came into his province, from
Ireland, a certain pontiff, by name Agilbert, by nation, verily, a Gaul
(or Frank), but then having remained no small time in Ireland, for
the sake of learning the Scriptures, joined himself to the king, assum-
ing the ministry of preaching, whose erudition and industry the
king seeing, asked him (an episcopal see being there accepted) to
tarry a pontiff to his nation, who assenting to his prayers, presided
over the same nation, by sacerdotal right, for many years.

At length the king, who knew only the language of the Saxon,
weary of his BARBAROUS SPEECH, † subintroduced into the province
another bishop of his own tongue, by name Viri, and himself ordained
in Gaul, and dividing the province into two parishes, offered to the
other an episcopal seat in the city *Venta*, which from the nation of the
Saxons is called *Vintancæster* (now Winchester), whence Agilbert
being grievously offended that the king should act in this matter
without consulting him, returned to Gaul, and (the bishopric of the
city of Paris being accepted) there died an old man, and full of days. ‡

---

* B. 3, ch. 3.

† In the original, "*pertæsus barbaræ loquelæ.*" This barbarous jargon would
seem to have been Latin, which the Saxon monarchs had not yet acquired.

‡ Bede, *Historia Eccl.*, l. 3, ch. 7.

The Saxons arrived in 449, as allies of the Britons, whom, having first defeated their enemies, they drove, after many a fierce engagement, into the mountainous parts of the west of England, where they have been suffered to remain. Though these treacherous strangers are not known to have brought over with them books or letters, or, in short, any kind of literary stock, while they continued pagans they were unquestionably a brave and warlike nation; but upon their conversion to Christianity, their kings became monks, the people cowards and slaves, unable to defend themselves, and a prey to every invader. The same effects had not long before been already produced upon the Romans, as they have in modern times upon the Mohawks, who, in consequence of a certain change, have lost all that was valuable in their national character, and are become the most despicable tribe that is left unexterminated. It will be in vain to expect any proofs of genius from such a savage and degraded people. If, as Warton pretends, "the tales of the Scandinavian scalds" flourished among the Saxons, who succeeded to the Britons, and became possessed of England in the sixth century, it may be justly presumed* they had been soon lost, as neither vestige nor notice is preserved of them in any ancient writer. They had a sort of poetry, indeed, a kind of bombaste or insane prose, from which it is very difficult to be distinguished. Alfred, it must be confessed, a great prince but a wretched bigot, upon the testimony of his chaplain or confessor, who wrote his life, though he allows him to have remained illiterate, through the unworthy neglect (for shame!) of his parents and nurses, until twelve years of age or upwards, says that the Saxon poems, being by day and night an attentive auditor, very often hearing from the relation of others, being docile, he retained by heart.† He had even formed a manual or commonplace book, called in Saxon his honobac, in which were several pieces of poetry by St. Aldhelm, who died in 709, and successfully cultivated that study, and particularly a song he had made, which in the time of Asser were still sung by the vulgar.‡ He translated the ecclesiastical history of Bede, Orosiuse's *Ormesta Mundi*, Boetius' *De Consolatione Philosophiæ*, Pope Gregory's *Pastorale*, and the *Psalms of David*, from Latin into his vernacular tongue. It has been pretended also that he paid the same attention to Æsop's fables, but this requires authority. Venerable Bede, who died in 731, had been a prodigy of learning, but only displayed his talents in Latin; at the commencement of Alfred's reign in 864, according to his own declaration, "there were very few on this side the Humber that could understand their daily prayers in English or translate any letter from the Latin. I think," he adds, "there

* I., c. 2, 6.   † Asser, 16.
‡ W. Malmes, 342. Asser says it was a collection of hours, and psalms, and prayers, which he carried in his bosom day and night. He says nothing of Aldhelm.

3

were not many beyond the Humber; there were so few that I, indeed,
cannot recollect one single instance on the south of the Thames
when I assumed the kingdom."* "Before everything," he says,
" had been ravaged and burned by the Danes, the churches, through
all the English nation, stood full of vessels and books and priests.
Of the use of their books, however, they knew very little, as they
were not written in the language which they spoke. So that though
they might see their treasures, they were unable to explore them."†

The Saxon language, after having been corrupted by the Danes,
who spoke a tongue of distant affinity, began to be infected by
the Norman-French before the conquest of England. We are
told by Ingulf that " Edward the Confessor, born in England,
but brought up and tarrying a very long time in Normandy,
had almost become a Frenchman, bringing over and attracting
a great many from Normandy, whom, being promoted to various
dignities, he raised very high.‡ . . . The whole land, there-
fore, being introduced under the king and the Normans, began
to dismiss the English customs, and in many things to imitate
the manners of the French, the Gallic idiom, that is, all the great
men in their courts to speak, their charters and deeds to make, and
their own custom in these and many other things to be ashamed of."
All the charters granted to Croyland by the English kings, accord-
ing to this learned abbot, were written in the Saxon hand " untill
these our times," he says, "which partly were written two ways,
as well in the *French* hand as in the *Saxon*. For the *Saxon*, by all
the Saxons and Mercians, until the times of King Alfred, who by the
French doctors was excellently instructed, used in all chirographs
from the time of the said lord the king, had become vile by disuse ;
and the *French hand*, because more legible, and very delectable to
the sight, excelled more frequently from day to day, pleased among
all the English."§ He says further " that a few years before the fire
of 1091 he took out of the chartary several chirographs, written in a
Saxon hand, of which they had duplicates and triplicates, and
delivered them to the chantor dom Fulmar, to be preserved in the
cloister, for teaching the younger monks to learn the *Saxon hand*,
forasmuch as such *letter*, for a long time, because of the Normans,
now neglected, had become vile, and was now known but to a few
elders, that the younger, instructed to read this *letter*, might be the

---

* Preface to the *Pastorale*, by himself.

† *Ibid.* There is but one single romance, and that in prose, extant in the Saxon
dialect ; it is the legend of Apollonius of Tyre, and has been translated from the
Latin, in the library of Bennet College.

‡ Gervase of Tillbury says he was educated with the Duke of Neustria (Nor-
mandy), for that, among the most noble English, a custom prevailed to bring up
their sons with the French, for the use of arms and taking away the barbarism of
their native language (*Otia Imperialia*).

§ *Ibid.*, 85.

more apt in their old age to allege the muniments of their monastery against its adversaries."*

The Saxon natives, a spiritless and cowardly race, who had been long accustomed to the conquest and ascendency of every neighbouring nation which thought proper to invade them, as the Scots, for instance, the Picts, and the Danes, the last of which had actually taken possession of the crown and kingdom of England, and held it for several reigns, were, after the Norman Conquest, reduced to a state of baseness and servility. They had been deprived of their native landlords, who were forfeited, banished, and put to death, and their estates confiscated, by the rapacious Normans; they had been deprived of their laws, and a final attempt was now made to abolish their language. This, however, though great pains were taken to enforce it, did not entirely succeed, owing chiefly, it may be, to the stupidity of the Saxon peasants.†

From the time of this conquest, the king, and the nobility, and the bishops, and most of the regular clergy, and every man, in short, of landed property, the whole kingdom having been parcelled out in knights' fees, under the feudal law, which was now for the first time introduced into the country, were Normans, and spoke the French, so that, long before his death, and ever afterward, we do not once meet with the name of one single Saxon nobleman; nor is there a single family now flourishing, however high in rank and opulence, that can prove a descent from the Saxon times by authentic documents; all were ruined, exiled, decapitated, or reduced to poverty, wretchedness, and distress, so that, in fact, like the Picts, they seem to have been cut off, all at once, by a single blow, without

---

* *Ibid.*, 98.

† It would, no doubt, have been a glorious matter for a conquered and enslaved people to boast that after they had lost the succession of their native sovereigns their laws, their possessions, their estates and property, and everything, in short that was really valuable, they were permitted to preserve their language, and continue a meagre and barren jargon, which was incapable of discharging its functions ; this, in fact, was the only measure of the Norman tyrants which was adapted to the benefit of their conquered subjects, and in this alone they were unsuccessful ; neither, on the contrary, did the Saxon commonality retain their primitive tongue ; they got, indeed, a barbarous mixture of Saxon, Danish, Norman, and one knows not what, which was no more Saxon than French, and is now known by the name of English, a term formerly synonymous with Saxon.

Hearne, indeed, contends that " the introduction of the French tongue was of very great disadvantage. It brought a disuse," he says, " of the Scriptures, which having been translated into Saxon, were commonly read among the vulgar till after the Normans came among us, who did all they could possibly to destroy everything that looked like Saxon ; and yet they were not able to bring their ill designs to perfection " (Preface to *Langtoft*, p. xxiv.). The loss sustained by the vulgar of their Saxon version would have been effectually remedied by the Latin Vulgate, which the priests continued to explain to them in their vernacular idiom (for, in fact, there was no French translation of the Bible) : and the reading of it might have contributed to the knowledge of the Latin tongue.

any progeny being left to represent them. "At length," says In‑
gulph, the Normans "so abominated the English, that whensoever
they excelled in merit, they were driven from their dignities, and
much less able foreigners, of whatsoever other nation which is under
heaven they were, would be taken willingly. The very idiom even
they so much abhorred, that the laws of the land and the statutes
of the English kings were treated in the French language.* And to
boys also, in schools, the grammatical principles of letters were
delivered in French, and not in English; the English mode also
of writing was omitted, and the French mode adopted, in all charters
and books." †

Henry of Huntingdon, relating the death of William the Con‑
queror, says that "now the Normans had accomplished the just

* The only laws promulgated by the Conqueror in Norman-French are those
that were found in a single MS. of Ingulph, now destroyed (a blank space being
left in other copies for their insertion), and have been printed by Selden in
Fulman's edition, and by Wilkins in *L.L. Saxonicæ*. If these laws be genuine,
a fact which is not intended to be disturbed, they must have been proclaimed, one
would think, in the Saxon language, being the old laws of the king's cousin
Edward, as he says, and intended for the benefit of his newly acquired Saxon
subjects; and this Norman version must be a work of later times, by some monk,
who preferred to get them translated for him by another who understood the
Saxon tongue, supposing him not to have done it for himself. But it seems
evident that the copyist of the MS. used by Sir Henry Saville had been unable to
write the Saxon character, and therefore obliged to leave a blank; and a Norman
monk, after Ingulph's death, would naturally prefer his native tongue. These laws,
no doubt, afford a very ancient specimen of the Norman-French; but it is the
height of absurdity to imagine that he would have restored them to his Saxon
subjects in a language they did not understand, particularly as we find in
Wilkins (p. 230) that, on other occasions, he had no objection to make use of
their own idiom. The laws in Latin, which immediately follow the above, are, like
many others, a manifest forgery. There are, in fact, several charters of the Con‑
queror, in the Saxon language, still extant, though the vulgar English, at that
period, seems to have been essentially different. William of Malmesbury, relating
the death of Aldred, Archbishop of York, who succeeded in 1060, and died in 1069,
says that the frankness of his mind shone very clear in one expression, which, he
adds, "I will give in English, because Latin words do not answer like the English
to the rhyme." One Urfus, who had been appointed by the king sheriff of
Worcester, having, in erection of his castle, committed a nuisance to the monks,
and their complaint being brought before the archbishop, as patron of that see, he,
as soon as he saw the sheriff, attacked him with these words:

"Hatest thou 1 Urse?
Have thou God's curse!"

which is, certainly, the most ancient and authentic vestige of the English tongue,
not being pure Saxon, that we are able to recover (*De Gestis Pontificum*, l. 3,
p. 271).

† Robert Holcot, as quoted by Selden, in his notes to Eadmer, says that the
Conqueror "deliberated how he might destroy the Saxon language, and accord
England and Normandy in idiom."

1 *I.e.*, dost thou call thyself.

will of the Lord over the nation of the Engles ; nor was there scarce any chief of the progeny of the Engles in England, but all were reduced to slavery and sorrow, so that it was a disgrace to be called an Englishman." *

"England," in the words of William of Malmesbury, contemporary with Henry the Archdeacon, "is made the habitation of strangers, and the dominion of aliens. No Englishman," he says, "at this day, is either duke,† or bishop, or abbot. The new-comers everywhere eat up the riches and bowels of England." ‡

Robert of Gloucester, in his rude provincial rhymes, says of this king William :

> " He yef londes in Engelond that lyghtlyche cam therto,
> That yut her eyrs holdest a londe mony on ;
> And deseryted mony kundemen, that he hulde his son ;
> So that the meste del of hey men that in Englond beth
> Beth ycome of the Normans, as ye nou yn feth ;
> And men of relygion of Normandye also ;
> So that vewe contreyes beth in Engelond,
> That monckes nabbeth of Normandye somthyng in her honde." §

John Rous, who, though not an ancient author, may have been acquainted with the work of one, remarks that " from the Conquest the English were everywhere trod under foot, and for a trivial offence, or none at all, most cruelly afflicted ; and, in the beginning of Henry I., the English were held in the greatest detestation." ‖

William, the only son of this Henry, who was drowned in the Channel, had boasted that if ever he should receive dominion over the Engles, he would make them draw the plough like oxen. ¶

After this how strange and weak a thing it was that so great a man as Sir Henry Spelman should, for the sake of a pitiful, forensic quibble, maintain that the name of *conquestor*, assumed by, or bestowed upon, William, Duke of Normandy, who routed the Saxon army in a pitched battle, and slew their native kings, signifies not *conquerour* in historical language, but *acquisitor*, or *purchaser*, in the feudal jargon, forgetting or contemning not only the old historians, but even the old Leonine : " *Gulielmus rex Anglorum* bello conquestor eorum."

It was still more weak and puerile in Sir William Blackstone, in a more enlightened age, to adopt such a groundless idea, though naturally enough to be expected from an ignorant reviewer.

---

* 370.

† In the original *dux*, but there was no duke in this kingdom before the eleventh year of King Edward III., when he created his eldest son duke of Cornwall. Ancient writers use *dux* and *comes* indifferently. Geoffrey Plantagenet, *duke* of Britany, is as frequently called *earl*.

‡ 459.   § 368.   ‖ 138.

¶ T. Walsingham, 444 ; H. de Knyghton. 23. 82 ; the latter cites William of Malmesbury.

"At more than a century after the Conquest," it is supposed,
"both the Norman and English languages would be heard in the
houses of the great, so that probably about this æra, or soon after,
we are to date that remarkable intercommunity and exchange of
each other's compositions, which we discover to have taken place
at some early period between the French and English minstrels;
the same set of phrases, the same species of characters, incidents,
and adventures, and often the same identical stories being found in
the old metrical romances of both nations."* This, though it
could not possibly take place at so early a period, nor more than a
century after, is by no means to be wondered at, as the English
minstrels, being far inferior, in genius and invention, to the Norman
or French *trouveres*, were obliged to content themselves with trans-
lating what had already become celebrated, and they were unable
to emulate. It is, at the same time, a gross misrepresentation and
imposition, however confidently or plausibly asserted or insinuated,
that any one English minstrel romance was ever translated into
French.

That William the bastard, his son Rufus, his daughter Maud,
or his nephew Stephen, did, or could, speak the Anglo-Saxon, or
English language, we have no information. The Saxon chronicle
ended in the last of these reigns; but, being imperfect towards the
conclusion, it is not certainly known how low it was actually brought,
and still less at what age it commenced. King Henry II., in his
progress to Wales, was addressed by a singular character "*in
Teutonica lingua*," very good English, it would seem, and it may
be also very good German, at least for the time; the three first
words of the speech delivered (all that is given in that language)
being "Gode olde kinge!" The king himself speaks French.†

In this reign, it is most probable, Layamon, the priest, made his
translation, in the style of Saxon poetry, without rhyme, from the
Brut of *Maistre Wace*, which affords a strange and singular
mixture of the Saxon and Norman idioms, both apparently much
corrupted. This curious work exhibits the progress of the English
language, properly so called, as we now have it, in its dawn or
infancy, if one may use such an expression.

The change of Saxon into English, however, was probably still
more rapid, as the Saxon chronicle terminated in the reign of King
Stephen, who died in 1154, and in FIFTEEN years after we have
English rhymes by St. Godric, a hermit at Finchal, who died in
1170, though it must be confessed there are specimens of a later
period in prose.

According to William of Malmesbury, in the time of King Henry I.,
the whole language of the Northumbrians, and most of all in York,

---

* *Essay on the Ancient Minstrels,* xxxii.
† J. Brompton, 1079.

creeked so rudely, that they of the south could understand nothing
of it, which happened on account of the vicinity of barbarous
nations,* and the remoteness of the kings, formerly English, then
Norman, "who are known," he says, "to sojourn more to the south
than to the north." †

Girald Barry, too, who resided frequently at the court of King
Henry II., says of the vulgar English idiom of his own time : "As
in the southern borders of England, and especially about Devon-
shire, the English language seems, at this day, rather discomposed,
it nevertheless, scenting far more of antiquity (the northern parts by
the frequent irruptions of the Danes and Norwegians, being greatly
corrupted), observes more the propriety and ancient mode of speak-
ing ; of which also not argument only, but likewise certainty, you
may have that all the English books of Bede, Rabanus, King Alfred,
or others whomsoever you will find written under the propriety of
this idiom." ‡

This seems to describe the Saxon into which Alfred translated
Bede's *Ecclesiastical History*, and many other Latin books.

"This apayring of the birthe tonge," says Higden, "is by cause
of tweye thinges ; oon is for children in scole, ayenes the usage and
maner of alle other naccouns, beth compelled for to leve her owne
langage, and for to construewe her lessouns and her thingis a
Frensche, and havith siththe that the Normans come first into
England. Allso gentilmennes children beth ytaught for to speke
Frensche, from the tyme that they beth rokked in her cradel, and
kunneth speke, and playe with a childes brooche. And uplondish-
men wole likne hemself to gentilmen, and fondeth with grete
bisynesse for to speke Frensche, for to be the more ytold of." §
Trevisa, the translator, in his addition to this passage, allows that
though "this maner was mych yused to fore the first moreyn," It
was "siththe som del ychaunged. So that now," he says, "the
yere of our lord a thousand thre hundrd four score and fyve, in all
the gramer scoles of Englond, children leveth French, and con-
strueth and lerneth an Englisch."

King Richard is never known to have uttered a single word of
English, unless one may rely on the evidence of Robert Mannyne
for the express words when of Isaac, King of Cyprus, "O dele,"
said the king, "this is a fole Breton." The latter expression seems
proverbial, whether it allude to the Welsh or to the Armoricans ;
because Isaac was neither by birth, though he might be both by
folly. Many great nobles of England in this century were utterly

---

* 258.
† The Picts and the Scots.
‡ Girald, *Cambriæ discriptio*, c. 6. He means pure Saxon, and not the jargon
of his own time.
§ Tyrwhitt's *Chaucer*, iv., 22.
‖ *Ibid*, iv., 23.

ignorant of the English language. A remarkable instance is related by Brompton, of William, Bishop of Ely, chancellor, chief justiciary, and prime minister, to Richard, and certainly at one time the greatest, at another the least, in the kingdom, who did not know a word of it.[*]

"Our nation," say King John's ambassadors to King Admiral of Morocco, "is learned in three idioms, that is to say, Latin, French, and English."[†] There is no specimen of the English language in this reign. It must, however, have been making its progress, as in the reign of his son and successor, Henry III., we find it, to a certain degree, mature and perfect. This, if we take the year 1188, the penultimate of Henry II., when the work of Jayamon may be thought to have been finished (the manuscript itself being of a not much later date), and the year 1278, when Robert of Gloucester completed his rhyming chronicle, no more than a single century, you find an entirely different appearance, with a considerable degree of rough energy, and a tolerably smooth and accurate metre, for the time, though it is generally thought to be conceived in a provincial dialect, and, in that case, may afford a far from favourable specimen of the English even at that time.

The King of England still adhered to the Norman-French, as far as one may rely upon Robert of Brunne, a good evidence in general, and who had the opportunity, in this instance, of knowing his authors' precise meaning, they residing only at a short distance from each other : " The kyng said on hie, ' *Symon, jeo vous defie !* ' " We never know him to speak a word of English. The last long expiring efforts of the Saxon language were made in the forty-third year of this

---

[*] A specimen of English poetry, apparently of the same age, is preserved by Benedict, Abbot of Peterborough (622), Roger de Hoveden (678), and in the manuscript chronicle of Lanercost. " In this year (1190)," says the former, "was fulfilled that prophecy, which of old was found written in stone tables, near the town of the King of England, which is called Here ; which Henry (the Second), King of England, had given to Randal (? William) FitzStephen, in which the same Randal (William) built a new house, in the pinnacle whereof he placed the effigy of a hart, which is believed to have been done that this prophecy might be fulfilled, in which it is said—

> " Whan thu sees in Here hert yreret,
> Than sulen Engles in three be ydeled,
> That an into Yrland al to late waie,
> That other into Puille mid prude bileve,
> The thridde into Airhahen herd all wreken drechegen."

As the inscription was set up when the house was built, before the death of Henry II., in 1189, it may be regarded as a very ancient and singular specimen of the English language, which had not yet, it would seem, at least universally, adopted rhyme to what is called poetry, though the example of St. Godric, already mentioned, will serve to prove that it was not altogether disused even at so early a period (see *Bibliotheca Poetica*, 1802).

[†] M. Paris, 204.

reign (1258-9), in the shape of a writ to his subjects in Huntingdon-
shire, and, as it is there said, to every other in the kingdom, in
support of the Oxford provisions. Certain it is, that this once famous
language had already become obsolete, and utterly incapable of dis-
charging its functions, being no longer either written or spoken :
and "there," as the worthy Lord Balcarres expressed himself, at
the close of his final speech on the dissolution of the Scotch Parlia·
ment, "is the end of an auld sang."

King Edward I. generally, or, according to Andrew of Wyntoun,*
constantly, spoke the French language, both in the council and in
the field, many of his sayings in that idiom being recorded by our old
historians. When in the council at Norham, in 1291-2, Anthony
Beck had, as it is said, proved to the king, by reason and eloquence,
that Bruce was too dangerous a neighbour to be King of Scotland,
his Majesty replied, " *Par le sang de Dieu vous aves bien eschanté ;*"
and accordingly adjudged the crown to Balliol ; of whom, refusing
to obey his summons, he afterwards said, "*A ce fol felon tel folie
fais ! S'il ne voult venir à nous nous viendrons à lui.*"†

There is but one instance of his speaking English, which was
when the great sultan sent ambassadors, after his assassination, to
protest that he had no knowledge of it. These, standing at a dis-
tance, adored the king, prone on the ground ; and Edward said in
English ("in Anglico"), "You indeed adore, but you little love
me ;" nor understood they his words, because they spoke to him by
an interpreter.‡

King Edward II., likewise, who married a French princess, used
himself the French tongue. Sir Henry Spelman had a manuscript, in
which was a piece of poetry, entitled, "*De le roi Edward le fiz roi
Edward, le chanson* qu'il fist mesmes," which Lord Orford was
unacquainted with. His son, Edward III., always wrote his letters
or despatches in French, as we find them preserved by Robert of
Avesbury ; and in the early part of his reign (1328), even the Oxford
scholars were confined in conversation to Latin or French.§ That
speech, however, soon afterwards began to decline. In the thirty-sixth
year of his reign (1362), an Act was made, the preamble whereof states,
"For this that it is oftentimes shewed to the king, by the prelates,
dukes, earls, barons, and all the commonalty, the great mischiefs
which are come to many of the realm, for this that the laws, customs,
and statutes of the realm are not commonly known in the same realm,
because that they are pleaded, shown, and judged in the French lan-
guage, which is too much unknown in the said realm, so that the
persons who plead, or are impleaded in the courts of the king, and the

* See ii., 46, 76, 83, 97.
† *Scoti Chronicon*, ii., 147, 156.
‡ Hemingford (Gale), 591.
§ Warton, i., 6, n. 6.

courts of others, have not understanding nor knowledge of that which is said for them, nor against them, by their serjeants and other pleaders, etc., ordains that all pleas, which shall be to plead in his courts, be pleaded in the *English language*, and that they be entered and enrolled in *Latin*;" which was not much better understood, it is presumed, by the suitors than the *French*.

This famous statute, at the same time, is itself in French, which, in fact, continued in use till the time of King Richard III. ; and if the serjeants and lawyers ceased to plead in that tongue, they certainly continued to write their year books, reports, abridgements, and summaries, in the same even so late as the last century, in which Chief Baron Comyns compiled his *Digest*. It likewise continued to be used in the mootings of the inns of court till a still later period, though it was certainly punishable to pronounce it properly.*

There is a single instance preserved of this monarch's use of the English language. He appeared, in 1349, in a tournament at Canterbury, with a white swan for his impress, and the following motto embroidered on his shield :—

> " Hay, Hay, the wythe swan !
> By godes soul, i am thy man " †

Lewis Beaumont, Bishop of Durham, 1317, understood not a word of either Latin or English. In reading the bull of his appointment, which he had been taught to spell for several days before, he stumbled upon the word *metropolitice*, which he in vain endeavoured to pronounce ; and having hammered over it a considerable time, at last cried out in his mother-tongue, " *Seit pour dite ! Par seynt Lowys, il ne fu pas curteis qui ceste parole ici escrit.*" ‡

Gower wrote much more in French and Latin than in English ; his *Speculum meditantis* is in the first of those languages ; his *Vox clamantis* in the second ; and his *Confessio amantis*, though in the third, a manifest version from both.

He even inserts pure French words in his English poetry ; for instance :—

> " To ben upon his *bien venu*,
> The first whiche shall him *salu* " (Fo. 35, *b*).
> " The dare not drede tant ne quant " (Fo. 41, etc.)

This, too, was the case with Chaucer, though disputed by Mister

---

* Barrington's *Observations on the Statutes*, 63. n. (*a*).

† See Warton's *History of English Poetry*, i., 251. He had another, "It is as it is ;" and may have had a third, " Ha St. Edward ! Ha St. George ! "

‡ Robert de Graystanes, *Anglia sacra*, i., 761 : "Take it as said ! By St. Lewis, he was not very civil who wrote this word here." The country schoolmasters in certain small villages of the north have recourse to a similar evasion when any of their little pupils are staggered at a difficult word : " It is a yowth," says Holofernes ; " pass it over."

Tyrwhitt,* who, however, allows in another place that "our
poets (who have, generally, the principal share in modelling a
language) found it their interest to borrow as many words as they
conveniently could from France, etc., etc. ;" * which is certainly as
true of Chaucer as of Gower or any other poet; more especially
in their translations, where, from a want of words, they take the
French as they find it. A striking proof of this fact, in the case of
both Gower and Chaucer, is that they adopted the mode of French
poetry, which ends one subject or sentence with half the rhyme, and
begins a new one with the other half; which few, if any, other
English poets are, at least constantly, known to do. Nothing is
more plausible than Warton's opinion that Chaucer imitated the
Provençal poets ; *His Dreme, The Flower and the Leaf, The
Assemblé of Ladies, The House of Fame,* and, it may be, others, are
very much in the manner of the *troubadours ;* even the *Roman de
la rose* is, apparently, an imitation of this kind ; which peradven-
ture might rather set him upon the translation. At any rate, the
English language, such as it is, or is esteemed to be, was by these
means greatly enlarged, as well as improved, in this reign, par-
ticularly by those two poets, not forgetting Robert of Brunne, to
whom Warton has done great injustice, and Lawrence Minot, whose
merit he was a stranger to.

The first instance of the English language which Mister Tyrwhitt
had discovered in the parliamentary proceedings was the Confession
of Thomas, Duke of Gloucester, in 1398.† He might, however,
have met with a petition of the mercers of London ten years earlier.‡
The oldest English instrument, produced by Rymer, is dated
1368 ; § but an indenture in the same idiom, betwixt the Abbot and
convent of Whitby and Robert the son of John Bustard, dated at
York in 1343,‖ is the earliest known ; the date of 1324, given in
Whatley's translation of Rapin's *Acta regia* (vol. i., page 394)
being either a falsification or a blunder for 1364, as appears by the
Fœdera, whence it was taken.

There is every reason, indeed, to believe that the English language,
before the invention of printing, was held by learned or literary men
in very little esteem. In the library of Glastonbury Abbey, which
bids fair to have been one of the most extensive in the kingdom,
in 1248 there were but four books in English, and those upon
religious subjects, all beside "*vetusta et inutilia.*" ¶ We have not
a single historian in English prose before the reign of Richard II.,

---

* See his edition of *The Canterbury Tales,* IV., i., etc., 45.
† IV., 25.
‡ Rot. Parl., III., 225.
§ VII., 526.
‖ Charlton's *History of Whitby,* 247.
¶ John of Glastonbury, 435.

when John Treviza translated the *Polychronicon* of Randal Higden. Boston of Bury, who seems to have consulted all the monasteries in England, does not mention one author who had written in English ; and Bale, at a later period, has, comparatively, but an insignificant number : nor was Leland so fortunate as to find above two or three English books in the monastic and other libraries, which he rummaged and explored under the king's commission. Gower, indeed, wrote well in all three languages, *Latin*, *French*, and English ; and there is sufficient reason to think that Chaucer, though he preferred his native tongue, was well acquainted with not only the other two, but with the *Italian* also, which was, at that time, little cultivated in his mother country.

§ 3.—ROMANCES.

No romances are to be expected among the Britons at the time they possessed the whole or the greater part of Britain, of which era the present Welsh are unable to produce the slightest literary vestige. They pretend, indeed, to have the poems of several bards of the sixth century, but they have no fabulous adventures or tales in verse of any age, and only a few, chiefly translations, heretofore specified, none of which can be proved anterior to the thirteenth century.

The Saxons, of whose learning or literature some account has been already given, as well as some idea of their poetry, being, for the most part, an ignorant and illiterate people, it will be in vain to hope for proofs among them of genius or original composition, at least in their native tongue. In consequence no romance has been yet discovered in Saxon, but a prose translation already noticed. So that if, as Warton pretends, the flourishing of the "tales of the Scandinavian scalds among the Saxons " may be justly presumed, it is certain they had been soon lost, as neither vestige nor notice is preserved of them in any ancient writer ; nor, in fact, would any but a stupid fool or rank impostor imagine that any of these supposititious Scandinavian tales existed in the middle of the fifth century, when the Saxons first established themselves in Britain. He pretends likewise that " they imported with them into England the old Runick language and letters ;" but whatever vestiges of either exist in the northern parts of the kingdom are by more learned writers attributed to the Danes.*

The most ancient romance now extant in the English language, if it may be so called, being a strange and apparently corrupt mixture of Saxon and Norman, in the style of the Saxon poetry, without

---

* I.. e., 2, b. The Runick characters exhibit proofs of Christianity, and must, consequently, be very late, and are, probably, forged.

rhyme, is a sort of licentious version, by one Layamon, a priest, at
Ernlye-upon-Severne, with great probability about the time of
Henry II. or Richard I., the manuscript itself being not later than
the commencement or at least the earlier part of the thirteenth
century, chiefly it seems from the *Brut* of *Maistre* Wace, Gace, or
Gasse, which was itself, in some measure, a translation from Geoffrey
of Monmouth's *British History*, and was finished in 1155. A curious
specimen of this singular production may be read to great advantage
in the elegant *Specimens of Early English Poetry*, published by
George Ellis, Esq.* The original is in the Cotton Library (Claudius,
A. ix.), in which invaluable collection was formerly a later and
modernised copy (Otho, c. xiii.), unfortunately destroyed in the
dreadful fire which happened in that invaluable repository, 1731. A
specimen of it, however, is luckily preserved in Wanley's *Catalogue
of Saxon MSS.*

Our King Richard I., in the first, as we are told by Du Verdier,
frequented the Court of Raymond Berenger, or Berenguier, Count
of Provence, the last of that name, and there fell in love with Leonore,
or Helyonne, one of the four daughters of that count, whom he
afterwards married. This princess sent him "*un beau romant, en
rime Provinçalle, des amours de Blandin de Cornaille et de
Guilhen de Myremas, des beaux faicts d'armes qu'ils firent l'un
pour la belle Bryand et l'autre pour la belle Irland, dames
d'incomparable beauté;*"† unfortunately now lost.

He had either a servant or a friend named Blondel de Nesle, who
was a minstrel, and discovered the king in the imperial prison, by
singing under his window the half of a Provençal song of his own
composition, and, pausing, the royal prisoner sung the other; which
certified Blondel where he was confined, and enabled his subjects to
obtain his ransom. The song is still extant. This gallant monarch,
himself a celebrated poet, as well in Norman as in Provençal, was the
subject of several romances. Leland found the *Historia de Ricardo
rege carmine scripta*, in the library of Croyland Abbey,‡ and in that
of the Abbey of Glastonbury, in 1248, were the *Gesta Ricardi*
registered. Both these, no doubt, were a romance, or two different
romances, in the French language. A copy of the same poem, or

---

* See i., 61.

† *Bibliotheque*, 1221. Nostredames, *Les vies des poetes Provençaux*, 1575, p. 140
Crescimbeni (II , 8) tells the same story, and adds that the king, when prisoner
composed sonnets, which he sent to Beatrix, the sister of this Leonora. It is well-
known, however, that he actually married Berengaria, daughter of Sancho, King of
Navarre, though some love affair between him and one of the princesses of Provence
may nevertheless have taken place. It may be observed at the same time that
Richard, Earl of Cornwall, King of the Romans, brother to Henry III., actually
married Sanchia, daughter of Raymond, Earl of Provence, and that he is
occasionally confounded by foreign writers with Richard I. Another daughter of
Raymond was married to Henry III.

‡ Coll. III., 30.

some other on the same subject, is in the library of Turin, and in the
national library at Paris (formerly the *Bibliotheque du roi*, 7532),
is the *"Histoire de Richard, roi d'Angleterre et de Maque-
more d'Irlande, en rime,"* fo. This Maquemore is Dermond Mac
Morough, King of Leinster, who, having ravished the wife of O'Rory,
King of Lethcoin, daughter of Melachlin MacColman, King of
Leinster, and being, on that account, attacked by Roderick O'Connor,
King of Connaught, implored and obtained the assistance of King
Henry II., which procured to him and his successors the dominion
of Ireland.* Ducange also cites the *Histoire de la mort Richard,
roy d'Angleterre*, meaning, it is presumed, this Richard, surnamed
Cœur-de-lion.

Kyng Richard Cuer du Lyon was printed by Wynkyn de
Worde in 1528, in quarto and black letter; and, according to Mister
Warton, an edition by the same printer in 1509 (C.R., 734, 8vo.)
"This," he says, "was in the Harleian library;" but unless there
were an edition beside No. 5933, he is probably mistaken. He
likewise mentions a third, "Impr. for W.C., 4to." Among the
"Englyshe boks off (Sir) John Paston" was "Kyng Ri cur de lion."†
The MS. copies of the English romance, doubtless a translation from
the French, contain many variations. One of these is in the library
of Caius College, Cambridge (D. 18); another Doctor Farmer had (im-
perfect); the fragment of a third is in the Harleian collection (No.
4690), in the British Museum; and another in the Auchinleck MS. in
the Advocates' Library, Edinburgh. "The victorious·achievements
of that monarch," according to Warton, "were so famous in the
reign of Henry the *Second*, as to be made the subject of a picture
(*duellum regis Ricardi*) in the royal palace of Clarendon" (1246,‡
in the time of Henry III.)

No romance in English rhyme has been hitherto discovered or
mentioned to exist before the reign of Edward I., towards the end of
which, as we may fairly conjecture, that of *"Horn-Child,"* a very con-
cise and licentious translation, or imitation, and abridgement, rather,
of the French original, nearly two centuries older, made its first
appearance. There is every reason to conclude that the other
romances mentioned by Chaucer, *Ypotys, Bevis, Sir Guy, Sir
Lybeaus, Pleindamour*, and, possibly, *Sire Percivell*, were in Eng-
lish verse, and in all probability much the same with those of which
copies have been preserved; except the last, which no one but
Chaucer ever notices. This sort of translation continued till at least the
time of King Henry VI.; in which reign the *St. Graal* was translated
into English by Henry Lonelish, skinner, at the instance of one Harry

---

* See, in Harris's *Hibernica*, what may with great probability be an abridgement
of a fragment of this identical poem; but why King Richard is introduced does not
appear.

† *Original Letters*, etc., ii.. 302.

‡ I., 114.

Barton,* and contains, though imperfect both at beginning and end, not less, according to Mister Nasmith, than 40,000 lines. Thomas Chestre gave a free and enlarged version of the *Lai de Lanval* of Mary of France; and Robert de Thornton produced *Morte Arthure* and *Percyvell of Gallwas*. *Yein and Gawin* seems to have been written at an earlier period, and very probably in the reign of King Richard II. There are not above two or three originally English, among which we may safely reckon *The Squyr of low degree*; unless *Sir Eglamour* and *Sir Tryamour* may likewise have that honour, till the originals be discovered.

It appears highly probable that the "rhyme" mentioned by Robert of Brun,† concerning Gryme the fisher, the founder of Grymesby, Hanlock the Dane, and his wife Goldeburgh, daughter to a King Athelwold, " who all now," exclaims the learned Tyrwhitt, together with their bard,—

Illacrymabiles
Urgentur ignotique longâ
Nocte,—

was an English romance, extant not only in the time of Henry de Knyghton, the historian, who wrote about the year 1400,‡ but also in that of Camden,§ and even made use of by Warner, who, in the twentieth chapter of his *Albion's England*, has told the same story in effect, though in a different manner, under the names of *Argentile* and *Curan*, in exquisite poetry. Whether this poem were originally composed in English, or were no more than a translation from the French, cannot be now ascertained, as it seems to be utterly destroyed; but in a part of a French metrical romance upon the history of England, by Geoffrey Gaimar, a poet anterior to *Maistre Wace*, to whose poem of *Le Brut* (though unfortunately mutilated) it serves as a continuation, in a manuscript of the King's Library in the British Museum (13 A. xxi.), the story itself is certainly preserved, though whether written originally by Geoffrey, or taken from some one of the " *liveres Engles, en romanze et en Latin*," of which he had purchased many a copy before he could draw his work to the end, particularly a book which, at the instance of the gentle dame Constance Fitz-Gilbert, Robert, Earl of Gloucester, who died in 1147,‖ and was sent for it to Helmsley, brought it away for him from Walter Espie, who was dead in 1140; or the English book of Washingburgh, in Lincolnshire, or how otherwise does not appear. It is, however, a great curiosity, though too imperfect, as well as too prolix, to insert here. In the meantime the paraphrase may be

---

* See his *Catalogus*, Bib. C.C.C.C., p. 54.
† Translation of *Langtoft*, 25.
‡ Co. 2320.
§ *Britannia*, 569; or Gibson's edition, 1695, 471.
‖ See the annals of Waverley, a house of his own foundation.

perused, with great pleasure and equal delicacy, in Warner's book
already mentioned.

Robert of Brunne alludes to a romance of *Dan Waryn*, which
was probably of this period, and being both in French and English,
appears to have been highly popular, and, from the extracts pre-
served of it, a very singular and curious omposition of extraordinary
merit. The passage is as follows :—

> " Wele I understonde, that the kyng Robyn *
> Has dronken of that blode the drink of Dan Waryn.
> Dan Waryn he les tounes that he held,
> With wrong he mad a res, and misberyng of scheld.
> Sithen in to the forest he yede naked and wode,
> Als a wilde beste, ete of the gras that stode :
> Thus of Dan Waryn in his boke men rede." †

In Leland's *Collectanea* (i. 230) are "Thinges excerptid" (by him-
self) "out of an old English boke, yn ryme, of the gestes of Guarine
and his sunnes." The story commenced, it seems, with the time of
William the Conqueror, and the extracts are exceedingly interesting.
Fulco, the real hero of the romance, by Leland called "*Fulco the
secunde*," was one of the four sons of Fulco *primus*, son of Guarine,
or Waryn, who appears to have been a lord-marcher, on the borders
of Wales, as his son and grandson were after him, the latter being
appointed by Richard I. "John, son to King Henry," it is said,
"and Fulco (the elder) felle at variance at Chestes, and John brake
Fulco hed with the chest-board ; and then Fulco gave him such a
blow that he had almost killid hym." ‡ "Morice," it seems,
"sunne to Roger, that had Whitington castel gyven him by the
Prince of Wales, was made govener of the Marchis by King John,
that yn nowise lovid Fulco Guarin. Moryce desired to have the title
of Whitington confermed to hym by the brode scale of King John, to
whom he sent a cursore welle trappid to Balduines castel, and ob-
teined his purpose." Upon this, "Fulco and his brethern, with
Balduine, desired justes of King John for Whittington ; but he could
have no gracious answer. Wherefore he and his brethern forsaked
their homage to King John, and went from Winchester." They
afterward "laid wait for Morice as he went toward Salisbury ; and
Fulco ther woundid hym ; and Bracy cut of Morice heed." The
whole of his adventures are too numerous to repeat ; but one, which
deserves to be noticed, is, that "Fulco resortid to one John of

---

* Robert de Brus, King of Scotland.

† P. 335.

‡ The like circumstance occurs in *Galyen le Rethord, Ogier le Dannoys,* and *Les
Quatre Fils Aymon.* Galyen receives a blow on the head from his uncle's chess-
board, which draws blood ; Baldwin, Ogier's bastard-son, had his head broke, and
was killed by Charlot, son of Charlemagne ; and Berthelot, his nephew, experiences
the same fate from Reynaud.

Raumpagne, a *sothsayer* and *jocular*, and made him his spy to
Morice at Whitington. He founde the meanes to caste them that
kept Bracy" (who, being sore wounded, had been taken and brought
by Audelegh to King John), "into a deadely slepe, and so he and
Bracy cam to Fulco to Whitington." Leland having stated that
" Fulco was taken by the Soldan (in Barbary), and brought onto
him," says, " Here lakkid a quayre or ii in the olde English booke
of the nobile actes of the Guarines ; and these thinges that follow
i translated oute of an olde French historie yn rime of the acts of
the Guarines onto the death of Fulco the 2." The popularity of the
French or English poem (the former being indisputably the original)
had caused some one to reduce or epitomise the story into French
prose ; and a fragment of this manuscript, apparently of the age of
Edward II., is fortunately preserved in the King's Library (12 C. XII.),
where the anecdote already mentioned from Leland's extracts will be
hereafter related.

The two most famous, if not the most ancient English metrical
romances now existing are those of *Guy of Warwick* and *Bevis
of Southampton.* Walter of Exeter, according to Bale (*Ex biblio-
thecis*, from the booksellers' shops), a native of Devonshire, and
professor of a sect of begging friars (a Dominican, as he thinks), at
the instance of one Baldwin, a citizen of Exeter, in the year 1301,
residing at St. Garrock in Cornwall, wrote the life of Guy, formerly
a famous Earl of Warwick, in one book; but Bale is a very dubious
authority. At any rate no such work is now extant, though Carew,
as if he had it in his library, says that this Walter " (de-)formed
the historie of Guy of Warwick." Hearne, in his appendix to
the *Annales de Dunstaple* has inserted " *Girardi Cornubiensis
Historia Guidonis de Warwyke*," from an old MS. in the library
of Magdalen College, Oxford, No. 147. This author, however, is
supposititious, and the MS., in all probability no older than the
fourteenth or fifteenth century, Lydgate translated from him. Guy
of Warwick is mentioned by no English historian before Robert of
Brunne or Peter de Langetoft, about 1340.* His story, at the same
time, is related in the *Gesta Romanorum*, c. 172 ; "and probably," as
Warton thinks, "this is the early outline of the life of that renowned
[but ideal] champion ;"† and in the Harley MSS. (No. 525) is an old
English poem, entitled *Speculum Gy de Warewyke per Alquinum
heremitam*, beginning "Herkenethe alle unto my speche." The
Alquinus here meant was *Albinus Alcuinus*, a Saxon-Englishman
(and not as Sir James Foulis asserts, a Scotch Highlander), who
was the preceptor to Charlemagne, being grounded upon his epistle
De virtutibus et vitiis ad Guidonem comitem, here called *Guy of*

---

* "That was Guy of Warwik as the boke says ;
 There he slouh Colbrant with hache Daness " (p. 32).
† III., 66.

Warwick. Warton relates that the *canticum Colbrondi* was sung by a juggler in the hall of Alexander, Prior of St. Swithin, Winchester, before Adam de Orleton, bishop of that see, in 1333; and in Bodley's MSS., Nos. 1731 and 3903, is a "*Disputatio inter priorem aliquem et spiritum Guidonis.*" The original French "*Romanz de Gui de Warwyk,*" extant in C.C.C.C.L. 6 (formerly in the library of St. Augustine's Abbey, Canterbury) in the public library (More, 690), and the Harleian and King's MSS. 3775, and 8 F. ix., is of the thirteenth century. The English translation, which exists in the library of Caius College, was first printed by William Copland before 1567, and afterward by John Cawood, before 1571. But, in fact and truth, famous as his name is, the man himself never existed. This likewise is the case with Sir Bevis, of whom Camden, with singular puerility says, "At the coming-in of the Normans, one Bogo or Beavose, a Saxon, had this title (of Earl of Winchester), who in the battle of Cardiff in Wales, fought against the Normans" (Gibson's Translation, 1695, co. 128). For this, however, in a way too usual with him, he cites no authority; nor does any ancient or veracious historian mention either *Bogo, Beavose,* or the battle of Cardiff, which, by the way, was not, as we learn from honest Caradoc of Llancarvan, contemporary with Geoffrey of Monmouth, in 1138, built before 1079. His *roman,* in French, however, is of the thirteenth century, and was extant in the magnificent library of the Duke de la Vallière, as it is at present in the late royal library at Turin. An English translation was printed by Pynson, Copland, East, and another, and three MS. copies are extant in the Public Library and that of Caius College, Cambridge, and in the Auchinlech Collection, Edinburgh; all three different from the printed copy, and at least two of them from each other.

Neither Bevis nor Guy is mentioned by Dugdale in his *Baronage,* and he must have been conscious that the latter's story was altogether fabulous when he introduced it into his *History of Warwickshire.*

"Bevis," as we are gravely told by the historian of English poetry, "was a Saxon chieftain, who seems to have extended his dominion along the southern coasts of England, which he is said [by whom?] to have defended against the Norman invaders. He lived at Downton in Wiltshire." This is highly ridiculous; Bevis and Guy were no more "English heroes" than Amadis de Gaule or Perceforest; they are mere creatures of the imagination, and only obtain an establishment in history because (like Mister Warton's) it was usually written upon the authority of romance. He accounts very ingeniously, however, for the fable of Dugdale, that the Saracens had the story of Guy "in bookis of their own language" (i., 145).

Chaucer, who mentions these two romances, notices, likewise, Horn-Child, Ypotis, Sire Lyb, and Pleindamour, none of which can, of course, be so late as the year 1380, when the *Canterbury Tales* are generally supposed to have been published, and one of them at least will be proved in another place to be nearly a century older. The last is unknown. "That of Sir ISEMBRAS," likewise, according to Warton, "was familiar in the time of CHAUCER, and occurs in THE RHYME OF SIR THOPAS," actually referring in a note to "v. 6." It is, however, a monstrous lie.

"The stories of Guy and Bevis, with some others, were probably the invention of English minstrels."* There are, doubtless, metrical romances, such as *Eglamour, Triamour, the Squyr of lowe degree*, and it may be one or two more, of which no French originals are known, and, therefore, may be fairly concluded to be of English invention; but it is absolutely impossible that this can be the case with *Guy, Bevis*, or the rest, of which these originals are extant, and no one who will take the trouble to compare them could have the slightest doubt upon the subject. The MS. French metrical romances are mostly of the twelfth or thirteenth century, the English of the fourteenth and fifteenth; obviously, therefore, they do not stand upon the same footing, and the originals are always superior, and sometimes to a very extraordinary degree.

Mister Tyrwhitt thinks it extremely probable that these romances (*Horn-Child, Sir Guy*, and *Bevis*), though originally written in French, were composed in England, and perhaps by Englishmen; for, says he, "we find that the general currency of the French language here engaged several of our own countrymen to use it in their compositions. He instances (doubtfully) Peter of Langtoft, as he is said "by some to have been a Frenchman"; Robert Grosseteste, Bishop of Lincoln in the time of Henry III., a native of Suffolk; Helis de Guincestre (*i.e.* Winchester); and a romance, also, in French verse, which he supposed to be the original of the English *Ipomedon*, by *Hue de Roteland*, and Gower. This, indeed, may be so, but it likewise may be otherwise; Andrew of *Wyntown*, which equally implies *Winchester*, was not, therefore, an Englishman, nor ever in England.

In the year 1361 appeared a singular allegorical and satirical romance in alliterative metre without rhyme, by one Robert Langeland, as it is alleged by some, without sufficient authority. It is, at any rate, however, a poem of great merit.

Geoffrey Chaucer, the famous poet, who passed his youth and the greater part of his life in the reign of Edward III., was a writer of romances, though in his *Rhyme of Sire Thopas* he attempts to burlesque and ridicule those of his predecessors and contemporaries, on account of what he calls their "drafty riming." The specimen, however, completely proves how successful he would have been in a

* III. xxii

more serious exertion of his lyrical and inventive powers.[*] His *Troilus and Cresside* was intended to be either read or sung, probably in public, or even in the latter case to the harp :

"And *redde* where so thou be, or ellis songe."[†]

A learned and judicious gentleman is inclined to believe that we have no English romance prior to the age of Chaucer which is not a translation of some earlier French one.[‡] After this decisive opinion, which may be supported, if necessary, by producing the original poems still extant in public libraries or private collections, as well in our own country as upon the Continent, it is very strange that Dr. Percy (for whose better information, it may be, the above observation of his worthy friend was intended as a gentle reprimand) should, in the last edition of his *Reliques of Ancient English Poetry*, published some years after that gentleman's death, venture to assert that *Horn-Child*, which he imagines, "although from the mention of Sarazens, etc.,[§] it must have been written after the first Crusade in 1096," a pretty moderate conjecture ; "yet from its Anglo-Saxon language, or which it would be somewhat difficult for any other critic to distinguish, can scarce," he says, "be dated later than within a century after the Conquest." As if this had not been sufficiently extravagant and ill-founded, as may be easily learned from the elegant *Specimens* of Mister Ellis, "it appears," he adds, "of genuine English growth, for after a careful examination I," he says, " cannot discover any allusion to French or Norman customs, manners, composition, or phraseology ;" as if such a circumstance were essential, or even observable, in a romance written by either French or Norman, where the scene is laid in a distant or imaginary country ; "no quotation," he proceeds, "as the romance saith."[∥] Not a name or local reference, which was likely to occur to a

---

[*] Doctor Hurd, Bishop of Worcester, has endeavoured to deprive old Geoffrey of the credit of this poem. "The *Boke* of the *Giant Olyphant and Chylde Thopas* was not," he asserts, " A FICTION OF HIS OWN, BUT A STORY OF ANTIQUE FAME, AND VERY CELEBRATED IN THE DAYS OF CHIVALRY," *Letters*, etc., iii., 218. This, however, is no more than a usual dash of the Warburtonian school, or, in the Gloucester prelate's own "warm language," a lie.

[†] B. 5, V. 1796.

[‡] Chaucer, C. T., iv., 68. Warton also has an argument to prove this, i., 38.

[§] The learned prelate does not appear to be aware that the name of *Saracens* is used by the old English writers for the pagan *Saxons* or Danes. See the forged laws of Edward the Confessor (Wilkins, 204), where Arthur is said to have "expelled the *Saracens* and enemies from his kingdom ;" and Warburton's note on Shakspere (v. 382). Geoffrey of Monmouth calls *Gormund*, a well-known King of *Denmark*, King of the Africans (B. II., c. viii., 11).

[∥] In *Horn-Child and Maiden Rimnild*, in the Auchinleck MS. in the Advocate's Library, a different poem on the same subject, and, doubtless, from the same original, the French is frequently referred to, as for instance :—

" Thus in *boke* as we rede,
In rime as it is told."

French RIMEUR. The proper names arc all of northern extraction, because the story is predicated of the Saxon and Danes in England and Ireland (though he mentions neither by that name). "So that this," he concludes (a manuscript of the fourteenth century), "probably is the original, from which was translated the old French fragment of *Dan Horn*, in the Harleyan MS. 527 (of, at least, a couple of centuries earlier), mentioned by Tyrwhitt (*Chaucer*, iv., 68), and by T. Warton (*Hist.*, i., 38), whose extract from *Horn-Child* is extremely incorrect." "O most lame and impotent conclusion!" The truth of this last assertion will be readily admitted. "Compare," he says, "the style of *Child-Horn* with the Anglo-Saxon specimens in short verses and rhymes, which are assigned to the century succeeding the Conquest, in Hickes's *Thesaurus*, Tom. I., cap. 24, pp. 224 and 231." The comparison, indeed, would be easy, but the result is not quite so certain. The Saxons, it is well known, had no rhyme, nor is there a single vestige in *Horn-Child* of a more intimate connection with the Saxon than was common to everything written in the English language at that period, about the year 1300, that is, and not "within a century of the Conquest." That the metre is Norman, if the writer were not, is manifest from a specimen given by Mister Ellis from M. de la Rue, of the kind of poetry used by Philip de Than, which does not, as those ingenious gentlemen choose to think, consist in making one-half (of a line rhyme) with another half, any more than the composer of *Horn-Child* has done ; but the truth is, that every two lines, being very short, are run together by the transcriber, for the salvation of parchment,—a practice of which the Harlein MS. (which contains the latter) affords abundant examples, many of the poems of that collection being written in prose ; and sometimes, as Warton observes, three or four verses together in one line, of which he gives instances.* That the English acquired the art of romance writing from the French seems clear and certain, as most of the specimens of that art in the former language are palpable and manifest translations of those in the other ; and this, too, may serve to account for the origin of romance in Italy, Spain, Germany, and Scandinavia ; but the French romances are too ancient to be indebted for their existence to more barbarous nations. It is, therefore, a vain and futile endeavour to seek for the origin of romance. In all ages and all countries where literature has been cultivated and genius and taste have inspired —whether in India, Persia, Greece, Italy, or France—the earliest product of that cultivation and that genius and taste has been poetry and romance, with reciprocal obligations, perhaps, between one country and another. The Arabians, the Persians, the Turks, and, in short, almost every nation in the globe, abound in romances of their own invention. The *Scander namch*, or history of Alexander, by Nezami,

---

* I. 35.

about the twelfth century, is a poem of considerable bulk, and much admired by the Persians, but has nothing in common with the European poetry on that subject. The Persick romance of *Mejnoun and Leila*, in prose and verse, is a most beautiful specimen of the art and genius of that extraordinary people. The enumeration of those specimens which are preserved in the Parisian and other great Continental libraries would be endless. The libraries of the monasteries, according to Warton, were full of romances ; but this is very doubtful.*

In that of Glastonbury, at any rate (already mentioned as probably the largest in England), we only find the four following :—the *Gesta Normannorum*, the *Liber de excidio Trojæ*, the *Gesta Ricardi Regis*, and the *Gesta Alexandri Regis;* all which, it is most probable, were in French verse, in which they are known to exist. The catalogue was taken in 1248.† In the appendix to Dart's *History of the church of Canterbury* is a meagre catalogue of books anciently in the monastic library, among which there are not two articles in either poetry or English. The monks at the same time appear to have made no use of their books, as Leland complained when he had to shake off the dust and cobwebs of Abingdon library.

In Madoxe's *Formulare* is a memorandum, or certificate, under seal, that on such a day, in the first year of King Edward III. (1315), was found "a book which speaks of the four principal gests, and of *Charles*; the romance (of) *Titus and Vespasian;* the romance of *Aygres;* the romance of *Marchauns;* the romance of *Edmund and Agoland;* the romance (of) *Girard de Vyeine;* the romance (of) *Williame de Orenges and Tabaud de Arabic;* the boke of *Life;* the romance of *Troy.*"‡ These were, doubtless, French metrical romances ; but where they had come from, or to whom they belonged, is not stated.

In a voluminous metrical version of Guido de Colonna, on the war of Troy, cited by Warton, and by him erroneously attributed to Lydgate, the translator, in his prologue, enumerates several popular romances of his own time

> "Many speken of men that romances rede, etc.,
>   Of *Bevys*, *Gy*, and *Gawayne*,
>   Of *kyng Rychard*, and *Owayne*,
>   Of *Tristram and Percyvale*,
>   Of *Rowland Ris*,§ and *Aglavayle*,

---

* I. 87.

† *John of Glastonbury*, by Hearne, 435.

‡ *Titus and Vespasian, Girard de Vienne, Williame D'Orenges*, and the romance of *Troy*, are all three in the British Museum.

§ *Rowland Ris* is a character in the romance of *Tristrem*, by Thomas Rymour ; doctor Percy, or the learned Scottish divine who inspected, on his account, the Auchinleck MS., has created another champion, called *Rowland Louth*, from the want of apprehension that *lough*, the identical word, meant *laughed !*

> Of *Archeroun*, and of *Octavian*,
> Of *Charles*, and of *Cassibedlan*,
> Of *Keveloke,** *Horne*, and of *Wade*,
> In *romances* that ben of hem bimade,
> That *gestours* dos of hem *gestes*,
> At maungeres, and at great festes,
> Her dedis ben in remembrance,
> In many fair romance." †

All these appear to have been in English rhymes, and most of them are extant at this day.

Another extract, of the same kind, is given by Warton, from the prologue to *Richard Cœur de Lion :*

> " Many *romayns* men make newe,
> Of good knightes, and of trewe ;
> Of ther dedes men make romauns,
> Both in *England*, and in *France ;*
> Of *Rowland* and of *Olyvere*,
> And of every doseperc ;
> Of *Alysaundre*, and of *Charlemagne*,
> Of *Kyng Arthur*, and of Gawayne ;
> How they wer knyghtes good and courtoys,
> Of *Turpin*, and of *Oger the Danois*,
> Of *Troye* men rede in ryme,
> Of *Hector* and of *Achilles*, etc." ‡

Again from a second prologue :

> " Herkene now how my tale gothe,
> Though I swere to you no othe,
> I wyll you rede romaynes none,
> Ne of *Partonape*, ne of *Ypomedon*,
> Ne of *Alisaunder*, ne of *Charlemayne*,
> Ne of *Arthur*, ne of *Gawayne*,
> Ne of *Bevis*, ne of *Guy* (ne) of *Sydrake*,
> Ne of *Ury*, ne of *Octavian*,
> Ne of *Hector*, the strong man ;
> Ne of *Jason*, neither of *Achilles*,
> Ne of *Eneas*, neither *Hercules*.§

---

* It should be Haveloke, see before.

† *History of English Poetry,* i., 119.

‡ *History of English Poetry,* i., 122. These must have been either wholly or principally romances in French metre ; as *Rowland, Oliver, Charlemagne, Turpin, Oger the Dane, Hector,* and *Achilles* never seem to have appeared in English verse.

§ *History of English Poetry,* i., 123. Warton, in a note, *perhapses Pertonape,* to be *Parthenope,* or *Parthenopeus,* whom, he elsewhere calls, " one of Statius's heroes " (ii., fig. *h, n, g*) but, in fact, it alludes to the romance of *Pertenopex, comte de Blois,* a famous *roman de féerie* in French rhyme, but which never made its appearance in English.

The romances of *Rouland, Olyvere, Gy of Warwyk, Wawayn,*
and *Tristram,* which, says the poet, "mockel is lesyngis," are,
likewise, mentioned in a sort of prologue to an old book of the *Lives
of the Saints,* written about the year 1200.*

"The anonymous author of an ancient manuscript poem, entitled
The boke of stories called Cursor mundi," translated from the French,
seems, as Warton observes, to have been of the same opinion. "His
work," he says, "consists of religious legends; but, in the prologue,
he takes occasion to mention many tales of another kind, which were
more agreeable to the generality of readers:"—

> "Men lykyn *jestis* for to here,
> And *romans* rede in divers maneree.
> Of *A lexandre* the conquerour,
> Of *Julius Cæsar* the emperour,
> *Of Greece and Troy the strong stryf,*
> Ther many a man lost his lyfe:
> Of *Brut,* that baron bold of hand,
> The first conquerour of Englond,
> Of *king Artour* that was so ryche;
> Was non in hys tyme so ilyche:
> Of wonders that among his knyghts felle,
> And auntyrs dedyn as men her telle,
> As *Gaweyn,* and othir full abylle,
> Which that kept the round tabyll,
> How *King Charles* and Rowland fawght,
> With Sarazins, nold thei be cawght;
> Of *Tristram* and Ysoude the swete.
> How thei with love first gan mete,
> Of *Kyng John,* and of *Isenbras,*
> Of Ydoine and Amadas." †

The fragment of a metrical romance, entitled *Le mort Arthure,*
preserved in the Harleian MSS., No. 2252, and of which Humphrey
Wanley has said that the writer "useth many Saxon or obsolete
words;" and doctor Percy, fancifully and absurdly, that "it *seems*
to be quoted in *Syr Bevis,*" is in fact nothing more than part
of the *Morte Arthur* of Caxton turned into easy alternate verse;
a very unusual circumstance, no doubt, in the time of Henry the
Seventh, to which Wanley properly allots it.‡ The antiquated words
used by this versifier are manifestly affected. Caxton's book is the
only one known by the name of *La mort D'Arthur,* which he took
as he found it.

It is no proof, because any metrical romances in English may not

---

* *Ibid.,* 123. See, also, a long passage, to the same purpose, in Skelton's works,
cited by mister Warton in his *Observations on the Fairy Queen,* ii., 42.

† *History of English Poetry,* i., 123, *n.*

‡ See Bedwell's preface to *The Tournament of Tottenham.*

happen to mention reading, they were not actually composed by writers at their desk. The minstrels were too ignorant and too vulgar to translate pieces of several thousand lines; though such pieces may have been translated or written for them, as many a minstrel, no doubt, could sing and play what he had not the genius to compose, nor even the capacity to write or read.

The "lytell geste of Robyn Hode" could not, it is true, have been composed by any *monk*, in his *cel*; but there can be no reason for supposing it not to have been composed by a *priest* in his *closet*: and, in fact, to an author of that description, this identical legend, or one of the same kind, hath been expressly ascribed.*

Sir Launsal is, certainly, a translation, the French original being extant in many libraries. It is not, however, by any means "the only piece of this sort, in which is inserted the name of the author."

There is not, however, one single metrical romance in English known to exist, which appears to have been written by a minstrel. The line adduced by Bishop Percy, from one in his folio MS.,

"Then is it time for *Mee* to carpe,"

by no means proves that the man who sung it had himself composed the words; it is sufficient that it had been originally intended to be sung by some minstrel, peradventure by many, or even by the whole body.

Several metrical romances, according to Bishop Percy's account, are extant in his lordship's celebrated folio manuscript, many of which are not to be now found in print; amongst these are the following :— *Sir Cauline, John the Reve, Guy and Colbronde, Libeaux Disconius* (a different copy from the one here printed), *King Arthur and the King of Cornwall, Sir Lionel, The Greene Knight, The Earl of Carlisle, Sir Lambwell, Merline, King Arthur's Death, The Legend of King Arthur, The Legend of Sir Guy, Eger and Grime*, and many songs and ballads. The MS. (compiled by Thomas Blount, author of *The Law-Dictionary*, etc., about the middle of the seventeenth century), as we are told by the right reverend prelate, † is a long narrow volume, containing 191 sonnets, ballads, historical songs, and metrical romances, either in the whole or in part, for many of them are extremely mutilated and imperfect.

"The first and last leaves," he says, "are wanting; and of 54 pages near the beginning half of every leaf hath been torn away, and several others are injured towards the end; besides that through a great part of the volume the top or bottom line, and sometimes both, have been cut off in the binding." . . . . The transcripts moreover

---

* There is another monk or priest, who has written several metrical romances.

† The "advertisement" is signed "Thomas Percy, fellow of St. John's College, Oxford," his lordship's nephew, whom the late Mister Steevens assured the present editor to have never seen a word of it.

" are sometimes extremely incorrect and faulty, being in such instances probably made from defective copies, or the imperfect recitation of illiterate fingers, so that a considerable portion of the song or narrative is sometimes omitted, and miserable trash or nonsense not unfrequently introduced into pieces of considerable merit :" the copyist, it seems, often growing " so weary of his labour as to write on without the least attention to the sense or meaning : so that the word which should form rhyme is found misplaced in the middle of the line ; and we have such blunders as these, *want and will* for *wanton will; even *pan and wale* for *wan and pale*, etc., etc." Certainly this is a most extraordinary, as well as unfortunate, book, and the labour of the right reverend editor in correcting, refining, improving, completing, and enlarging the orthography, grammar, text, style, and supplying the chasms and hiatuses, *valdè deflenda !* must have equalled that of Hercules in cleansing the Augean stable : so that a parcel of old rags and tatters were thus ingeniously and haply converted into an elegant new suit.

The existence and authenticity of this famous MS. in its present mutilated and miserable condition is no longer to be denied or disputed ; at the same time, it is a certain and positive fact, that, in the elegant and refined work it gave occasion to, there is scarcely one single poem, song, or ballad, fairly or honestly printed, either from the above fragment or other alleged authorities, from the beginning to the end ; many pieces, also, being inserted, as ancient and authentic, which there is every reason to believe never existed before its publication.   To correct the obvious errors of an illiterate transcriber, to supply irremediable defects, and to make sense of nonsense, are certainly essential duties of an editor of ancient poetry, provided he act with integrity and publicity ; but secretly to suppress the original text, and insert his own fabrications for the sake of providing more refined entertainment for readers of taste and genius, is no proof of either judgment, candour, or integrity.

In what manner this ingenious editor conducted himself in this patched-up publication will be evident from the following parallel, which may be useful to future manufacturers in this line :—

THE MARRIAGE OF SIR GAWAINE.*

The original (printed in large type) from *Reliques*, edition 1795, iii., 350.   The improvement (printed in small type) from *Reliques*, edition 1775, iii., 11.

> " King Arthur lives in merry Carleile,
>   And seemely is to see ;

---

* The lines or words marked with elevated *commas* are substitutions in place of the old readings.   The whole in italics is his own.

And there he hath with him queen Genever,
    That bride so bright of blee.

> King Arthur lives in merry Carleile,
>   And seemely is to see ;
> And there " with him queene Guenever,
>   That bride so bright of blee.

And there he hath with him queen Genever,
    That bride so bright in bower,
And all his barons about him stoode,
    That were both stiffe and stowre.

> And there " with him queene Guenever,
>   That bride so bright in bowre ;
> And all his barons about him stoode
>   That were both stiffe and stowre.

The king kept a royall Christmasse
    Of mirth and great honor,
. . . . . when . . . . .
            [About nine stanzas wanting].

> The king "a royale Christmasse kept,"
>   " With " mirth and "princelye cheare,"
> *To him repaired many a knighte,*
>   *That came both farre and neare.*
>
> *And when they were to dinner sette,*
>   *And cups went freely round ;*
> *Before them came a faire damselle.*
>   *And knelt upon the ground.*
>
> *A boone, a boone, O kinge Arthure,*
>   *I beg a boone of thee ;*
> *Avenge me of a curlish knighte,*
>   *Who hath shent my love and mee.*
>
> *At Tearne-Wadling his castle stands,*
>   *Near to that lake so fair,*
> *And proudlye rise the battlements,*
>   *And streamers deck the air.*
>
> *Noe gentle knighte, nor ladye gay,*
>   *May passe that castle-walle ;*
> *But from that foule discourteous knighte*
>   *Mishappe will them befalle.*
>
> *Hee's twyce the size of common men,*
>   *Wi' thewes, and sinewes stronge,*
> *And on his backe he bears a clubbe*
>   *That is both thicke and longe.*
>
> *This grimme baròne 'twas our hard happe,*
>   *But yester morne to see ;*
> *Went to his bowre he bare my love,*
>   *And sore misused mee.*
>
> *And when I told him, king Arthure,*
>   *As lyttle shold him spare ;*
> *Goe tell, sayd hee, that cuckold kinge,*
>   *To meete mee if he dare.*

Upp then sterted king Arthure
And sware by hille and dale,
He ne'er wolde quitt that grimme baròne,
Till he had made him quail.

Go fetch my sword Excalibar ;
Goe saddle mee my steede ;
Now, by my faye, that grimme baròne
Shall rue this ruthfulle deede.

And when he came to Tearne Wadlinge,
Benethe the castle walle :
Come forth ! come forth ! thou proude baròne,
Or yielde thyself my thralle.

On magicke grounde that castle stoode,
And fenced with many a spelle :
Noe valiant knighte could tread theron,
But straite his courage felle.

Forth then rush'd that carlish knight,
King Arthur felte the charme,
His sturdy sinewes lost their strengthe,
Downe sunke his feeble arme.

Nowe yield thee, yield thee, king Arthùre,
Now yield thee, unto mee,
Or fighte with mee, or lose thy lande,
No better termes maye bee.

Unlesse thou sweare upon the rood,
And promise on thy faye,
Here to returne to Tearne Wadling,
Upon the new-yeare's daye ;

And bring me word what thing it is
That ? a woman most desire.
This shal be thy ransome Arthur, he sayes,
For Ile have noe other hier.

And bring me worde what thing it is,
"All" women moste desyre ;
This "is" thy ransome, Arthur, he sayes,
Ile have noe other hyre.

King Arthur then held up his hand
According thene as was the law,
He tooke his leave of the baron there
And homword can he draw.

King Arthur then held up his hande,
"And sware upon his faye,"
"Then" tooke his leave of the "grimme barone,"
And "faste hee rode awaye."

And when he came to merry Carlile,
To his chamber he is gone,
And ther cam to him his cozen, Sir Gawaine,
As he did make his mone.

And there came to him his cozen, Sir Gawaine,
    That was a curteous knight,
Why sigh you soe sore unckle Arthur, he said,
    Or who hath done thee unright ?

O peace, O peace, thou gentle Gawaine,
    That faire may thee befall ;
For if thou knew my sighing soe deepe,
    Thou wold not mervaille att all.

For when I came to Tearne Wadling,
    A bold barron there I fand,
With a great club upon his backe
    Standing stiffe and strong.

And he asked me wether I wold fight,
    Or from him I shold be gone,
O[r] else I must him a ransome pay,
    And soe depart him from.

To fight with him I saw noe cause,
    Me thought it was not meet,
For he was stiffe and strong with all,
    His strokes were nothing sweete.

Therfor this is my ransome Gawaine,
    I ought to him to pay,
I must come againe as I am sworne,
    Upon the new yeers day.

> *And he rode east, and he rode west,*
> *And did of all inquyre,*
> *What thing it is all women crave,*
> *And what they most desyre.*

And I must bring him word what thing it is
    [About nine stanzas wanting].

> *Some told him riches, pompe, or state,*
> *Some rayment fine and brighte ;*
> *Some told him mirthe, some flatterye ;*
> *And some a jollye knight.*

Then king Arthur drest him for to ryde,
    In one so rich array,
Toward the foresaid Tearne Wadling,
    That he might keepe his day.

> *In letters all king Arthur wrote,*
> *And sealed them with his ringe ;*
> *But still his mind was helde in doubt,*
> *Each told a different thinge.*

And as he rode over a more,
  Hee see a lady where shee sate,
Betwixt an oke and a greene hollen,
  She was cladd in red scarlett.

> "As ruthfulle" he rode over a more,
>   He "saw" a ladye "sette,"
> "Betweene an oke, and a greene "holléye,"
>   "All" clad in red scarlette.

Then there as shold have stood her mouth,
  Then there was sett her eye ;
The other was in her forehead fast,
  The way that she might see.

> Her nose was crookt and turnd outward ;
>   Her "chin" stood "all" awrye ;
> "And where" as sholde have "been" her mouthe,
>   "Lo"! there was set her eye.

Her nose was crooked and turned outward
  Her mouth stood foule awry,
A worse formed lady then shee was,
  Never man saw with his eye.

> *Her haires, like serpents, clung aboute,*
>   *Her cheekes of deadlye hewe :*
> A worse-formed lady than she was,
>   No man "mote ever viewe."

To halch upon him, king Arthur,
  The lady was full faine ;
But king Arthur had forgott his lesson,
  What he should say againe.

> To "haile the king in seemelye sorte,"
>   "This" ladye was fulle faine ;
> But king Arthure "at fore amaz'd,"
>   "No aunswere made" againe.

What knight art thou, the lady sayd,
  That wilt not speake to me ?
Of me thou nothing [be] dismayed
  Tho I be ugly to see.

> What "wight" art thou, the ladye sayd,
>   That wilt not speake to mee ;
> "Sir, I may chance to ease thy paine,"
>   Though I be "foule" to see.

For I have halched you courteouslye,
  And you will not me againe,
Yett I may happen, sir knight, shee said,
  To ease thee of thy paine.

Give thou ease me, lady, he said,
  Or helpe me anything,

Thou shalt have gentle Gawaine, my cozen,
  And marry him with a ring.

> "If" thou (wilt) ease "my paine," he sayd,
>   "And " helpe me " in my neede ";
> "Ask what " *thou wilt, thou grimme ladye,*
>   *And it shall be thy meede.*

Why if I helpe thee not, thou noble king Arthur,
  Of thy owne hearts desiringe,
Of gentle Gawaine . . . .
          [About nine stanzas wanting].

> *O sweare mee this upon the roode,*
>   *And promise on thy faye ;*
> *And here the secrette I will telle,*
>   *That shall thy ransome paye.*

> *King Arthur promised on his faye,*
>   *And sware upon the roode ;*
> *The secrette then the ladye told,*
>   *As lightlye well she con'de.*

> *Now this shall be my paye, sir king,*
>   *And this my guerdon bee,*
> *That some yong, fair, and courtlye knighte,*
>   *Thou bringe to marrye mee.*

> *Fast then pricked king Arthure,*
>   *Ore hille, and dale, and downe ;*
> *And soone he founde the barone's bowre ;*
>   *And soone the grimme barōune.*

And when he came to Tearne Wadling
  The baron there cold he frinde (finde),
With a great weapon on his backe,
  Standing stiffe and stronge.

> " He bare his clubbe " upon his backe,
>   " He stood bothe " stiffe and stronge ;
> "And when he had the letters reade "
>   Awaye "the lettres flunge."

And then he tooke king Arthurs letters in his hands,
  And away he cold them fling ;
And then he puld out a good browne sword,
  And cryd himself a King.

And he sayd, I have thee and thy land, Arthur,
  To doe as it pleaseth mee ;
For this is not thy ransome sure
  Therfore yeeld thee to mee.

> "Nowe yielde " thee, Arthur, and thy "lands,"
>   " All forfeit unto mee";
> For this is not thy "paye, sir king,
>   Nor many thy ransome bee."

And then bespoke him, noble Arthur,
  And bad him hold his hands ;
And give me leave to speak my mind
  In defence of all my land.

> "Yet hold thy hand, thou proude baròne,
> "I pray thee " hold "thy " hand ;
> And give me leave to speak "once moe "
> In "reskewe " of my land.

' He ' said as I came over a more,
  I see a lady where she sate,
Betweene an oke and a green hollen,
  She was clad in red scarlette.

> "This morne," as I came over a more,
> I "saw " a ladye "sette,"
> Between an oke, and a greene hollèye,
> "All " clad in red scarlètte.

And she says a woman will have her will,
  And this is all her chief desire,
Doe me right as thou art a baron of sekill,
  This is thy ransome and all thy hyer.

> She sayes "all women " will have "their " wille,
> This is "their " chief desyre ;
> "Now yield," as thou art a barone "true,"
> "That I have payd mine hyre."

He sayes, an early vengence light on her,
  She walkes on yonder more,
It was my sister that told thee this,
  She is a mishappen hore.

> An earlye vengeaunce light on her!
> "The carlish baron swore ; "
> "Shee " was my sister tolde the this,
> And "shee 's " a mishapen whore.

But heer Ile make mine avow to god,
  To do her an evill turne;
For an ever I may thate fowle theefe ge[t],
  In a fyer I will her burne.

> [About nine stanzas wanting.]

> But here I will make mine avowe,
> To do her "as ill a " turne,
> For an ever I may that foule theefe gette,
> In a fyre I will her burne.

PART THE SECOND.

Homewarde pricked king Arthure,
  And a wearye man was he ;
And soon he met queene Guenever,
  That bride so bright of blee,

What newes ! what newes ! thou noble king,
    Howe, Arthur, hast thou sped ?
Where hast thou hung the carlish knighte ?
    And where bestow'd his head ?

The carlish knight is safe for mee,
    And free fro mortal harme ;
On magicke grounde his castle stands,
    And fenc'd with many a charme.

To bowe to him I was fulle faine,
    And yielde mee to his hand ;
And but for a lothly ladye, there,
    I sholde have lost my land.

And nowe this fills my hearte with woe,
    And sorrowe of my life ;
I swore a yonge and courtlye knight
    Sholde marry her to his wife.

Then bespake him sir Gawàine,
    That was ever a gentle knighte ;
That lothly ladye I will wed ;
    Therefore be merrye and lighte.

Nowe naye, nowe naye, good sir Gawàine ;
    My sisters sonne yee bee ;
This lothlye ladye 's all to grimme,
    And all too foule for yee.

Her nose is crookt and turn'd outwàrde ;
    Her chin stauds all awrye ;
A worse formed ladye than she is,
    Was never seen with eye.

What though her chin stand all awrye,
    And shee be foule to see,
I'll marry her, unkle, for thy sake,
    And I'll thy ransome bee.

Nowe thankes, nowe thankes, good sir Gawàine,
    And a blessing thee betyde,
Tomorrow wee'll have knights and squires,
    And wee'll go fetch thy bride.

And wee'll have hawkes and wee'll have houndes,
    To cover our intent ;
And wee'll away to the greene forèst,
    As wee a hunting went.

Sir Lancelot and Sir Steven bold,
    They rode with them that day,
And the formost of the company
    There rode the steward Kay.

Sir Lancelot, Sir Stephen bolde,
    They rode with them that daye ;
And foremost of the companye,
    There rode the stewarde Kaye.

Soe did Sir Banier and Sir Bore,
    Sir Garrett with them soe gay,
Soe did Sir Tristeram that gentle knight,
    To the forrest fresh and gay.

Soe did sir Banier and sir Bore
    "And eke sir Garratte keene";
Sir Tristram "too" that gentle knight,
    To the forest freshe and "greene."

And when he came to the green forèst,
    Underneath a green holly tree,
There sate a lady in red scarlett
    That unseemly was to see.

> And when "they" came to the greene forrèst
> Beneathe a "faire" holley tree,
> There sate that ladye in red scarlètte,
> That unseemelye was to see.

Sir Kay beheld this ladyes face,
    And looked upon her suire;
Whosoever kisses this lady, he sayes,
    Of his kisse he stands in feare.

> Sir Kay beheld "that" lady's face,
> And looked upon her sweere;
> Whoever kisses "that" ladye, he sayes,
> Of his kisse he stands in feere.

Sir Kay beheld the lady againe,
    And looked upon her snout,
Whosoever kisses this lady, he sayes,
    Of his kisse he stands in doubt.

> Sir Kay beheld "that" ladye againe,
> And looked upon her snout;
> Whoever kisses "that" ladye, he sayes,
> Of his kisse he stands in doubt.

Peace, cozen Kay, then said Sir Gawaine
    Amend thee of thy life;
For there is a knight amongst us all
    That must marry her to his wife.

> Peace, "brother" Kay, sayde Sir Gawaine,
> And amend thee of thy life;
> For there is a knight amongst us all,
> Must marry her to his wife.

What wedd her to wiffe! then said Sir Kay,
    In the divells name anon;
Get me a wiffe where-ere I may,
    For I had rather be slaine.

> What "marry this foule queene, quoth" Kay
> I "the devil's" name anone;
> Get mee a wife wherever I maye,
> 'In sooth she shall be none."

Then some tooke up their hawkes in haste,
  And some tooke up their hound s,
And some sware they wold not marry her,
  For citty nor for towne.

> Then some took up their hawkes in haste,
>   And some took up their houndes;
> And "sayd" they wolde not marry her,
>   For cities, nor for townes.

And then bespake him noble king Arthur,
  And sware there by this day,
For a litle foule fight and misliking
    (about nine stanzas wanting).

> *Then bespake him king Arthüre,*
>   *And sware there by this daye;*
> *For a little foule fight and mislikinge,*
>   *Yee shall not say her naye.*
>
> *Peace, Lordings, peace, Sir Gawaine sayd;*
>   *Nor make debate and strife;*
> *This lothlye ladye I will take,*
>   *And marry her to my wife.*
>
> *Nowe thankes, nowe thankes, good sir Gawaine,*
>   *And a blessinge be thy meede!*
> *For as I am thine owne ladye,*
>   *Thou never shalt rue this deede.*
>
> *Then up they took that lothly dame,*
>   *And home anone they bringe;*
> *And there Sir Gawaine he her wed,*
>   *And married her with a ringe.*
>
> *And when they were in wed-bed laid,*
>   *And all were done awaye;*
> *"Come turn to mee mine owne wed-lord,*
>   *Come turn to mee I praye."*
>
> *Sir Gawaine scant could lift his head,*
>   *For sorrowe and for care;*
> *When, lo! instead of that lothelye dame,*
>   *Hee sawe a young ladye faire.*
>
> *Sweet blushes stayned her rud-red cheeke,*
>   *Her eyen were blacke as sloe;*
> *The ripening cherrye swellde her lippe,*
>   *And all her necke was snowe.*
>
> *Sir Gawaine kissed that lady faire,*
>   *Lying upon the sheete;*
> *And swore, as he was a true knighte,*
>   *The spice was never soe sweete.*
>
> *Sir Gawaine kissed that lady bright,*
>   *Lying there by his side;*
> *"The fairest flower is not soe faire;*
>   *Thou never can'st bee my bride."*
>
> *I am thy bride, mine owne dear lorde,*
>   *The same which thou didst know,*
> *That was so lothlye, and was wont*
>   *Upon the wild more to goe.*

Then shee said, choose thee, gentle Gawaine,
  Truth as I doe say,
Wether thou wilt have (me) in this likenesse,
  In the night or else in the day.

> "Nowe, gentle Gawaine, chuse, quoth shee,"
>   "And make thy choice with care";
> Whether "by night, or else by daye,"
>   "Shall I be foule or faire?"

And then bespake him gentle Gawaine,
  With one soe mild of moode,
Sayes, well I know what I wold say,
  God grant it may be goode,

To have thee fowle [still] in the night,
  When I with thee should playe,
Yet I had rather, if I might,
  Have thee fowle in the day.

> To have thee foule (still) in the night,
>   When I with thee should playe,
> "I had rather—farre, my lady deare,"
>   (To) have the foule 'by' daye.

What when lords goe with ther feires, shee said,
  Both to the ale and wine,
Alas! then I must hyde myself,
  I must not go withinne.

> What when "gaye ladyes" goe with their "lordes,"
>   To (drinke) the ale and wine;
> Alas! then I must hide myself,
>   I must not go with "mine?"

And then bespake him gentle Gawaine,
  Said, Lady thats but a skill,
And because thou are my owne lady,
  Thou shalt have all thy will.

> "My fair ladyè sir Gawaine sayd,"
>   "I yield me to thy" skille,
> Because thou art mine owne ladyè,
>   Thou shalt have all thy wille.

Then she said, blessed be thou, gentle Gawaine,
  This day that I thee see,
For as thou see me att this time,
  From henceforth I wil bee.

> "Now" bless'd be thou, "sweete" Gawaine,
>   (And) "the" day that I thee see;
> For as thou seest me at this time,
>   "Soe shall I ever bee."

My father was an old knight,
  And yett it chanced soe,
That he marryed a younge lady,
  That brought me to this woe.

My father was an "aged" knight,
  And yet it chanced soe,
He "tooke to wife" a "false" ladyè,
  "Whiche" broughte me to this woe.

Shee witched me, being a faire young lady,
  To the greene forrest to dwell,
And there I must walke in womans liknesse,
  Most like a feeind of hell.

  Shee witched me, being a faire yonge "maide,"
    "In" the greene forèst to dwelle;
  And there " to abide " in lothlye shape,
    Most like a fiend of helle.

  Midst mores and moses; woods and wilds,
    To leade a lonesome life;
  Till some yong faire and courtlye knight
    Wolde marreye me to his wife.

  Nor fully to gaine mine owne trewe shape,
    Such was her devilish skille,
  Until he wolde yielde to be rul'd by mee,
    And let mee have all my wille.

She witched my brother to a carlish b . . . .
    [About nine stanzas wanting.]

  She witched my brother to a "carlish" *boore,*
    And made him stiffe and stronge;
  And built him a bowre on magicke grounde,
    To live by rapine and wronge.

  But now the spelle is broken throughe,
    And wronge is turnde to righte;
  Henceforth I shall bee a faire ladyè,
    And he be a gentle knighte.

  .   .   .   .   .   .

That looked soe foule and that was wont
  On the wild more to goe.

Come kisse her, brother Kay, then said sir Gawaine,
  And amend thee of thy life,
I sware this is the same lady
  That I marryed to my wiffe.

Sir Kay kissed that lady bright,
  Standing upon his feete:
He swore, as he was trew knight,
  The spice was never soe sweete.

Well, cozen Gawaine, saies sir Kay,
  Thy chance is fallen arright,
For thou hast gotten one of the fairest maids,
  I ever saw with my sight.

It is my fortune, said sir Gawaine,
    For my unckle Arthurs sake :
I am as glad as grasse wold be of raine,
    Great joy that I may take.

Sir Gawaine tooke the lady by the one arme,
    Sir Kay tooke her by the tother ;
They led her straight to King Arthur,
    As they were brother and brother.

King Arthur welcomed them there all,
    And soe did lady Genever his queene,
With all the knights of the rounde table,
    Most seemly to be seene.

King Arthur beheld that lady faire,
    That was soe faire and bright,
He thanked Christ in trinity
    For Sir Gawaine that gentle knight.

Soe did the knights, both more or lesse,
    Rejoyced all that day,
For the good chance that hapened was
    To sir Gawaine and his lady gay.

This mode of publishing ancient poetry displays, it must be con-
fessed, considerable talent and genius, but savours strongly, at the
same time, of unfairness and dishonesty.   Here are numerous
stanzas inserted which are not in the original, and others omitted
which are there.   The purchasers and perusers of such a collection
are deceived and imposed upon ; the pleasure they receive is derived
from the idea of antiquity, which, in fact, is perfect illusion.

If the ingenious editor had published all his imperfect poems by
correcting the blunders of puerility or inattention, and supplying the
defects of barbarian ignorance, with proper distinction of type (as,
in one instance, he actually has done), it would not only have
gratified the austerest antiquary, but also provided refined entertain-
ment "for every reader of taste and genius."   He would have acted
fairly and honorably, and given every sort of reader complete
satisfaction.   Authenticity would have been united with improve-
ment, and all would have gone well ; whereas, in the present editions,
it is firmly believed, not one article has been ingeniously or faith-
fully printed from the beginning to the end ; nor did the late eminent
Thomas Tyrwhitt, so ardent a researcher into ancient poetry, and
an intimate friend of the possessor, ever see this curious, though
tattered, fragment, nor would the late excellent George Stevens, on
the bishop's personal application, consent to sanction the authenticity
of the printed copy with his signature.*

---

* The Bishop of Dromore (as he now is), on a former occasion, having himself,
as he well knows, already falsified and corrupted a modern Scottish song, " This

A change similar to that which is before represented to have taken place in France, took place in England at a somewhat later period. Caxton, our first printer, had so little taste for poetry that he never printed one single metrical romance, nor, in fact, any poetical compositions whatever, beside Gower's *Confessio amantis, The Canterbury Tales*, and a few other pieces of Chaucer, Lydgate, etc. He translated, indeed, Virgil and Ovid, out of French into English prose, and we are indebted to him, by the like mean, for several venerable black-letter romances in folio or quarto, such as *Mort D'Arthur*, compiled, it seems, by Sir Thomas Malory; *Charlemagne, Reynard the Fox*, and others; the first of which, though most abominably mangled, became exceedingly popular, and was frequently reprinted; although no copy of the original edition is now known to exist. Several of the old English metrical romances were, afterward, printed by Wynken de Worde, Pinson, Copland, and others, chiefly in the earlier part of the sixteenth century, many of

---

line," he says, " being quoted from memory and given as old Scottish poetry, is (by no one, in such a case, except himself) now usually printed " (*Reliques*, 1775 I., xxxviii.*)

> " Come ye frae the border ? "

to give it a certain appearance of rust and antiquity. This identical song being afterward, faithfully and correctly printed in a certain *collection* of such things, from the earliest copy known, which, like all the rest, was accurately referred to

> " LIVE YOU upo' the border ? "

(*Scottish Songs* printed for J. Johnson, 1794, I., 266), the worthy prelate thought proper, in the last edition of his already recited compilation, to assert that his own corruption " would have been readily corrected by that copy, had not all confidence been destroyed by its being altered in the *Historical Essay*, prefixed to that publication to

> " 'YE LIVE upo' the border ;'

the better," he adds, with his usual candour, " to favour a position, that many of the pipers might live upon the borders, for the conveniency of attending fairs, etc., in both kingdoms." This, however, is an INFAMOUS LYE ; it being much more likely that he himself, who has practised every kind of forgery and imposture, had some such end to alter this identical line, with much more violence, and, as he owns himself, actual "CORRUPTION," to give the quotation an air of antiquity, which it was not entitled to.

The present editor's text is perfectly accurate, to a single comma, but, "this line," as he pretends to apologise for his own, " being quoted (in the *Essay*) from memory," having frequently heard it so sung, in his younger days, by a north country blacksmith, without thinking it necessary, at the moment, to turn to the genuine text, which lay at his elbow, and which his lordship DARE NOT IMPEACH. "Thou hypocrite, first cast out the beam out of thine own eye, and then shalt thou see (more) clearly to cast out the mote out of thy brother's eye " (*Gospel according to* ST. MATTHEW, chap. vii., verse 5).

---

* Scottish poetry, of the fifteenth or sixteenth century, has been so printed, but not that of the eighteenth, unless by impostors.

which are still preserved in public libraries, and a few private collections.

"When we consider," says Mister Warton, "the feudal manners, and the magnificence of our Norman ancestors, their love of military glory, the enthusiasm with which they engaged in the crusades, and the wonders to which they must have been familiarised from those eastern enterprises, we naturally suppose, that their retinue abounded with minstrels and harpers, and that their chief entertainment was to listen to the recital of romantic and martial adventures. But I have been much disappointed in my searches after the metrical tales which must have prevailed in their times. Most of those old heroic songs are perished with the stately castles in whose halls they were sung. Yet they are not so totally lost as we may be apt to imagine. Many of them still partly exist in the old English metrical romances,* yet divested of their original form, polished in their style, adorned with new incidents, successively modernised by repeated transcription and recitation, and retaining little more than the outlines of the original." This, it must be confessed, is not only a just and accurate, but also a beautiful and interesting description of the old English romances. Many, however, in the French language still remain, correct and perfect as they came from the hands of the poet or minstrel, and preserved in contemporary manuscripts, more or less, in most of the public libraries in Europe, being likewise infinitely superior, in point of style and expression, to their translations into English; of the comparative merit whereof it is highly probable our learned historian had a very imperfect idea.

It is no slight honour to ancient romance that so late as the seventeenth century, when it was become superannuated and obsolete, the expansive and enlightened mind of our British Homer was enraptured with the study, as is manifested by frequent and happy allusions in his two principal poems :

> "——— and what redounds
> In fable or romance of Uther's son,
> Begirt with British and Armoric knights,
> And all who since, baptised or infidel,
> Jousted in Aspramont or Montalban,
> Damasco, or Marocco, or Trebisond,
> Or whom Biserta sent from Afric shore,
> When Charlemain with all his peerage fell,
> By Fontarabbia."†

---

* But many more in the French, some of which were actually written in England.

† *P. L. B.*, I., v., 579. "Next," he says, "I betook me among those lofty fables and romances which recount in solemn cantos the deeds of knighthood. . . . So that even those books . . . . proved to me so many inticements to the love and steadfast observation of . . . . virtue. . . ."

See Toland's *Life*, p. 35.

("Though like a covered field, where champions bold
Wont ride in armed, and at the soldans chair
Defied the best of Panim chivalry
To mortal combat or career with lance.")[*]
"Such forces met not, no so wide a camp,
When Agrican, with all his northern powers
Besieged Albracca, as romances tell,
The city of Gallaphrone, from thence to win,
The fairest of her sex, Angelica,
His daughter, sought by many prowest knights,
Both Paynim, and the peers of Charlemane:
Such and so numerous was thir chivalrie." [†]

He had even meditated a metrical romance, or epic poem, upon the story of Arthur, which would, doubtless, have excelled in sublimity and interest everything he has left us, had not his increasing attachment to the puritanical superstition of the times perverted his intention.

" Since first this subject for heroic song
Pleased me long choosing, and beginning late,
Not sedulous by nature to indite
Warrs, hitherto the only argument
Heroic deemed chief maistrie to dissect,
With long and tedious havoc, fabled knights
In battels feigned ;—
Or tilting furnature, emblazoned shields,
Impreses quaint, caparisons and steeds ;
Bases and tinsel trappings, gorgeous knights
At joust and tourneament, then marshaled feast,
Served up in hall with sewers, and seneshals," [‡]

Notwithstanding his religious enthusiasm, he still appears to regard the favourite pursuits of his earlier days with a kind of melancholy sensation :

And casts a long and lingering look behind.

To the above design he himself alludes in his *Epitaphium Damonis*, v., 161, etc.

" *Ipse ego Dardanias Rutupina per æquora puppes
Dicam, et Pandrasidos regnum vetus Inogeniæ,
Brennumque Arviragumque duces, priscumque Belinum,
Et tandem Armoricos Britonum sub lege colonos ;
Tum gravidam Arturo, fatali fraude, Iogernen,
Mendaces vultus assumptaque Gorlois arma,
Merlini dolus.——*"

---

[*] *Ibid.*, v., 762.
[†] *Paradise Regained*, Bk. 3, v., 336. See the *Orlando inamorate* of Boiardo.
[‡] *P. L. B.*, 8 (edition 1667) ; see *Toland's Life*, pp. 16, 17.

So that, it seems, the fabulous history of Geoffrey of Monmouth was to have been the platform of his sublime poetical structure ; but this project, whether wisely or not, he abandoned. Pope likewise had an intention of writing a poem on the subject of *Brutus*.*

§ 4.—MINSTRELS AND MINSTRELSY.

Homer, who, as it hath been already observed, composed romances in Greek verse, was a rhapsodist bard or minstrel, who resorted to feasts, at which he sung his compositions to the lyre. He says of himself, in one of his hymns : " Hail, heavenly powers, whose praises I sing ; let me also hope to be remembered in the ages to come, and when any one, born of the tribe of men, comes hither, a weary traveller, and inquires, Who is the sweetest of singing men that resort to your feasts, and whom you most delight to hear ? then do you make answer for me : It is the blind man that dwels in Chios ; his songs excell all that can ever be sung." †

An anecdote, communicated to Herodotus by the Lesbians, savours, likewise, very strongly of the minstrel character. Arion of Methymna (near three hundred years after Homer), who was second to none of the harpers of his age, and made, and named, and taught, the dithyrambick at Corinth, having desired to sail into Italy and Sicily, and wishing, much money being acquired, to return back to Corinth ; and whereas he was about to go to Tarentum, because he trusted none more than the Corinthians, hired a ship of some of those men. When, therefore, they were out at sea, these conspired against Arion, that, he being got rid of, they might enjoy his money. He, understanding this, prayed, the money being offered to them, that his life might be spared. Not prevailing upon the mariners, they ordered that he should either lay violent hands upon himself, that so he might obtain sepulture upon the shore, or, immediately, leap into the sea. Arion, at this difficulty, besought that forasmuch as such was their pleasure, they would suffer him to sing, standing upon the deck ; and when he should have sung, he promised that he would lay violent hands upon himself. These, therefore (for the desire of hearing the most excellent performer had seized them), retired from

---

* See his *Life*, by Ruffhead.

† Blackwell's *Enquiry into the Life of Homer*, p. 110. Huet to the same purpose observes, " It is necessary to remark, for the honour of the troubadours, that Homer has been one before them, and that he went about reciting his verses from town to town " (*De l'origine des romans*, Paris, 1678, p. 128). Dr. Bentley says, " He wrote a sequel of songs and rhapsodies, to be sung by himself, for small earnings and good cheer, at festivals and other days of merriment ; the *Ilias* he made for the men, and the *Odysseïs* for the other sex. These loose songs were not collected together in the form of an epic poem till Pisistratus's time, about five hundred years after." (*Remarks upon a late Discourse of Free-Thinking*, p. 18). This ancient bard, as it is supposed by some learned men, could neither write nor read.

the poop to the midst of the ship. He, being dressed with every ornament, and the harp taken up, standing upon the deck, awaked the song which is called Orthian; and that being sung, he cast himself, as he was with all his finery, into the sea ; and these, truly, held their course for Corinth ; but he, received, they say, by a dolphin, was carried to Tænarus ; and, when he had descended from the dolphin, he went in that same habit to Corinth, and when he arrived there he related everything that had happened. These things the Corinthians and Lesbians were wont to say ; and there was extant at Tænarus the moderate gift of Arion, in brass, a man above, carried by a dolphin.*

It is highly probable, as Huet has remarked, that other illustrious poets of Greece imitated Homer ; he particularly mentions Simonides, who, he expressly says, exercised the profession of a *trouveur* and *chanteur*.†

The *histriones* of the Romans were theatrical performers, who delivered the oral parts ; the *mimi* dumb actors, who expressed everything by dancing and gestures ; neither of these, of course, bore the least resemblance to a minstrel ; except that it has been suggested by mister Ledwich to doctor Percy upon a reference of Salmasius (Notes to *Historiæ augustæ scriptores*, Paris, 1620, fo. p. 385) ; whence the latter infers that the imitative minstrel of Geoffrey of Monmouth shaved himself by classical authority.†

Both names, however, seem, after the decline of the empire, to have been, erroneously, conferred upon the minstrels or musical performers of those times. Since at least the *mimes*, or jugglers, are allowed, by the laws of James II., King of Majorca, to be lawfully admissible in courts, as their office affords pleasure ; wherefor that prince ordains, that in his palace the number of *mimes* should be *five*, of whom two were to be *trumpeters*, and the third, a *tabourer* ; so that the minstrel who made use of the phrase "*Mimia et cantu victum acquiro*" must, necessarily, have intended two distinct functions.§

Whether the Lombards brought the minstrel arts into Italy, or acquired them from the old inhabitants, is a question of difficult solution : but, in the year 774, it happened that a *joculator*, or juggler, came to Charles the emperour, usually called Charlemagne, and,

---

* Clio., § 24.

† *De l'origine*, etc., as before.

‡ Dio, indeed, in the time of Nero, says, that "It was most filthy and grievous to see, that men and women, not only of the equestrian, but, even, of the senatorial order, entered into the orchestra, and circus, and amphitheatre, like the vilest men ; and some of them sung to pipes, danced, acted tragedies and comedies, sung to the harp, etc. Even Nero himself, frequently at the voice of the common crier, in the habit of a harper, sung to the harp. (Refer to the article *Citharoedos* in the index to Reimar's edition).

§ *Reliques*, etc., I. lxxiv.

turning round in the sight of his followers, sung a song composed by himself.*

Philip Mouskes, in the time of Philip the august, feigns this emperour to have formerly given, to his parasites and mimes or mimicks (*scurris et mimis suis*), the county of Provence; whence, afterward, so great a number of poets grew up in this country :

> " *Quar quant li buen rois Karlemaigne*
> *Ot toute mise à son demaine,*
> Provence, *qui mult iert plentive,*
> *De vins, de bois, d'aigue, de rive,*
> *As* laccours, *as* menestreus,
> *Qui sont au ques luxurieus*
> *Le donna toute & departa.*"†

The anecdote, at the same time, seems to require more ancient testimony than that of Philip Mouskes.

Sainte-Palaye is of opinion that chivalry, considered merely as a ceremony by which young persons, destined to the military profession, received the first arms they were to carry, was known from the time of Charlemagne : but that, regarded as a dignity which gave the first rank in the military order, and which was conferred by a species of investiture, accompanied by certain ceremonies, and a solemn oath, it would be difficult to carry it higher than the eleventh century.‡

Henry I. however, emperour of Germany, surnamed *The fowler*, appears to have established tournaments in 930.§ There is likewise an instance of a just or single combat, on horseback, at Paris, in 978, between Grey-coat, Earl of Anjou, and Bertold, brother to the Duke of Saxony.‖ Chivalry and minstrelsy, it is generally thought, had some sort of connection, and, possibly, a coëtaneous origin ; but little or nothing is known for a certainty respecting the latter, till about a century after the establishment of the former. According to a contemporary historian, Henry III., surnamed *The Black*, or *Blackbeard*, emperour of Germany, celebrating his nuptials with Agnes, daughter of William earl of Poictou, at the town of Ingelenheim, in 1043, permitted an infinite multitude of minstrels and jugglers, to the accumulation of his praise, empty and hungry, without food and rewards, to depart sorrowing.¶

---

* Muratori, *Antiquitates Italiæ*, ii., 2.

† Du Cange, " Ministrellus *et* Lecator."

‡ *Memoires sur l'ancienne chevalerie*, i., 65.

§ See his *Leges Hasti ludiales, sive de torneamentis in Goldasti Imperatorum recessus, Hanoviæ*, 1609, fo. II., 41.

‖ *R. de Diceto*, 459.

¶ *Hermanni Contracti chronicon*. Basileæ 1529, fo. 218, b. John Bromto, abbot of Jervaux, says, that the money which he had been before accustomed to give to the minstrels, he distributed to the poor : but this was robbing Peter to pay Paul.

" The minstrels," as defined by the ingenious and respectable author of an essay on the ancient English ones prefixed to *Reliques of Ancient English Poetry*, were an order of men in the middle ages, who united the arts of poetry and music, and sung verses to the harp of their own composing. They also appear to have accompanied their songs, he says, "with mimicry and action ; and to have practised such various means of diverting as were much admired in those rude times, and supplied the want of more refined entertainments." Thus stood the passage in the first, second, and third editions ; but the learned author not having brought any proof that these characters composed their own songs, and still less that the singers themselves used mimicry and action, it appears in the last edition, thus altered, "who subsisted by the arts of poetry and music, and sang to the harp verses composed by themselves or others." But that those minstrels, who sung to the harp, " accompanied their songs with mimicry and action," still appears to stand in need of authority.

Maistre Wace, in his account of the coronation feast of King Arthur, is careful to enumerate the various orders of minstrelsy, which he supposes to have been present on that occasion :—

> " *Mult ost à la cort* jugleors
> Chanteors, *et* rumenteors.
> Mult *poissez oir* chançons,
> Rotuenges *et* voialx sons,
> Vileors, lais, *et* notex,
> Laiz *de* vieles, lais *de* rotez,
> Laiz *de* harpez, laiz *de* fietalx,
> Lires, tempes, *et* chalemealx
> Symphoniez, psalterious,
> Monacors, *des* cymbes, chorous,
> *Assez i ot* tregetours,
> Joieresses, *et* joicors,
> *Li uns disoent* contes *et* fables, etc."[*]

The manners of a company of minstrels are thus described in an old *fabliau*, probably of the thirteenth century :

> " *Li quens manda les menestrels ;*
> *Et si a fet crier entre els,*
> *Qui la meillor truffe sauroit*
> *Dire, ne faire, qu'il auroit*

---

[*] " . . . Many *juglers* had they at the court, *singers*, and *rimers* ; many *songs* might you hear, *Rote-songs* (see *Fabliaux ou contes*, B, 323), and *vocal songs*, *fiddlers*, *lays* and *notes* ; *Lays* for *fiddles*, lays for rotes, *lays* for harpes, *lays* for *sytols* ; *lyres*, *and corn-pipes* ; *symphonics*, *psalteries*, *monochords*, *cymbals*, *choirs*. Enow there were of *tregetours*, female and male performers (*joueurs*, F.). Some said *tales* and fables, etc."

Sa robe d' escarlate nuove.
L'uns menestrels à l'autre reuve
Fere son mestier tel qu'il sot,
Li uns fet l'yvre, l'autre sot,
Li uns chante, li autre note,
Et li autres dit la riote ;
Et li autres la jenglerie ;
Cil qui sevent de ' jouglerie '
Vielent par devant le conte ;
Aucuns ja qui fabliaus conte ;
Il i ot dit mainte risee, etc."*

In another extract from a romance, written in 1230, we are told
that :

" *Quand les tables ostées furent*
Cil juggleurs in pies esturent
S'ont vielles, et harpes prisées,
Chansons, sons, vers, et reprisés,
Et gestes chanté nos ont."†

The minstrels certainly were not always an order of men "who
united the arts of poetry and music and sung verses to the harp of
their own composing." as the worthy divine who formerly made that
assertion has been compelled to acknowledge.

At the nuptials of Robert. brother to St. Lewis, in 1237, "those
who are called minstrels," according to Alberic, " in this spectacle
of vanity did many things there ; as he who on a horse rode upon a
rope in the air ; and as those who rode two oxen clad in scarlet,
blowing their horns at the several messes which were served up to
the king at table.‡

In the ancient *Roman de Berthe au grand pied*, written by King
Adenés, a well-known poet, so-called, in the thirteenth century, it is
related that during the grand feast given by Pepin on his marriage
there was executed a magnificent concert composed by three min-
strels, of whom one played upon the *vielle* (or fiddle), another upon
the *harp*, and the third upon the *lute*.§

---

* *Fabliaux et contes,* ii., 161. " The count commanded the minstrels, and so he
has caused to be cried among them, that he who should say or do the best gibe
should have his new scarlet robe. Some of the minstrels prayed another to do his
business such as he knew. Some sung, others noted, and others had recourse to
scolding, and others to raillery ; those who knew juglery fiddled before the count
Some they were told *fabliaus*. There was said many a laughable thing."

† " When the tables were taken away, the juglers stood up on their feet, so have
they taken violins and harps, and we had songs, tunes, verses, and reprises, and
gests sung."

‡ " *Illi qui dicuntur ministelli (l. ministrelli) in spectaculo vanitatis multa ibi*
fecerunt, sicut ille qui in equo super cordam in aere equitabat, et sicut illi qui
duos boves de scarlate vestitos equitabant cornutantes ad singula fercula quæ appone-
bantur regi in mensa."—*Chro.,* p. 462 ; *Memoires sur l'ancienne chevalerie,* i.,
245. I.

§ *Bib. des Romans* Avril, 1777, p. 147.

It is certain that many persons in France bore the title of "*Roy de ministraux*," instances whereof are given by Du Cange; but, in England, though Anstis has mentioned several *minstrels* who are distinguished by the title of *king* (as *Rex Robertus ministrallus,* etc. in the time of King Edward I.), none of them is expressly called *rex ministrallorum* or *King of the minstrels* (except John Caumz, king of Richard II.'s, in 1387); neither does his *Rex juglatorum* belong to this country. Adenés, a celebrated poet, who lived in the thirteenth century, says of himself, in one of his romances:

> "*Ce livre de* Cleomades
> *Rimé je le* roy Adenez,
> Menestre *au bon* duc Henry:"

meaning, it seems, Henry Duke of Brabant, who died in 1247. He elsewhere calls himself *Roy Adenés* and is so called by others; but still the reason is unknown. Pasquier is quite at a loss to account for the word *king* as applied to a *minstrel;* remarking only that the word *jouingleur* (*jouglerie*) had, by succession of time, turned into *slight-of-hand*. "We have seen," he says, "in our youth the *jouingleurs* meet at a certain day every year, in the town of Chauny in Picardy, to shew their profession before the people, who could do best; and this," adds he, "that I here say of them is not to depreciate these ancient *rimers*, but to shew that there is nothing so beauteous which is not annihilated with time:"* where, by the way, he seems, by the expression "*anciens rimeurs*," to allude rather to what they had formerly been, than to what they were in his own time, when, as he has already told us, they were sunk into mere *jugglers.*

That the different professors of minstrelsy were, in ancient times, distinguished by names appropriated to their respective pursuits, cannot reasonably be disputed, though it may be difficult to prove.

The *trouveur, trouverre,* or *rymour,* was he who composed *romans, contes, fabliaux, chansons,* and *lais;* and those who confined themselves to the composition of *contes* and *fabliaux,* obtained the appellation of *conteurs, conteours,* or *fabliers.* The *menetrier, menestrel,* or minstrel, was he who accompanied his song by a musical instrument, both the words and the melody being occasionally furnished by himself, and occasionally by others.† The *jogelour, jougleor,*‡ *jugleor, jogelere,* or jugler, amused the spectators with slight-of-hand tricks, cups and balls, etc.

---

* *Recherches*, etc., Paris, 1633, fo. p. 611.

† Le Grand distinguishes the *menestrier* who played and sung from the *menestrel* who was the chief or head of the troop; but without being able to adduce any authority for proving such a distinction.

‡ Not *jongleur*, as the ignorant or inattentive French printers of the fifteenth century, who could not, it is probable, read the manuscripts, and mistook the *u* for an *n*, there being, in fact, little or no distinction between them, uniformly orthographised it; and as every French author, historian commentator, etymologist, glossarist, or dictionary-maker, with the whole herd of copyists and printers, from

Again, in *The Frere's Tale*, v. 7049 :
          " A lousy *jogelour* can deceiven thee."

This appears clear from the conduct of John de Raumpayne, who,
when he sets out to deceive Moris of Whitington, takes with him a
male, which contains his jugleries, and out of which, most likely, he
had already so blackened, inflated, and deformed his visage, that
his most intimate acquaintance did not know him.   The *chanteour*,
or *chanterre*, was one who sang ; the *vielere* or *harpere*, he who
accompanied the *chanterre*, when he did not perform himself, and
would be called indifferently by either name, or the general one of
minstrel, etc.   A *histrio*, or mimus, should properly have been the
buffoon of a play, as he was among the Romans ; but these names,
in fact, appear to have been given by affected pedants, who mistook
their meaning.   There were, likewise, *flutours*, *timbesteres*, and
sailours, dancers, all three mentioned by Chaucer in his translation
of *Romant of the Rose*, v. 762, etc.

          " There mightist thou se these *flutours*,
          Minstrallis and eke *jogelours*,
          That well to singin did ther paine—
          There was many a *timbestere*,
          And *sailours*, that i dare well swere,
          Ycothe ther craft full parfitly
          The *timbris* up full subtilly
          Thei castin, and hent them full oft
          Upon a finger faire and soft."

---

that time to the present, have constantly written, printed, etymologised and explained
it.   In every manuscript, however, French or Norman, of the thirteenth or four-
teenth century, or, at least, wherever the *u* occurs, and can be distinguished from
an *n*, it is uniformly written *jougleour*, or *jougleor* (*Roman de Troye*, Harley MS.
4482), but generally without a *u* *joglere* (*Roman de Fitz-Guarine*, in the king's MS.
12, c. xii.), and frequently without an *o*, as jugleour (Harley MS. 2253), *jugclere* (*Le
Brut, passim*).   Many hundred of such instances could have been easily added, but
the scrupulous reader had better consult the originals.   The same propriety was
observed in England, where the corrupt orthography, *jongler*, has never been
made use of, either in manuscript or print, till within these few years, and pro-
bably for the first time in the *Reliques of Ancient English Poetry*.   Thus in Davies'
Lyf of Alysander:
          " The minstrelles synge, the *jogelours* carpe."
Again in Robert Mannyngs translation from Peter of Bridlington.
          " *Jogelours* were there inouh."
But though he names both, he does not give them several employments.   *Carp-
ing* seems synonymous to *singing ;* though it is said above—
          " The *minstrels sing*, the *jogelours carpe ;*"
and may, therefore, imply *talking* or *reciting*.
     Again in Chaucer's *Romant of the Rose*, v. 764—
          " *Ministrallis* and eke *jogelours*.'
All evidently and immediately from the Latin *joculator*.   He is however, in other
places, repeatedly called a *jogelor*.   Carpentier, says Warton, mentions a joculator
qui sciebat tombare , a *jugler* who knew how to tumble (I.G).

The *farceurs*, or buffoons, were, possibly, the proper *histriones* or *mimi*, who acted ridiculous and burlesque dramas of a single part, whence the term *farce* is still used for a short and laughable entertainment ; *baladins* or *dancers; tabourers*, or *tabereres*, who performed on the tabour or tabourine :* and, peradventure, several other distinctions. All these, however, in process of time, appear to have been confounded under the common name of minstrels or juglers, and by Latin writers, *ministri, ministrelli, joculatores, histriones, mimi, leccatores, scurræ, vaniloqui, citharistæ or citharædæ, cantores, or cantatores, parasitæ, famelici, nebulones, epulones*, and the like.

Their peculiar appellations, however, may doubtless have been preserved among themselves, without being much attended to by those who only considered them as a body of men whose profession was to please ; or, at least, by their own corruption in later times, when one did all, and the whole system sunk into insignificance and contempt.

" Sometimes," says Fontenelle, "during the repast of a prince, you would see arrive an unknown *trouverre*, with his minstrels or juglers, and make them sing, upon their harps or violins, the verses which he had composed ; those who made the *sounds* as well as the *words*, being the most esteemed."†

Le Grand having already spoken of these troops of rambling musicians, who in the great feasts, in the plenary courts, and at marriages ran together to amuse the nobility, says, " This profession, which misery, libertinism, and the vagabond life of this sort of people, have much decried, required, however, a multiplicity of attainments and of talents, which one would, at this day, have some difficulty to find reunited, and who has much more right to be astonished, moreover, in the ages of ignorance : for beside all the songs, old and new, beside the current anecdotes, the tales, and *fabliaux*, which they piqued themselves upon knowing ; beside the romances of the time, which it behoved them to know, and to possess in part, they could declaim, sing, compose in music, play on several instruments and accompany them. Frequently, even, were they authors, and made themselves the pieces which they uttered.

---

* In an old *fabliau*, in the Harleian MS. 2253, a minstrel setting out from London and meeting the king,

> " *Entour son col porta soun* tabour
> *Depeynt de ore riche acour.*"

The king, who addresses him with "*sire* joglour," is treated with very little ceremony. Fauchet remembered to have seen Martin Baraton (then old minstrel of Orleans), who at feasts and nuptials beat a tabour (tabourin) of silver, set with plates, also of silver, graven with the armorial bearings of those whom he had taught to dance (*Recueil*, p. 73). " Here," observes doctor Percy, " we see that a minstrel performed sometimes the function of a dancing-master " (p. xlviii).

† *Histoire du theatre.*

6

"In fine, there were some who, to all these talents, joined the science of the cork-balls, of juglery, and of all the tricks known." *

The following curious narrative of these singular characters is related in an old *fabliau :* "Two troops of minstrels met in a castle, and willed to amuse the lord by a quarrel. One said he could tell tales (conter) in *Romance* (*i.e.*, French), and *Latin*. He knew more than forty *lays* and *songs* of *gests*, and all the songs you could possibly ask for. He knew, also, the romances of *adventure*, and in particular those of the *round table*. He knew, in fact, how to SING a great many romances, such as *Vivien*, *Reynaud* (r *Oger*), *le Danois*, etc., and to TELL *Floris* and *Blancheflower*. He finished the enumeration of his talents by some pleasantries ; and pretended that if he had taken to the profession he followed, it was not that he had not many others to procure him a considerable fortune ; for he knew very well how to hoop an egg, to bleed cats, to cup an ox, and cover houses with omelettes, etc., and if anyone would give him two harps, he felt himself capable of producing music such as no one ever heard the like. At length, after some new insults, he advised the minstrel whom he had attacked to go out of the castle without further trouble : despising him too much to dishonour himself and his comrades by striking a man so contemptible. This fellow undervalued him in his turn, and demanded of him how he dared to say he was a good minstrel who knew neither pleasant tales nor *dits*. As for me, said he, I am not one of these ignoramuses whose whole talent is to play the cat, the fool, the drunken man, or to say foolish things to their comrades ; I am of the number of these good *trouverres*, who invent all that they say :

> "*Ge suis* juglere *de* viele ;
> *Si sai de* muse *et de* frestele,
> *Et de* harpe, *et de* chiphonie
> De la gigue, *de l'*armonie,
> *E el* salteire, e en *la* rote."†

I know how to sing a song; I know tales, I know *fabliaux*, I know how to tell fine new *dits*, *rotruenges* ‡ old and new, and *sirvantes* and pastorals; I know how to counsel love, and to make chaplets of flowers; and a girdle for lovers ; and to speak courteously." After this detail of his talents, as the musician

---

* A., 47.

† "I am a player of the *violin*,
    So know I the *bagpipe*, and the *frestele*
    And the *harp*, and the *symphony*,
    The *gig*, the *harmony*,
    And the *psaltery* and the rote."
  The translation of the whole passage was so absurdly faulty, I have been compelled to alter it considerably.—E.G.

‡ A species of song sung to the rote.

and fine fellow, he passes to those which he has for the tricks of
dexterity, and the play of cork-ball (*a song*) ; " Well know I the cork-
ball ; and to make the beetle come alive and dancing on the table ;
and so I know many a fair table game the result of dexterity and
magic ; well I know how to make an enchantment ; I know how to play
with the cudgels ; and so I know how to play with the cutlasses ; and
with the cord, and the rope." He boasts himself to know all *the
songs of gests* which the first knew ; he knows all the good serjeants,
and renowned champions of his time ; and the most celebrated
minstrels, to whom he gives ridiculous nick-names. In fine, ad-
dressing himself to his rival, he advises him, if he have a little shame,
never to enter into the places where he shall know him : "And you,
sir," says he, "if I have spoken better than he, I pray you to put
him out of doors, and thus prove to him that he is a sot." *

The musical instruments of the French minstrels were chiefly the
viele,† the *clavicorde*, the *rote*,‡ the *tabour*, and others, it is pro-
bable, not only to accompany the voice, but to perform sprightly airs,
and exhilarate the lively dance.

None of the minstrel melodies, or chants, are supposed to be now
existing, unless, it is possible, in some ancient manuscript of the
French National Library. Sainte Palaye, in fact, says that the
beautiful tale of *Aucassin and Nicolette* occurs in a MS. near five
hundred years old, and that what was preceded by the words "on
chante," was set to music, but whether the poetical part be in the
minstrel-metre does not clearly appear. The *Chansons du chatelain
de Coucy*, in 1200, likewise *Du roy de Navarre*, have been printed
with the original music. It is a plain chant, in square notes, ranged
upon four lines, under the clef C. *sol ut* (*Fabliaux ou contes*, A. 48).§

Some idea of the dress or manners of a French minstrel in the
fourteenth century may be conceived from the following anecdote :
" A yonge man cam to a feste, where were many lordes, ladyes, and
damoysels, and arrayed as they wold have sette them to dyner, and
had on hem a coote hardye after the manner of Almayne. He cam
and salewed the lordes and ladyes, and whan he had done to them
reverence, syre Geffroy (de Lyege) called hym before hym, and
demanded hym where his *vyell* or *clavycordes* were, and that he
should make his craft : and the yonge man answered, Syre, I cannot

---

* Le Grand, B., 313, etc. Those who, in the north of England, cheat the poor
ignorant graziers, farmers, and horse-cosers, who come to the fair, by the delusion
of the cork-ball, are called *thimblers*.

† Doctors Percy and Burney mistake this for the *rote* or *mandolin* (*Reliques*, I.,
lxxv) ; but that it was clearly the *violin* is proved by M. Le Grand (*Fabliaux ou
contes*, A. 49 ; B. 319). Fauchet writes it " viole."

‡ The *rote*, from *rota*, a wheel, in modern French *vielle*, and in vulgar English
hurdy-gurdy, which is seen so frequently both in Paris and London in the hands
of Savoyards.

§ I presume Ritson means the clef of C.—E. G.

medle therwith. Haa, said the knyght, I cannot byleve it ; for ye be contrafaytted and clothed lyke a *mynystrell.*" *

"Helgaud, the lord of Joinville, and other authors, remark," according to Du Cange, "that at these solemn feasts were made public banquets where the kings eat in the presence of their whole suite, and were there served by the great officers of the crown, and of the Hotel,† every one according to the function of his charge. There was with them the divertisements of the *minstrels* ("*des* menestrels *ou des* menetriers"). Under this name were comprised those who played with the *nakairs*, with the *demicanon*, with the *cornet*, with *guiterne Latine*, with the *fluste Behaigne*, with the *trompette*, with the *guiterne Moresche*, and with the *vieille;* which are all named in an account of the hotel of the duke of Normandy and Guienne of the year 1348." A curious species of concert, no doubt ; though there be not a single minstrel of them who "sings" to the harp songs of his own making. "They had, moreover," he says, "*far-ceurs, jongleurs* (*rectius* jougleurs) (*joculatores*), and *plaisantins,* who should divert the companys by their jokes and their comedys, for the entertainment of whom the kings, the princes, and the simple Lords, made such prodigous expences, that they gave occasion to Lambert *d' Ardres*, and to the cardinal James *de Vitry*, to inveigh against these superfluities of their time, which had ruined whole families : which St. Augustine had done before them, in these terms : "*Donare res suas* histrionibus, *vitium est immane, non virtus. Illa sanies Romæ recepta, et favoribus aucta, tandem collabefecit bonos mores, et civitates perdidit, coëgitque imperatores saepius eos expellere.*"‡

With respect to the melody, or intonation, to which the French metrical romances were usually sung, being accompanied by some musical instrument, either in the hands of the singer, or in those of his companion, it is conjectured to have been little or nothing else than a sort of recitative, or chant, the performer sustaining his voice,

* *The booke of thenseynementes and techynge that the knights of the towre made to his doughters* (translated and printed by Caxton), c., 115.

† This useful dissyllable, HOSTEL, we obtained from the French soon after the Norman conquest ; and it remains with its old anglicised pronunciation, *hostel,* in the University of Cambridge to this day, but having become obsolete, for some centuries, in every other place it has lately returned to us *à la mode de la France moderne,* and is written and pronounced *hôtel.*

‡ *Dissertation* v. *sur* Joinville, 161. Warton, who professes to give this very passage, and cites this very page, instead of 1348, says "before the year 1300." The *nakair* he explains "the *kettledrum,*" and the demi-canon "the flagellet" ; for what reason does not appear. *Nacaires* is explained by Du Cange (*Observations sur l'histoire,* 59) to mean a kind of *tambour,* which is in use among the German cavalry, which the French call, vulgarly, *tymbales.* There was some essential difference, it may be fairly presumed, between the *histriones* of King Philip de Valois' time and those of St. Augustine. John of Salisbury reprobates those of his own age who, for the redeeming their fame, and extending their name, threw away their riches on "*histriones et mimos*" (Epis. 247).

as the ingenious mister Walker has expressed it, "with arpeggios swept over the strings of his harp." *

Almost all the French poets of the twelfth and thirteenth century, according to M. Laborde, composed the airs of their songs, but these airs were nothing more than the Gregorian chant; and even it was often merely the chants of the church, which they parodied.†

This kind of chant or recitative continued in use upon the French stage even to a late period. Voltaire, having observed it to be highly probable that the *Melopée*, regarded by Aristotle, in his *Poeticks*, as an essential part of tragedy, was an even and simple chant, like that of the *preface to the mass*, which is, in his opinion, the Gregorian chant, and not the Ambrosian, but which is a true *melopée*, adds, that "when the Italians revived tragedy in the sixteenth century, the recitation was a *melopée*, but which could not be noted ; for who can note inflexions of the voice, which are eighteenths or sixteenths of tone ? They were learned by heart. This usage was received in France, when the French began to form a theatre, above a century after the Italians."

The *Sophonisba* of Mairet was chanted like that of Trissino, but more rudely. All the parts of the actors, but especially of the actresses, were noted *memoriter* by tradition. Mademoiselle Bauval, an actress of the time of Corneille, of Racine, and of Molière, recited to me, more than sixty years ago, the beginning of the part of *Emilie* in *Cinna* such as it had been delivered in the first representations by Beaupré.‡

All this, it must be confessed, will not be apt to convey a very correct or conspicuous idea of the musical performances of a French minstrel ; it is, nevertheless, by no means improbable that there was a considerable degree of resemblance ; but the misfortune is, that no historian or other writer, who flourished in the time of the minstrels, has ever thought them deserving of much attention. The author of *Gerard de Rousillon* says, at the commencement of his romance, that he has made it upon the model of *The song of Antioch*, that is, as Le Grand conceives, he wrote it in the same measure, and sung it to the same tune.§

About the commencement of the fifteenth century the profession of minstrel was rapidly declining ; and before its expiration, was to all appearance totally extinct, except it may be in a few instances,

---

* *Historical memoires of the Irish bards*, p. 17. Cormac Common, a blind *fins-gealaighthe*, or tale-teller of the modern Irish, living in 1786, at the age of eighty-three, of whom this gentleman has, in his appendix to that interesting work, inserted a curious account, did not, like the tale-teller mentioned by Sir William Temple, chant his tales in an uninterrupted even tone : the monotony of his modulation was frequently broken by cadences introduced with taste at the close of stanza. " In rehearsing any of Ossian's poems (which in Ireland are genuine and ancient), or any composition in verse, (says mister) now Sir William (Ousley), he chants them pretty much in the manner of our Cathedral-service" (p. 57).

† *Essai sur la musique*, ii., 146 (note).

‡ *Questions sur l' Encyclopédie*, Chant, Musique, etc. § 13, 317.

where common fiddlers, or the like, might retain the name. No
metrical romance, however, appears to have been composed or sung
in any part of France after the fourteenth century, nor is the least
mention made, or notice taken, of a profession which had made so
much noise in the kingdom during the three preceding ones. The
old rhyming romances had already been begun to be converted into
prose ; in which many others, upon the same or similar subjects,
were now composed by a very different set of authors ; many of
whom, however, are not entirely devoid of merit ; though Warton,
with great reason, considers the change among the French as " a
proof of the decay of invention."

Most of these prose romances, after the invention of printing, made
their appearance in large and beautiful folios and quartos, which are
at present become very rare, but are still eagerly pursued by collec-
tors, and highly esteemed by those who are fortunate enough to
possess them. The national library at Paris is peculiarly rich in
this species of literary treasure.

It certainly may be presumed there were in the last age of the Saxon
kingdom men who professed and exercised the minstrel-art. King
Edgar, about the year 960, enjoined in one of his canons, that
no priest should be an *ale-drinker*, nor, in any wise, a *minstrel*
(zliyize, Saxon ; *scurra*, Latin,—properly a parasite) either by himself
or with others ;* and in his oration to St. Dunstan grieves that the
houses of clerks were become a brothel of *whores*, and a *conciabulum*
of *minstrels* (*histriones*); and says, in the same oration, that the
mimi SING and DANCE :† this, however, is, most probably, a term of
the historian's time, and not of the king's, and, therefore, not of
equal authority.

According to Ingulph, King Alfred feigning himself to be jugler
(*joculatorem*), a harp being taken up, went to the tents of the Danes,
and being received into the more secret places, learning all the secrets
of his enemies, when he had satisfied his desire, unknown and safe,
returned to Athelney : and now, his army being collected, having
suddenly attacked, he slew his enemies with incredible slaughter.

King Godrum (whom we call Gurmound), with a very great
multitude of noblemen and also of his people, taken alive, received
baptism, and being taken out of the sacred font by the king, was
endowed with East-England, that is Norfolk, to inhabit with his
people, by the royal gift. The rest refusing to be baptised, England
being abjured, sought France in a ship.‡

---

* Spelman's *Concilia*, i., 228.   † Spelman's *Concilia*, i., 246.

‡ 26. William Malmesbury, who enlarges this anecdote and differs in some
respects from Ingulph, whom, however, it is certain he had made use of, being not
only a less ancient authority, but even adopting several of his words which would
not otherwise have occurred to him, at the same time, describes Alfred's disguise
as that of a mime or mimic (*mimus*), though, apparently, a synonymous term.

So that Malmesbury, a very honest and faithful historian upon most occasions,
is, in this, a mere copyist, and the echo of Ingulphus. It is certainly a somewhat

This defeat of the Danes and subsequent baptism of Gormund took place in the year 878.* Athelstan, the son of Edward, began to reign in the year 924, and held the kingdom sixteen years. His

suspicious adventure. It is mentioned neither by Asser, not only the contemporary but also the chaplain and confessor, and even the biographer of Alfred, nor in the Saxon chronicle, nor by Henry of Huntingdon, nor Simeon of Durham, nor Roger de Hoveden, all of whom, however, notice the battle in which Godrum was defeated and his final conversion ; nor, in fact, by any other ancient or authentic writer, except the two already cited. It militates still more forcibly against such a romantic and improbable incident that a pious, warlike, honourable and glorious monarch, who conquered his enemies in the field and not by treachery, should assume the infamous character of a spy.[1] It is not less extraordinary, at the same time, that Geoffrey of Monmouth, the contemporary of Malmesbury, who never saw his book, has introduced a third actor of the same foolery by the name of Baldulph, a Saxon, who, having been defeated by the Britons under the command of Cador, Duke of Cornwall, and anxious to relieve or speak with his brother, Colgrin, who was besieged in York by Arthur, "shaved his hair and beard, and took the habit with the harp of a jugler (*joculatoris*). Then walking up and down within the camp, by the musical notes he composed on his lyre, he showed himself to be a harper ; and when he was suspected of no man, he approached to the walls of the city, effecting his commenced simulation by little and little. At last, when he was found by the besieged, he was drawn up by ropes within the walls, and conducted to his brother " (B. 9, c. 1).[2] Though, in reality, there is scarcely a single word of truth in this pretended history, yet every flagrant impostor is sure, at some time or other, to obtain belief, favour, and justification. " Although the above fact," according to a right reverend prelate, who mixes his romance with his history, it must be confessed in a very pleasing and ingenious manner, especially for those who are quite indifferent to truth or falsehood, " comes only from the suspicious pen of Geoffrey of Monmouth, the judicious reader will not too hastily reject it ; because if such a fact really happened, it could only be known to us through the medium of British writers. . . . And Geoffrey, with all his fables, is allowed to have recorded many true events that have escaped other annalists " (*Essay on the Ancient Minstrels*, xxvi.) Now it is certain that this impudent forger, bishop as he was, lived, according to his own fanciful chronology, about six hundred years after King Arthur. Who then are " the British writers," through whose " medium" these absurd and monstrous lies "could only be known to us " ? Is it Nennius ? Is it Gildas ? Is it any newly-invented British historiographer, who has never yet been heard of? Who are they, likewise, if not fools, knaves, or madmen, who have followed this rank forger, and impostor, "with all his fables, . . . to have recorded many true events that have escaped other annalists "? Where is there any one such event to be found throughout his ample legend ? And how is it possible, with this inconsistent admission, that the " events recorded " by Geoffrey, "with all his fables," can be ascertained to be true ?

* Asser, 34, and the Saxon chronicle. The veracious Geoffrey, as we have already seen, makes this Gormund King of the Africans, "who had arrived in Ire-

[1] If "the Anglo-Saxons had such strong prejudice against the minstrels " as is supposed in the *Essay on the English* ones (lxxii.), is it at all probable that such a profession would have been permitted to exist among them? Neither Alfred, nor Anlaf, did anything more than play on the harp.

[2] *Maistre* Wace adds a certain circumstance to Geoffrey's account, which is very whimsical :

> Al sege a lui cume jugelere,
> Si se feiust kil esteit harpere
> Il aveit apris à chanter
> E lais e notes à harper,
> Par aler parler à son frere.
>
> Si fist par mi la barbe rere,
> E le chef par me ensement
> E un des germuns sulement,
> Ben sembla lecheur e fol."
>
> Le Brut.

last battle was with Analaf,* the son of Sithrick, who, in the hope of
invading the realm, had passed over the boundaries ; and Athelstan
advisedly yielding, that he might the more gloriously conquer him
who now insulted, the youth, greatly daring, and breathing in his
mind illicit thoughts, had proceeded very far into England, at length
by the great skill of his generals, and great force of soldiers, was met
at Bruneford.† He who discerned so great a danger to impend at-
tempted a benefit by the art of a spy ; and having put off his royal
ensigns, and taken in his hand a harp, proceeded to the tent of our
king ; where, as he was singing before the doors, he would occasion-
ally also shake the strings with a sweet irregularity, he was easily
admitted, professing himself a mime (or mimic, *mimus*), who by such
kind of art earned his daily stipend. The king and his guests he
for some little time gratified with his musical performance : though
during his singing and playing, he examined all things with his eyes.
After ;that satiety of eating had put an end to pleasures, and the
severity of administering the war began afresh in the discourse of
the peers ; he being ordered to depart, received the price of his
song ; which loathing to carry away, he hid under him in the earth.
This was observed by some one, who had formerly been a soldier,
and immediately told it to Athelstan. He, blaming the man, for
that he had not seized an enemy placed before his eyes, received
this answer : " The same oath, which I lately, O King, made to thee,
I formerly gave to Anlaf ; which if thou hadst seen me violate in
myself, thou might'st also beware of a like example regarding thy-
self. But deign to hear the advice of a servant, that thou remove
thy tent hence, and remaining in another place until the parties left
shall come, thou wilt disappoint the enemy, petulantly insulting by
modest delay." The speech being approved, he thence departed.‡
    After all, it is highly probable that those three anecdotes of
Baldulph, Alfred and Anlaf, have been derived and improved from a
story related by *Saxo-Grammaticus*, the Danish historian, who died
in 1204, upon the authority, no doubt, of some ancient *saga*, con-
cerning an adventure of Hother, King of Sweden and Denmark,

---

land with a very great fleet, and had subdued that country (B. II., c., 8) ; this, too,
may be one of the many true events that have escaped other annalists."
    * More correctly, it is conceived, *Aulaf* or *Olave.* He is, however, generally
called *Anlaf* by our ancient historians.
    † Or *Brunanburgh,* a town upon the Humber, now unknown ; but certainly not,
as Camden absurdly conjectures, *Bromeridge* in Northumberland. Robert Mannyng
says expressly : " *At Brunesburgh* on *Humber* thei gan tham assaile" (p. 31).
    ‡ W. of Malmesbury, 48. Anlaf, unconscious of the change which has taken
place in the situation of the king's tent, makes his attempt in the night, and slays
the whole family he found in the place where he had performed his minstrelsy and
been entertained. He then penetrates to the real tent of Athelstan, who was indulg-
ing in rest ; and making what exertions he was able, his sword falls out of the
sheath, he is relieved by a miracle, and in the morning obtains a decisive victory.
The whole story, therefore, is nothing more than a legend and a lie.

who, at a certain time, as he was hunting, misled by the error of
a cloud, fell into the cave of the Sylvestrian virgins, of whom
being saluted by his own name, he inquired who they were.
These virgins affirmed that by their conduct and their auspices,
they chiefly governed the fortune of wars. For, oftentimes
they were present in battles, seen by no man, to afford by secret
aids the wished-for successes to their friends ;* and exhorting
him not to harass Balder, the son of Othin (although worthy of the
most deadly hatred) by arms ; affirming him to be a demi-god,
procreated by the secret seed of superior beings. These things
being received, Hother, in a swoon, by the roof of a falling house,
beheld himself in the open air, and destitute of all cover, exposed on
a sudden in the midst of fields. But he chiefly wondered at the
swift flight of the damsels, and the versatile site of the place, and the
delusive figure of the house. For he was ignorant that the things
which had been done about him were nothing but mockery, and the
vain device of juggling arts. But Hother, harassed by his unfor-
tunate wars with Balder, having wandered into remote and devious
ways of places, and passed through a forest unaccustomed to mortals,
found the cave inhabited, peradventure, by the unknown virgins
They appeared to be the same who had formerly given him an im-
penetrable vest ; by whom being asked why he came thither of all
places, he declared the fatal events of war. Therefore their faith
being condemned (or their promise violated), he began to bewail the
fortune and sorrowful chances of things unhappily conducted. But
the nymphs said that he himself, although he were rarely victor,
nevertheless poured in equal mischief upon the enemies, nor had he
been the author of less slaughter than his accomplice. Hencefor-
ward the grace of the victory in readiness would be his, if he could
snatch a meat of a certain unusual sweetness, invented to augment
the force of Balder. For nothing to be done would be difficult, so
long as he should enjoy the victuals destined to the enemy for the aug-
mentation of his strength.

Therefore, arriving at the camp of the enemies, he knew that the
three nymphs, bearers of the secret meat, had departed from the
camp of Balder : whom hastily following (for their footsteps in the
dew betrayed their flight), he, at length, came to the houses to
which they had accustomed themselves. Therefore, being asked by
these nymphs what he was, he said he was a harper. Nor was the
experiment dissonant to his profession : for, tuning the harp he had
brought, with inflected strings, to a song, and the chords being com-
posed by the quill, he poured forth a melody grateful to the ears by the
most prompt modulation. As to the rest, three female snakes were
with them, with the poison thereof they were wont to make a dish
of solidative confection for Balder : and much poison now flowed from

---

* These nymphs seem to have been the *valkyriur* of the *Edda*, and the three
weird (or wizard) sisters of Macbeth.

the open jaws of the snakes. But some of the nymphs, also, studious of humanity, would have acquainted Hother with the meat, if the chief of the three had not forbid it, protesting that a fraud would be done to Balder, if they should augment his very enemy with the increase of corporeal strength. He said he was not Hother, but a companion of Hother, and, therefore, these nymphs gave him a girdle of exquisite splendour, and the potent zone of victory. On a future day Balder renewed the battle, and the third being elapsed, too much excruciated with the wound he had before received, was utterly destroyed. *

In the time of William the Conqueror, Berdic, the king's jugler (*joculator regius*), had three vils, and there five carucates, in Gloucestershire without rent ;† but the nature of his office or employment is not ascertained ; nor does the existence of this man after the conquest afford any proofs, " that the minstrel was a regular and stated officer in the court of our Anglo-Saxon kings."‡ Though the minstrels are, elsewhere, said to have been considered in a very unfavourable light " by the Anglo-Saxon clergy."§

One Royer, or Raher, the first founder of the hospital of St. Bartholomew, in London, is designed by Leland the mime or mimic (*mimus*) of King Henry I.||

And that *mimus* is properly a minstrel is proved by an extract in the *History of English Poetry*,¶ from the accounts of the priory of Maxtock, near Coventry, in 1441 : "*Dat. sex* minis *domini Clynton* cantantibus, citharisantibus, ludentibus, etc. iiii, f." In his legend, cited by doctor Percy, from the *Monasticon*, "his minstrel profession," it appears, "is not mentioned : there is only a general indistinct account that he frequented royal and noble houses, where he ingratiated himself *suavitate joculari*."** Hence Stow, who cites no authority, describes himself as " A man of a singular and pleasant wit, and therefore of many called the king's jester or minstrel ;"†† and Deloné, in the *History of Thomas of Reading*, says that he " was a great musician and kept a company of MINSTRELS, *i.e.* FIDDLERS, who played with silver bows."‡‡

King Henry may have had a harper named Galfrid or Jeffrey, who, in 1180, received a corrody or annuity from the Abbey of Hide: but as we by no means know that " in the early times every harper was

---

* *Historia danica*, L. 3, p. 39, 43.
† Domesday Book, fo. 162, co. I.
‡ *Reliques*, I., xxviii.
§ *Ibid.*, lv. (edition 1775).
|| Leland's *Collectanea*, i., 61, 112. In another part of the same work is this entry : " *Prioratus S. Bartolomei de Smethefeld.* Henricus I., fundator procurante Raherio, ejus fideli CLERICO " (ibid. 99).
¶ II., 109, n.q.
** *Reliques*, I., lxxxi.
†† *Annales*, 1592, 186, *Survey*, 1598, 308.
‡‡ Hawkins, iii., 85.

expected to sing," we may reasonably doubt that this reward was
given him for his songs, as well as for his music,* and still more that
it was " undoubtedly on condition that he should serve the monks in
the profession of a harper on public occasions."†

To show what John of Salisbury, in the reign of King Henry II.,
thought of this numerous body of men, it will be necessary to adduce
his own words, and for certain nameless reasons, after the laudable
example of the worthy historian of English poetry,who has furnished us
with the extract, to give them in Latin. " At cam (*desidiam*)," says
he, " *nostris prorogant* histriones *Admissa sunt ergo* spectactula, *et
infinita lenocinia vanitatis.—Hinc mimi salii, vel* saliares, bala-
trones, æmiliani, gladiatores, palæstritæ, gignadii, præstigiatores,
malefici quoque multi, et tota joculatorum scena *procedit.
Quorum adeo error invaluit, ut à* præclaris domibus *non areantur
etiam illi, qui* obscœnis partibus corporis, oculis *omnium eam in-
gerunt* turpitudinem, *quam erubescet videre vel cynicus. Quodque*
magis *mirere, nec* tunc *ejiciuntur*, quando *tumultuantes inferius
crebro sonitu aërem fœdant, et, turpiter inclusum turpius pro-
dunt.*"‡

In the reign of this king, William surnamed Longchamp, a
Frenchman, Bishop of Ely, or his chancellor, great justiciary, and
according to the language of modern times, prime minister, who did
not understand a word of English, and was a monster of vice and
iniquity, " to the augmentation," as we learn from a contemporary
epistle of Hugh, Bishop of Coventry, "and fame of his name, pur-
chased begged songs and adulatory rimes and had enticed with
rewards, out of the kingdom of France, singers and juglers, that they
might sing of him in the streets : and now was it everywhere said,
that there was not such a one in the world."§

Geoffrey of Vinesauf says that when Richard arrived at the Chris-
tian camp before Ptolemais, he was received with POPULAR SONGS
(*populares cantiones*), which recited THE FAMOUS GESTS OF THE
ANCIENTS (*Antiquorum præclara gesta*).‖ These, apparently
were parts of metrical romances, and must have been in French.

Ela, the wife of William Longespee the first, was born at Ambres-
bury, her father and mother being Normans. Her father, therefore,
being decayed with old age, migrated to Christ, in the year of the
Lord 1196 ; her mother dyed two years before. . . . In the mean-
time the most dear lady was secretly by her relations conveyed into

* *Reliques*, etc., I., xxvii.
† Warton, i., 92.
‡ II., 205, n.
§ Benedictus, 702. Mister Warton, who, at first, mistook this act of William,
Bishop of Ely, for that of the king himself, a mistake which the more accurate
Tyrwhitt taught him to correct, adds, of his own accord, that "These gratuities
were chiefly arms, cloaths, horses, and sometimes money " (I., 113, II., 62 b).
‖ Warton, I., 62 b.

Normandy, and there brought up under safe and straight custody. In the same time in England was a certain knight, by name William Talbot, who assumed the habit of a pilgrim, passed over into Normandy, and stayed for two years, wandering here and there, to find out the lady Ela of Salisbury : and she being found, he put off the habit of a pilgrim, and dressed himself as if he were a harper, and entered the court where she stayed : and as he was a jocose man, wel skilled in the *gests* * of the ancients, he was there kindly received as an inmate : and when he found a fit time, he returned into England, having with him that worshipful lady Ela, heiress of the county of Salisbury ; and presented her to King Richard : and he most joyfully took her, and married her to his brother William Longespee. †

The anecdote related by Doctor Powell, "who," according to Bishop Percy, "is known to have followed ancient Welsh MSS." which, at the same time, he neither quotes nor pretends to, and, after him, by Camden, and Sir William Dugdale, is not to be relied on, it being better known that the Welsh have no such MSS., except Caradoc, who was dead before it happened, as containing misrepresentation and falsehood ; Sir Peter Leycester, who cites an ancient parchment roll, written above two hundred years before, gives the story thus : " Randle (the third, surnamed Blundevill, Earl of Chester), among the many conflicts he had with the Welsh, was forced to retreat to the castle of Rothelent, in Flintshire, about the reign of King John, where they besieged him : he presently sent to his constable of Cheshire, Roger Lacy, "surnamed *Hell*," for his fierce spirit, that he would come with all speed, and bring what forces he could towards his relief. Roger, having gathered a tumultuous rout of *fidlers, players, coblers, debauched persons, both men and women*, out of the city of Chester (for 'twas then the fair-time in that city),—marcheth immediately towards the earl. The Welsh perceiving a great multitude coming, raised their siege and fled. The earl, coming back with his constable to Chester, gave him power over all the *fidlers* and *shoemakers* in Chester, in reward and memory of this service. The constable retained to himself and his heirs, the authority and donation of the *shoemakers*, but conferred the authority of the *fidlers* and *players* on his steward, which then was *Dutton* of *Dutton*, whose heirs enjoyed the same power and authority over the minstrelcy of Cheshire even to this

---

* *Gesta*, romances. Doctor Percy has strangely confounded the *gests* of the minstrels with those of the sovereign in his progresses, the word, he says, having at length come " to signify *adventures* or *incidents* in general " (1. clii.) This is amazingly ridiculous, as it is well known that when our kings used to travel, the *gest* (*giste*, F.) was the resting-place for every night to which the whole party was to be apprised. Charles I. seems to have been the last of them who proceeded by *gests*.

† Vincent's *Discovery of Errors*, etc., 445, etc.

day; who in memory hereof keep a yearly court upon the feast of St. John the Baptist at Chester, where all the minstrels of the county and city are to attend and play before the lord of Dutton, &c." * After all, it is to be wished we could have had coeval authority for so interesting an event.   Doctor Percy, who has worked it up with his usual eloquence and ingenuity, into a fine minstrel story, says : " These men (MINSTRELS, he calls them, assembled at Chester fair) LIKE SO MANY TYRTÆUS'S, BY THEIR MUSIC AND THEIR SONGS SO ALLURED AND INSPIRED the multitudes of loose and lawless persons then brought together, that they resolutely marched against the Welsh." This, to be sure, as a beautiful hyperbole, might have properly remained, "had not," in his lordship's own language, "all confidence been destroyed,"† by its being printed between inverted commas as the genuine words of Sir William Dugdale, whom he actually quotes in the margin : in consequence of which detection, his lordship has been so ingenuous, as, in the last edition, to suppress the whole passage.   There may, however, have been some foundation for the above narrative, as the worthy baronet has inserted the original charter of John Constable of Chester, by which he gave, says he, "*dedi & concessi, & hâc presenti chartâ confirmavi,* Hugoni de Dutton, *& hæredibus suis*, magistratum omnium LECCATORUM & MERETRICUM *totius* Cestershiriæ, *sicut liberius illum magistratum teneo de comite.*" These *leccatores*, it seems, which Sir Peter translates *letchers*, may, upon the authority of Du Cange, still mean *minstrels*; and, from the company they are here found in, it is very properly applied.   It is not, however, very probable· that these *letchers* (or *minstrels* if it must be), with *fiddles* at their necks, instead of *bills*, and accompanied by a parcel of prostitutes, would or could have gone to attack a body of Welshmen, who had already put to flight the noble and valiant earl of Chester, among whose gallant actions recorded in the old rimes mentioned by the author of *Piers Plowman,*‡ this may be one.

It appears, in fact, that, in the fourteenth year of King Henry VII., "a *quo warranto* was brought against Laurence Dutton of Dutton, Esquire, why he claimed all the *minstrels* of Cheshire, and in the city of Chester, to meet him at Chester yearly, at the feast of St. John Baptist, and to give unto him at the said feast four bottles of wine and a lance; and also every *minstrel* to pay unto him at the said feast fourpence-halfpenny; and why he claimed from every *whore, officium suum exercente,* four pence, to be paid yearly at the feast aforesaid : whereunto he pleaded prescription."

At the court held annually for the manor of Dutton, the steward having called every *minstrel*, and impanelled a jury, charged them

---

* *Historical Antiquities,* 141.

† See *Reliques,* etc., I., xxxi., etc.

‡ *Iean rimes of Robin Hood and Randal Earl of Chester.*

§ *Ibid.,* 142.

to enquire, "whether any man of that profession had exercised *his instrument* without license from the lord of the court, &c." *

Dugdale, who describes the congress of all the minstrels of Cheshire at midsummer, and the procession of these minstrels "two and two, and playing on their several sorts of musical instruments," says not a word of their songs.

" Forthwith came John of Rampayne, and saw Foukes make such sorrow. ' Sir,' said he, ' suffer this sorrow to depart, and, if it please God, before tomorrow prime, you shall hear good news of Sir Andulf de Bracy, for I myself will go to speak to the King." John of Rampaygne knew enough of the *tabour*, the *harp*, *violin*, *sitole*, and *juglery*, so he drew much abundantly with earl or baron ; and caused stain his hair and his whole body entirely as black as jet, so that nothing was white but his teeth ; and caused hang about his neck a very handsome *tabour* ; afterward he mounted a fair palfrey, and rode toward the town of Salisbury, as far as the gate of the castle. John came before the King, and put himself on his knees, and saluted the King very courteously ; the King returned him his salutes, and asked him whence he was. ' Sire,' said he, ' I am an Ethiopian minstrel, born in Ethiopia.' Said the King, ' Are all the people of your country of your colour.' ' Yes, my lord, man and woman.' ' What say they in those strange realms of me ?' ' Sire,' said he, ' you are the most renowned king of all Christendom ; and for your great renown am I come to see you.' ' Fair sir,' said the King, ' welcome.' ' Sir, my lord, many thanks.' (John said that he was renowned more for his badness than his bounty ; but the King could not understand him.) John made that day many a minstrelsy with tabour and other instruments. When the King was gone to bed, he made Sir Henry de Audeley go for to see the minstrel, and he led him into his chamber, and they made great melody : and, when Sir Henry had well drunk, then he said to a varlet, ' Go seek Sir Andulf de Bracy, whom the King will slay tomorrow, for he shall have a good night before his death.' The varlet soon brought Sir Andulf into his chamber, then they talked and played. John commenced a song which Sir Andulf used to sing. Sir Andulf raised his head, so he regarded in the middle his visage, and with great difficulty knew him. Sir Henry asked to drink, John was very serviceable, danced lightly on his feet, and before all served of the cup. John was brisk, cast a powder in the cup, that no one perceived him, for he was a good jugler, and all that drank became so sleepy, that, very soon after the draught, they lay down to sleep ; and, when all were asleep, John took a fool that the king had, so he put him between the two knights, that they might save Sir Andulf. John and Sir Andulf took the towels and sheets that were in the chamber, and by a window toward the

* King's *Vale Royal of England*, 29.

Severne they escaped, and went on toward Blanchemolt, which is twelve leagues from Salisbury."*

On the marriage of King Henry III. with Eleanor of Provence, in 1236, such a multitude of nobles of each sex, such a number of religious, such a populousness of the commons, such a variety of *histriones* (musicians, it is presumed), assembled, that scarcely could the city of London contain them in her capacious bosom.†

We meet with no other anecdote of the minstrels during the reigns of John, (unless it be the romance of Fulco-Fitz-Warim already noticed), nor any at all in that of his son Henry, or his grandson Edward. The last, indeed, when prince, and in the Holy Land, appears to have had a harper among his servants, who, on his master's attempted assassination, and even after the king himself had slain the assassin, had the singular courage to brain a dead man with a trivet, or *tripod*, for which act of heroism he was justly reprimanded by Edward.‡ It may be, likewise, observed that *The geste of Kyng Horn* was, apparently, written in his reign.

His son, Edward the Second, was much addicted to buffoons, singers, tragedians, waggoners, ditchers, rowers, sailors, and other such low company :§ under some or one of which respectable designations are, doubtless, included minstrels and juglers. Adam Davie, the author of *Alisaundre*, a romance of great merit, and of considerable length, was marshal of Stratford-le-Bow at the same period.

Seventy shillings were expended on minstrels, who accompanied their songs with the harp, at the feast of the installation of Ralph, abbot of St. Augustin's at Canterbury, in the year 1309. At this magnificent solemnity, six thousand guests were present in and about the hall of the Abbey.‖

---

* King's MSS., 12 C. xii.

† M. Paris, p. 355.

‡ Walter Hemingford (Gale), 591. Robert of Brunne, however, tells us, that Edward himself *raukt* the *trestille*, "als his romance sais :" adding,

"The Carazin so he smote, in the hede, with that *treste*,
That brayn and blode alle hote, and igen alle out, gan brest."

According to Doctor Percy, Heminford lived in the time of Edward I. (*Reliques*, III., xl.) ; which, if living implies writing, is somewhat unlikely, as he lived to write the life of that monarch's grandson, and did not die, as Bale hath it, before 1347, 40 years after the death of Edward I., and 70 from the event in question. Matthew Paris, likewise, who relates the story, and certainly wrote about the time, has made no mention of the harper. There appears to have been some metrical narrative, either in French or English, of Edward's expedition to the holy land ; as Robert of Brunne says of the assassin : "To, I wene he lauht, als his romance says," p. 229. Warton, by one of his habitual blunders, asserts "the *harper* . . . . *killed* the assassin," (11, sig. b2, *b*.)

§ Warton, i., 89.

‖ H. de Knyghton, co. 2532.

In the year 1217 the King celebrated the feast of the Pentecost in the great hall of Westminster, where, as he royally sat at table, the princes of his realm being present, there entered a certain woman adorned with the habit of a minstrel (*histrio*), sitting upon a good horse, caparisoned jugler-wise, who went round the tables in the manner of juglers, and at length ascended by the steps to the King's table, and put a certain letter before the King, and pulling back the rein (having saluted those everywhere sitting), as she had come, so she departed. The King, however, caused the letter to be opened, that he might know its tenor, which in sense was such : "The lord the King too uncourtly hath regarded his knights, who, in his father's time and his own, exposed themselves to several dangers, and, for their honour, either lost or diminished their substance ; and too abundantly enriched others, who never bore the burthen of busyness." These words being heard the guests, regarding each other, wondered at so great feminine boldness, and severely blamed the porters or doorkeepers that they had permitted her to enter ; who, excusing themselves, answered, that it was not the custom of the king's house that juglers should, in any wise, be prohibited from entry, and especially in such great solemnities, or feast days. It was, therefore, sent to seek the woman, who was easily found, taken, and committed to prison, and was forced to tell why she had so done, and answered the truth, that she had been induced to do it by a certain knight for an adequate reward. Then the knight was sought, found, taken, and led before the King, and examined upon the premises ; who, nothing at all fearing, boldly confessed that he was author of the letter, and had done it for the King's honour. The said knight, therefore, by his constancy, obtained the King's favour, with abundant gifts, and liberated the young woman from prison.[*] This was, manifestly, a woman pranked up like a minstrel, not a real one, for, notwithstanding the pains Doctor Percy has taken to prove that some ladies, in former times, played upon the harp, as many do at this day, there is no instance to be found of their doing it, as a minstrel, in public and for the sake of reward, nor of their being called female *minstrels* or *harpers*. Neither can this be fairly inferred from the female terminations of *jengleresse* (which is very suspicious), *joculatrix*, *ministralissa*, *femina ministralis*, etc., unless it were known in what sense the word was used, and whether this female minstrel sung to the harp verses of her own composing, or composed by others, or what particular branch of minstrelsy she exercised. That there were women who *danced* and *tumbled* is manifest from Chaucer :

" And right anon in comen *tombesteres.*"

So, again, in *The Testament of Love* (Urry's edition, 493 *a*), " his dame was a *tombystere*"; which seems properly explained in

---

Mister Thomases *Glossary*, "*A tumbler*, a woman dancer, or stage-player." Mister Tyrwhitt, who derives the word from the Saxon *tumban*, to dance, explains it,—" A dancing-woman," or " Women-dancers." The following passage, however, from the ancient *Roman de Perceval*, will put the existence of female *dancers* and *tumblers* out of all doubt :

> " Harper y faisoit harpeors,
> Et vieler vieleors,
> Et les baleresses baler
> Et *les Tumbleresses Tumber*."

The *baleresses*, or female dancers, are here plainly distinguished from the *tumbleresses*, which, therefore, cannot have the same identical meaning ; and *Tomber*, in Cotgrave's *Dictionary*, is explained to *fall*, or *tumble down*, and refers from *Tumber* to *Tomber*.

When Adam de Orleton, Bishop of Winchester, visited his cathedral priory of St. Swithin in that city, a jugler named Herbert sung *The Song of Colbrond*, and also *The gest of queen Emma, deliver'd from the plough-shares*, in the hall of the prior, Alexander de Herriard, in 1338.[*]

At the feast of Pentecost, which King Henry V. celebrated in 1416, having the emperor and the Duke of Holland for his guests, he ordered rich gowns for sixteen of his minstrels : and, having before his death orally granted an annuity of one hundred shillings to each of his minstrels, the grant was confirmed in the first year of his son, Henry VI., and payment ordered out of the Exchequer.[†]

Men thus distinguished by such singular marks of royal favour must have been in some office about the King's person very different from that of singers or performers of instrumental music.

The commission issued in 1456, " for impressing *boys* or *youths* to supply vacancies by death among the King's minstrels," sufficiently proves that by the latter we are to understand the singing men in the chapel-royal. This idea is confirmed by Tusser :

> " Thence for my voice, I must (no choice)
> Away of forse, like posting horse,
> For sundrie men had placards then
>   Such child to take :
> The better brest, the lesser rest,
> To serve the queere, now there now heere,
> For time so spent, I may repent,
>   And sorrow make."

In the margin he calls these *placards* " singing men's commissions."

---

* Warton, i., 89.
† *Reliques*, I., xliv., from Rymer's *Fœdera*.

That "minstrels sometimes assisted at divine service," appears from the charter of Edward IV. for creating a fraternity or guild of those persons; in which it is recited to be their duty "to sing in the king's chapel, and particularly for the departed souls of the king and queen when they shall die, etc."[*] There are such kind of minstrels in it to this day, though they have long ago lost the name.

Lydgate, in a passage of his poem entitled *Reson and Sensualitie*, as quoted by Warton, enumerates a variety of entertainments comprehended under the name of minstrelsy :

> " Of all maner of *mynstralcye*
> That any man can specifye :
> For there were *rotys* of Almayne,
> And eke of Arragon and Spayne :
> *Songes, stampes*, and eke *daunces*,
> Divers plenté of plesaunces ;
> And many unkouth *notys* newe
> Of swiche folke as loved trewe ;
> And instrumentys that did excelle,
> Many moo than I kan telle ;
> *Harpys, fythales*, and eke *rotys*,
> Well according with her notys,
> *Lutys, ribibles*, and *geternes*,
> More for estatys than tavernes ;
> *Orguys, citolis, monacordys.*—
> There were *trumpes*, and *trumpettes*,
> Lowde '*shalmys*' and *doucettes*."[†]

The instruments of the English minstrels appear to have been the harp, fiddle,[‡] bagpipe, pipe and tabour, cittern, hurdy-gurdy, bladder (or cannister), and string,[§] and, possibly, the Jews-harp, [||]

---

[*] *Ibid*, I., iv.

[†] *History of English Poetry*, ii., 225, No. x. "*Orguys* is organs."

[‡] In *The Life of St. Christopher*, as quoted by Warton (i., 17) from an ancient MS. in the Bodleian Library (Laud, L. 70), is this passage :

> " Cristofre hym served longe ;
> The kynge loved melodye much of FITHELE and of songe,
> So that his JOGELER on a dai biforen him gon to play faste,
> And in a time he nemped in his song the devil at laste."

[§] A venerable old man, the melancholy representative of an ancient minstrel, appeared a few years ago in London streets, with a *cannister and string*, which he called a *humstrung*, and chanted to it the old minstrel ballad of *Lord Thomas* and *fair Eleanor;* but having, it would seem, survived his minstrel talents, and

> " Forgot his epick, nay pindarick art,"

he was afterward seen begging. The death of a person of this description, we had known in Derbyshire, was, about the same time, announced in the papers.

[||] Henry Chettle says : "There is another *jugler*, that beeing well skild in the *Jewes trumpe*, takes upon him to bee a dealer in *musicke:* especially good at mending instruments."—*Kind-Harts Dreame*, Sig. F, 46.

and a variety of vulgar inventions, the nature and name of which have long since perished. Little notice can be added to that which has been already given of the French minstrels, of their melody or music; not a single particle of any one romance in English metre, being found accompanied with musical notes, though it is possible that the chants of the few minstrel-songs already mentioned may be preserved by vocal or vulgar tradition, that of *John Dory* alone being found in printed characters. All, in short, that is known of the minstrel-music of this country is that it was very unrythmical or irregular. "Your ordinarie rimers," says Puttenham, "use very much their measures in the odde, as nine and eleven, and the sharpe accent upon the last syllable, which, therefore, makes him go ill-favouredly, and like a MINSTRELS musicke."[*]

"The minstrels," as Doctor Percy observes "seem to have been in many respects upon the same footing as the heralds: and the king of the minstrels, like the king at arms, was both here and on the continent an usual officer in the courts of princes. Thus we have in the reign of King Edward I. mention of a King Robert, and others: and in 16 Edward II. is a grant to William de Morlee 'the King's minstrel, stiled *Roy de North*,' of houses which had belonged to another king John le Boteler." Rymer hath also printed a licence granted by King Richard II., in 1387, to John Caumz, the king of his minstrels, to pass the seas.[†]

The "minstrells" of the King's household, in the time of Edward III., were "trompeters, cytelers, pypers, tabrete, mabrers, clarions, fedelers, wayghtes."[‡]

Those of King Edward IV. were musicians "whereof some 'were' *trompets*, some with the *shalmes* and *smalle pypes*, and some, strange mene coming to the court at [the] fyve feastes of the year, and then take their wages . . . . after iiij. d. ob. by day," etc.[§]

The "mynstrals" of the earl of Northumberland, in the time of King Henry VIII., were no more than "a *tabaret*, a *luyte*, and a *rebec*."[||]

Among the household musicians of King Edward VI. are enumerated "*harpers, singers*, MINSTRELLES;"[¶] what was the peculiar office of the last does not appear; but it must be evident that they were neither *singers* nor *harpers*.

In the feast of Alwyn the Bishop, and during *pietancia* in the hall of the convent of St. Swithin, Winchester, six minstrels, with four

---

[*] *Arte of English Poesie*, 1589, p. 59.

[†] *Reliques*, I., xliii.

[‡] Hawkins's *History of Music*, ii., 107. *Wayghtes* were players on the hautboy or other pipes during the night, as they are in many places at this day.

[§] *Ibid.*, 290.

[||] *Reliques*, I., lxxiv.

[¶] Hawkins, iii., 479.

harpers, made their minstrelsies; and after supper in the great
bowed chamber of the lord prior, sang the same gest; in which
chamber was suspended, as was the custom, the great arras of the
prior, having the pictures of the three kings of Cologne.*

In an account-roll of the priory of Bicester, in Oxfordshire, Mister
Warton found a parallel instance under the year 1432, by which it
appears that four shillings were given to six minstrels of Bucking-
ham, singing in the refectory *The Martyrdom of the Seven Sleepers*,
at the feast of the Epiphany.†

In the fourth year of King Richard II. (1380), John King of
Castille and Leon Duke of Lancaster, by a charter in the French
tongue, ordained, constituted, and assigned his well beloved N.N.,
the king of the minstrels, within his honour of Tutbury, which now
is or who for the time shall be to take and arrest all the *minstrels*
within his same honour and franchise, who refused to do their
services and minstrelsy to them appertaining to do from ancient
time at Tutbury aforesaid, annually the day of the assumption of
our lady: giving and granting to the said king of the minstrels
for the time being full power and command to make them do reason-
ably, justify and constrain to do their services and minstrelsies in
manner as belongs, and as it there has been used and from ancient
times accustomed.‡ These minstrels, like those in Cheshire, appear
to have been a very disorderly and licentious set of men, who
required a court of justice to keep them in order. Plot, who was
a spectator of their procession in the reign of Charles the Second,
thus describes it: "On the court-day, or morrow of the assumption,
what time all the *minstrels* within the honor come first to the
bayliff's house, where the steward or his deputy meeting them they
all goe from thence to the parish church of Tutbury, two and two
together, *musick playing before them, the king of the minstrells*
for the year past walking between the steward and bayliff, etc."§

One of the articles of enquiry in the steward's charge to the
inquest was, whether any of the minstrels within the honour had
"abused or disparaged their honorable profession, by drunkenness,
profane cursing or swearing, SINGING LEWD OR OBSCENE SONGS,
etc.," which is all the information we can obtain of their minstrel
talents. There was a custom in this manor that the *minstrels* who
came to matins thither on the Feast of the Assumption should have
a bull given them by the prior of Tutbury, if they could take him on
that side of the river Dove which is next Tutbury; or else the prior
should give them forty pence; for the enjoyment of which custom

---

* *Registr. Priorat. S. Swithini Winton*, quoted in the *History of English
Poetry*, ii., 174, *n. m.*
† II., 175.
‡ Blount's *Law Dictionary*, king of the minstrels.
§ *Natural History of Staffordshire*, 437.

they were to give to the lord at that feast twenty. This bull, being, by inexpressible barbarities, "rendered as mad as 'tis possible for him to be," was turned out of the abbey-gate where these respectable personages, "who subsisted by the arts of poetry and music, and sang to the harp verses composed by themselves, or others," were waiting to satiate their savage cruelty; and, if they could take this poor mutilated animal, and hold him so long as to cut off some of his hair, the bull was brought to the bailiff's house, "and there collared and roped, and so brought to the bull-ring in the high street, and there baited with dogs!"*

The worthy and pious editor of *The Reliques of Ancient English Poetry* observes, with a *nota bene*, that "The barbarous diversion of bull-running was no part of the original institution, etc., as is fully proved by the Rev. Dr. Pegge in *Archæologia*, vol. ii., No. xiii., p. 80." But whether part of "the *original* institution" or not, it was practised by these infamous fiddlers or ballad-singers (whom that editor is desirous to treat with so much delicacy and respect) for upwards of three hundred years, at the least, being confirmed by *inspeximus* in the time of King Henry VI., and having continued, to the disgrace and infamy of those who were concerned in it, down to the year 1778, when the minstrel-court, bull-baiting, etc., were abolished by the Duke of Devonshire, lessee of the honor.†

By an order of the Chancellor of the Duchy-court, dated the 10th of May in the sixth year of Charles I. (amongst other orders to the like purposes): "*Item*, it is ordered, that no person shall use, or exercise, the art and science of music within the counties of Stafford and Darbie, as a common musician or minstrel for *benefit and gain*, except he have served or been brought up in the same art and science, by the space of seven years, and be allowed and admitted so to do at the said court, called the minstrels' court, by the jury of the said court for the time being, or the greater part of them, being xii. in number, by the consent of the steward of the said court, for the time being, on pain to forfeit, for every month that he shall so use, or exercise the said art, or science, iii*s*. iiij*d*."

"What feast, I pray," exclaims Thomas of Elmham, describing the coronation of King Henry V., "can be said to be more solemn than that which such a royal presence honoured, such a multitude of princes and ladies adorned, where the tumultuous noise of so many trumpets forced the æthereal parts to rëecho with the thundering roar, and the hyperlyrical melody of the harpers, by a certain most velocious touch of the fingers, shaking long notes with short ones, softly tickled the ears of the guests by a most sweet and gentle whisper. The musical concert, also, of the other instruments, which learned to jar by the strife of no dissonance, invited them to

---

* Plot's *Natural History of Staffordshire*, pp. 437, 439.
† See the edition of Blount's *Ancient Tenures*, by Beckwith, p. 313.

congruous joys."* Warton, who has mentioned this ceremony, tells
us he did it to introduce a circumstance very pertinent to his
purpose, "which is, that the number of harpers in the hall was
innumerable, who, UNDOUBTEDLY, accompanied their instruments
with heroic rhymes;"† although Elmham, his sole authority,
neither says that "the number of harpers was innumerable, nor
that there was any singing at all; all sorts of instrumental per-
formers striving to make as loud a noise as possible;" but this is
his manner of writing history.

On his return from France, after his glorious victories, and his
magnificent entry into London, he, according to the same historian,
"utterly prohibited that songs should be made of his triumph, to be
sung by harpers, or any other whatsoever." ‡

In despite, however, of this proclamation, some audacious minstrel
actually composed a metrical romance on his conquests, which is
still extant, § being the same with "The battayle of Egyngecourt,"
likewise mentioned by Mr. Wharton, and printed by John Skot, if
not, also, by Wynken de Worde, both in quarto and black letter;
another poet of a more humble description producing a song on the
same victory, also in print. It is not, at the same time, at all pro-
bable, that the minstrels who had been required to accompany him
in his invasion of France, were composers or singers of romance, or
even performers on the harp; since, as Cassius observes, "What
should the wars do with these jiging fools?"||

"Even so late as the time of Froissart," according to Bishop
Percy, "we find *minstrels* and *heralds* mentioned together, as those
who might securely go into an enemy's country."¶

In *The Noble History of King Ponthus*, 1511, it is said, "Than
beganne *mynstrelles* for to *play* all manner of *mynstrelsy*, and
also the *herauldes* began to cry, etc." These minstrels, therefore,
would seem to have been the musicians of the army, or military
band: *trumpeters*, it is probable, who, in modern times, are entitled
to the same privilege.

Edward IV., in 1496, granted a charter, by which he in-
corporated Walter Haliday marshal, and seven others of his min-
strels, to be a fraternity or perpetual guild (such as, he understood, the
brothers and *sisters* of the fraternity of minstrels had in times past)
to be governed by a marshal and by two warders, who were to

---

* *Vita Henrici quinti*, p. 23.
† *History of English Poetry*, ii., 35.
‡ P. 72.
§ See Hearne's *Appendix to Elmham*, No. vi.
|| Shakespeare's tragedy of *Julius Cæsar*, Act iv., scene 3.
¶ *Reliques*, i., 63. In the sixteenth year of Edward II., William de Morlee has
a grant with the addition of "the kings minstrel, styled, *Roy de North*; and, in the
twelfth of his successor, *Andrew Norris*, his "*chier sergeaunt*." Andrew Norris
was "roy d'armes de North." Anstis, ii., 300.

admit *brothers* and *sisters* into the said guild, and are authorised to examine the pretensions of all such as affected to exercise the minstrel profession ; and to regulate, govern, and punish them throughout the realm (those of Chester excepted).* " This," Doctor Percy thinks, " seems to have some resemblance to the Earl Marshal's Court among the heralds, and is another proof of the great affinity and resemblance which the minstrels bore to the college of arms."†

This fraternity is never mentioned by any English historian ; and it is certainly difficult to conceive for what purpose these minstrels, brothers and sisters, were thus incorporated, unless they were to attend the king's army, in the nature of heralds, whenever it went abroad. Alexander Carlile, an officer, it would seem, of this fraternity, called " sarjaunt of the mynstrellis," came, it is said, to the king as he lay in bed in the north, in the same year, in great haste, "and badde hym aryse, for he had enemyes cummyng for to take him."

This gild appears to have continued down to within the reign of King Henry VIII.‡ It would seem from the above circumstance that it was the duty of a party of the minstrels to accompany the king in his progresses.

The English minstrels, as they were called, though the names of *jestours* or *gestours*, jogeloures, jugloures, or *juglers, glewemen,* or *gleemen, magiciens, tregetours,*§ disours, seggers,‖ *fiddlürs, harpers,* etc., were by no means uncommon, appear to have undergone a mutation similar to that heretofore observed in the French, the names of the particular branches being confounded in that of the general profession. Chaucer, as we have already seen, defines the *jogelour,* of his own time, to be a wonder-worker, or sleight-of-hand

---

* *Fœdera,* xi., 642.   † *Reliques,* i., xlv.   ‡ *Reliques,* i., xlvi.

§ *Tregetours* are mentioned by Gower (fo. 38) :

> "With *sleightes* of a *tregetour* ;"

and both *tregetours* and *magicians* by Chaucer, in *The House of Fame,* iii., 169. Lydgate, in *The Dance of Machabree,* supposes *Death* to address thus :

> "Maister John Rykell, sometime *tregitour*
> Of noble Henri king of Englelond,
> For all the *sleyghtes* and turnyng of *thyne honde.*
> Thou must come near this dame to understonde :
> For Deth shortly, nother on see nor londe,
> Is not dysceyved by noon *illusions.*"

This word is derived by Tyrwhitt from *treget,* deceit, imposture.

‖ These two words occur in Robert of Brunnes' version of *The Manuel de Peche*

> "I mad nought for no *disours,*
> Ne for *seggers,* no harpours."

Thus, too, Gower, speaking of the coronation-festival of a Roman emperor :

> "When he was gladest at his mete,
> And every minstrel had *plaide*
> And every *disour* had *saide,*
> Which most was pleasaunt to his ere." (B. 7, fo. IV.)

man, as the *juggler* or *juglour* is at present. Again, in *Piers Plow-
man*, fo. 32:

> " Save Jake the *jugloure*, and Jonet of the stewes,"
> " And *japers*, and *juglers*, and janglers* of gests."

This author, however, generally uses *minstrel* and *gleman*, as
synonymous.

Sir John Mandeville, describing the exhibitions he saw at the
court of the *Grete chan*, says, "And than comen *jogulours* and
enchantoures, that don many marvaylles, etc."

William of Nassyngton, in his prologue, warns his readers,—

> "——furst at the begynnyng,
> That i will make na vayn *carpynge*,
> Of *dedes of armys*, ne of *amours*,
> As dus *mynstrallis* and *jestours*,
> That makys *carpyng* in many a place,
> Of *Octovyane*† and of *Isambrase*,
> And of many other *jeestes*,
> And namly, when thai come to feestes." ‡

But though he names both *minstrels* and *jestours*, he does not
give them several functions; as *carping* seems synonymous with
singing. Yet it must be admitted that Adam Davie, actually or
apparently, makes a distinction on this subject:

> " The *minstrels singe*, the *jogelours carpe*."

In a narrative of " The departure of the princess Katherine out of
Spaine, together with her arival and reception in England," 1501,
printed in the new edition of Leland's *Collectanea* (V., 352), we read
that " she and her ladyes called for their *minstrells* . . . and solaced
themselves with the disports of *dauncing*.

If "mynstrells" at that period were neither "trompetts" nor
"sakebowtts," they were clearly instrumental musicians of no very
dissimilar nature.§ In the progress of the new Queen of Scotland,
elder daughter of Henry VII., to meet her husband in the year
1502-3 : "Apon the gatt [of Berwick]," as we are told by an eye-

---

* *Janglers*, which frequently occurs in Chaucer's *Canterbury Tales*, is explained,
by his learned editor, a *prater* or *babbler*, and has, therefore, no sort of connection
or analogy with *jougelour*. It is, at the same time, from the French ; as in an old
fabliau in the Harley MS. 2253 :

> " *Vus estez tenuz un* janglers."

Thus, too, in Chaucer's *Troilus and Cressida*, v., 755, jonglerie is a corruption of
janglerie :

> " No force of wickid tongis *jonglerie*."

† An abridgement of *The Romance of Octavian* was printed by the Aungervyle
Society, Series I.

‡ King's MSS., 17, c. viii.

§ See Leland's *Collectanea*, iv., 272, 285.

witness, "war the MYNSTRAYLLS of the capitayn, playnge of their INSTRUMENTS."* "After the soupper . . . MYNSTRELLS begonne to *blowe*, wher daunced the qwene accompayned of my lady of Surrey."† After . . . the MYNSTRELLS begonne to play a basse daunce ; " and "after thys doon, they playde a rownde."‡ These, it may be, were the regimental band.

It would seem that the minstrels of this era had a dress to distinguish their profession. The company described by the old author, whose words are quoted, being seated in a tavern, " in comes a *noise of musicians*, IN TAWNEY COATS, who taking off their caps, asked if they would have any MUSIC ? The widow answered, No ; they were merry enough. "Tut!" said the old man, " let us hear, good fellows, what you can do ; and PLAY ME *The beginning of the world*."§ With respect to these *tawney coats*, it is well known to have been the livery of the Bishop of Winchester, within whose manor of Southwark, and under whose patronage, licence, and authority, the PUBLIC STEWS at that period flourished. This circumstance is even alluded to in *The First Part of King Henry VI.*, where the cardinal-bishop of Winchester enters " attended by a train of servants IN TAWNY coats ; " and is addressed by the Duke of Gloucester :—

" Thou, that givest whores indulgences to sin,
Draw, men, for all this privileged place ;
Blue-coats to tawny coats ! "
" Winchester-goose,‖ I cry, a rope ! a rope !
Out, tawny-coats ! Out, scarlet hypocrite !"

Henry Chettle describes *Anthony Now-Now*, a famous minstrel of his own time (not Anthony Munday), as "an od old fellow, low of stature, his head covered with a round cap, his body with a *tawney coate*, his legs and feete trust uppe in leather buskins, his gray haires and furrowed face witnessed his age, his *treble viol* in his hande, assured me of his *profession*. On which (by his continuall sawing having left but one string) after his best manner, hee gave me a *hunts-up*."¶

The Beginning of the World appears to have been a favourite tune. It is mentioned, with others, in Heywood and Broome's tragi-comedy of *The Witches of Lancashire*, 1634.

---

* *Ibid.*, 279.
† *Ibid.*, iv., 283.
‡ *Ibid.*, 284. See also 296.
§ *History of Jack of Newbury*, by Tho. Delony. *A noise of musicians* was a *company* of them. In *The Second Part of King Henry IV.* one of the drawers of *The Boar's Head* bids his fellow see if he can find out " Sneak's *noise ;*" mistress Tearsheet being desirous to have some music.
‖ A *Winchester-goose*, according to Doctor Johnson, was "*a strumpet*, or *the consequences of her love.*"
¶ *Kind-Harts Dreame*, sig. B, 2.

A curious account of the minstrel romances, and their vocal and instrumental performers, in the time of Queen Elizabeth, is transmitted to us by master Puttenham, a courtier, it would seem, and in his own conceit a most elegant and polished writer.

"That rime or concord is not commendably used both in the end and middle of a verse . . . albeit these common rimers use it much . . . . so on the other side doth the over-busie and too speedy returne of one maner of tune, too much an annoy and as it were glut the eare, unless it be in small and popular musickes song by these *cantabanqui* upon benches and barrels heads, where they have no other audience than boys or countrey-fellowes that passe by them in the streete, or else by blind harpers, or such like taverne minstrels that give a fit of mirth for a groat; and their matter being for the most part stories of old time, as the tale of Sir Topas, the reportes of Bevis of Southampton, Guy of Warwicke, Adam Bell, and Clymme of the Clough, and such other old romances, or historicall rimes, made purposely for recreation of the common people at Christmasse diners and brideales, and in tavernes and alehouses, and such other places of base resort."*

The rewards of the minstrels for their musical and vocal performances appear to have been, at least on many occasions, considering the superior value of money in those times, by no means contemptible. In the year 1306, William Fox, and Cradock his associate, for singing in the presence of the prince, and other great men, being in his company at London, received 20*s.* The minstrel of the Countess Mareschal, doing his minstrelsy before the prince at Penrith, 4*s.*† In an annual account-roll of the Augustine priory of Bicester, for the year 1431, among the *Dona prioris*, is to a harper, 8*d.* ; to another, 12*d.* ; to a certain minstrel of the Lord Talbot at Christmas, 12*d.* ; to the minstrels of the Lord Strange in the Epiphany, 20*d.* ; to two minstrels of the Lord Lovel in the morrow of St. Mark, 16*d.* ; to the minstrels of the Duke of Gloucester, in the Feast of the Nativity, 3*s.* 4*d.* ; and to a certain bearward, 4*d.* ‡ The Prior of Maxtoke, in Warwickshire, in various years of King Henry VI., gave to a juggler in the week of St. Michael, 4*d.* ; to a harper and other jugglers at Christmas, 4*d.* ; to the mimes of Solihul, 6*d.* ; to those of Coventry, 20*d.* ; and at another time, 12*d.* ; to the mime of Lord Ferrers, 6*d.* ; to the mimes of the Lord Astely, 12*d.* ; to those of the Lord of Warwick, 10*d.* ; to a blind mime, 2*d.*, etc.§ In the time of Queen Elizabeth, as we are told by Puttenham, the usual fee of a chanting

---

* Puttenham, *Arte of English Poesie*, p. 68.
† Warton, i., 116 ; from the Wardrobe-roll.
‡ *Idem*, i., 89.
§ Warton, i., 90.

harper was "a groat," which Doctor Percy seems to think no bad thing.*

"Many of our old metrical romances," as Doctor Percy says, "whether originally English, or translated from the French, to be sung to an English audience, are addressed to persons of *high rank*, as appears from their beginning thus—"Listen *Lordings*," and the like (P. lxxxiii.) He elsewhere observes that "*our nobility* are often addressed therein by the title of *Lordings*" (P. ciii.). *Lordings*, however, by no means implies nobility, and is merely equivalent to *sirs* or *masters*. Thus Chaucer's *pardonere* addresses his fellow-pilgrims, who certainly were not persons of high rank :

"*Lordings*, quod he, in chirche when i prade."

John Derrick, also, in his *Image of Irelande*, 1581, repeatedly addresses his readers by the same title.

The like address to the auditory frequently recurs in the *Chester-Whitsun-plays*, which appear to have been performed before an immense number of people.

It has been maintained elsewhere that the minstrels, whether singers or instrumental performers, were held in very little if any kind of estimation. That the word *minstrel*, whatever it might have originally or anciently signified, meant no more, in comparatively modern times, than a *fiddler*, a *crowder*, a musician, is evident from all the glossaries and dictionaries which mention them ; as, for instance, those of Florio, Spelman, Cotgrave, and Blount. Their true character, however, or peculiar accomplishments, will sufficiently appear from the author of *Piers Plowman*, who composed that work in 1362, and seems to have been very well acquainted with them, and thus introduces one of this respectable fraternity, speaking for himself :

" I am MYNSTRELL, quod that man, my name is *Activa Vita*,
All idle iche hate, for All-Active is my name.
A wafrer well ye wyt, and serve manye lordes.
And fewe roobes I fong, or furred gownes :
Can I lye to do men laughe, than lachen I should,
Other mantell or money, amonges lord or minstrels.
And for I can neither *taber* ne *trumpe*, ne *tell no gests*,
Farten,† ne fysten, at feastes, ne harpen,

---

* That this was the common price, long after Puttenham's time, appears from Jonson's *Masque of the Metamorphosed Gipsies*, 1621, where, on the introduction of Cheeks the piper, or Tom Ticklefoot the tabourer, one of the company says : "I cannot hold now, there's my *groat*, let's have a fit for mirth-sake." These *groats* gave rise to the expression of *fiddler's money*, though, as that coin is no longer current, it has since been applied to *testers*.

† See before, at the end of a passage from John of Salisbury.

Jape, nc *juggle*, nc gentilly *pype*,
Nc neither *saylen*, nc *saute*, nc *syng to the gyterne*,
I have no good gystes of these great lordes.* "

This poor fellow, however, could do none of these things. He
was, in fact, a sort of *cake-baker*, and dealt in *wafers;* but the
allegory cannot be easily separated from the costume.
He elsewhere (fo. 43, b) speaks of

> " gods *gleman*, and a game of heaven,
> Would never the faithful father his *fidle* were untempered,
> Nc his *gleman a gedlyng, a goer to a tavern*."

Again, fo. 7, b :

> " Some chosen chaffer, they cleveden the better,—
> And myrthes to make as *mynstrelles* kunneth,
> And getten golde wyth her *glee*, synles I leve,
> As japers and janglers, Judas chyldren."

Again, fo. 47, b :

> " And glader then the *gleman* that golde heith to gyfte ; "

Again, fo. 45, b :

> " Harlots for her harlotry may have of her goods,
> And japers, and *juglers*, and *janglers of gestes*,"

Again, fo. 32 :

> " Save Jake the *juglourre*, and Junet of the stewes."

Again, fo. 26 :

> " And than he go, lyke a *glewemans lytch*,
> Sometyme asyde, and sometime arere."

It may be inferred from this passage that the minstrel-harpers
were frequently blind ; and, in fact, the phrase of "blind harper"
has become proverbial. So, in Cotton's *Virgile travestie*, B. 7 :

> " Whilst a *blind harper* did advance,
> That wore queen Didos cognizance,
> A *minstrel*, that Jopas hight,
> Who played and sung to them all night."

Again, fo. 13, b :

> " As common as a cart-waye to eche a knave that walketh,
> To monkes, and to *minstrels*, to *mesels* in hedges."

It must be owned we frequently meet them in very good company.
The minstrels were also *bagpipers*   Thus in the *Coventry
Corpus-Christi* play :

> " Ye *mynstrell* of myrth, *blowe up* a good blast,
>   Y Whyll i go to *chawmer*, and chaunge myn array."

---

* Fo. 68.

Again, in Sir David Lindsay's *Satyre of the thrie estaits*, 1602
(but written in 1539) :

> " *Minstrell, blaw up* ane brawl of France,
> Let see wha hobbils best."

Again, in John Heywood's *Play of the wether* :

> " For the most part all maner *mynstrelsy*,
> By wynde they delyver theyr sounde chefely,
> Fyll me a *bagpype* of your water full,
> As sweetly shull it sounde, as it were stuffyd with woll."

Again, in *The popish kingdome*, from the Latin of Thomas
Meogeorgus, by Barnabe Googe, 1570, fo. 56 :

> " The table taken up they rise, and all the youth apace,
> The minstrell with them called, go to some convenient place,
> Where, when with *bagpipe* hoarce, he hath begon his music fine,
> And unto such as are prepared to *daunce* hath given signe,
> Comes thither streight, etc."

Sometimes their instruments were a drum and fife : for so Robert
Greene, in his *Orlando furioso*, 1594 :

> " I'll be his *minstrell* with my *drum* and *fife*,
> Bid him come forth, and *dance* it, if he dare."

Many other instances, of the same kind, might be added, but
these may suffice.

Stubs, in his *Anatomie of Abuses*, 1583 and 1595, describes the
minstrels of his time as a parcel of drunken sockets and baudy para-
sites, "that," says he, "raunge the countries, rhyming and singing
of unclean, corrupt, and filthy songs in taverns, ale-houses, inns, and
other public assemblies. . . . There is no ship," he exclaims, "so
laden with merchandise, as their heads are pestered with all kinds of
baudy songs, filthy ballads, and scurvy rhymes, serving for every pur-
pose and for every company. For proof whereof," adds he, "who
be baudier knaves than they ? who uncleaner than they ? who more
licentious and looser minded than they ? who more incontenent than
they ? and, brieflie, who more inclined to all kind of insolency and
leudness than they ? . . . I think that all good minstrels, sober, and
chaste musicians, may dance the wild Moris through an eedle eye."

This same puritanical snarler allows that, " notwithstanding it
were better (in respect of worldly acceptation) to be a piper, or a
baudie minstrel, then a divine, for the one is loved," he says, " for his
ribauldrie, the other hated for his gravity, wisdom, and sobriety. Every
town, city, and county," he adds, " is full of these minstrelles to pipe a
daunce to the devil ; but of devines, so few there be as any may hardly
be seen." It would have been much the better, indeed, if there had
been none at all, for certainly a piper is preferable to a parson.*

---

* The present Editor is not, of course, responsible for Mr. Ritson's opinions.

It is, at the same time, no small compliment to the minstrels of
former ages that, as they were, doubtless, much more active and
useful, they were infinitely better paid than the idle and good-for-
nothing clergy.

"The fraternity of the holy cross in Abingdon, in Henry the sixth's
time. . . . did every yeare keepe a feast, and then they used to
have twelve priests to sing a *dirige*, for which they had given them
foure pence a peece. They had also twelve minstrells, some from
Coventré, and some from Maydenhith, who had two shillings three
pence a piece, besides theyre dyet and horsemen. . . Observe that,
in those days, they payd theyre minstrells better than theyre
preistes." *

The employment of these minstrels may be collected from a sub-
sequent passage, in which the writer says that they had "pageantes,
and playes, and May-games to captivat the sences of the zelous
beholders, and to allure the people to the greater liberality."
Another instance of the same kind of disparity is related by
Warton, where four shillings were given to the six *mimi*, or
minstrels, and only two shillings to the eight priests. In the same
year (1441), the prior gives no more than sixpence to a preaching
friar.†

"From the following entry," says Mr. Steevens, "on the books
of the stationers company in the year 1560, it appears that the hire
of a *parson* was cheaper than that of a *minstrel* or a *cook*:—

"Item, payd to the preacher—vi *s.* 11 *d.*
Item, payd to the minstrell—xii *s.*
Item, payd to the coke—xv *s.*

(*Shakspeare*, 1793, xiv., 529.)

It should be remembered, at the same time, that the parson's
business would be finished in an hour, whereas the cook and the
minstrel would be employed the whole of the day, and peradventure
all night too.

The only genuine minstrel-ballads which are known to exist at
present (except such as may have been published with great in-
accuracy and licentiousness by the Right Reverend the Lord Bishop
of Dromore, or remain concealed in his lordship's folio manuscript)‡
are *The Ancient battle of Chevy-chace, The battle of Otterbourne,
John Dory, Little Musgrave and Lady Barnard, Lord Thomas
and fair Eleanor,* and *Fair Margaret and sweet William,* to
which one may possibly venture to add *John Armstrong,* and
Captain Care; all which are somewhere or other in print.

A singular and whimsical writer, named Robert Lancham, or
Langham, a *Nottinghamshire* gentleman, who appears to have
accompanied Elizabeth in some of her progresses, as "clark of the
councel chamber door," in a letter: "whearin part of the enter-

---

* *Liber Niger*, p. 598.   † II., p. 106.   ‡ Since published.

tainment untoo the Queenz Majesty at Killingworth castle, in Warwick Sheer, in this soomery progrest, 1575, iz signified : from a freend officer attendant in the coourt, unto hiz freend (Master Humfrey Martin, mercer) a citizen and merchant of London," and there printed in the above year, in a small volume in a black-letter, gives the following curious narrative of "a ridiculous devise of an auncient minstrell and his song," which "waz prepared to have been profferd, IF MEETE TIME AND PLACE HAD BEEN FOOUND FOR IT ; " so that this intended exhibition (in flat contradiction to doctor Percy's misrepresented account) did not actually take place ; but, as good luck would have it, " Ons, in a woorshipful company, whear, full appointed, he recoounted his matter in sort az it should have been uttered," master Langham, in person, "shaunsed to bee ; and what i noted," says he, " heer this i tell yoo. A parson very meet seemed he for the purpose ; of a xlv. years olld, apparelled partly as he woold himself : Hiz cap of hiz hed seemly rounded tonster-wyze ; sayr kembd, that with a spoonge devoutly dipt in a little caponz greas, was finelye smoothed to make it shine like a mallards wing ; hiz beard smugly shaven ; and yet his shyrt after the nu trink, with ruffs fayr starched, sleeked, and glistering like a payr of nu shooz : marshalld in good order : with a stetting stick, and stoout that every ruff stood up like a wafer. A side gooun of Kendal green, after the freshness of the year now ; gathered at the neck with a narro gorget fastened afore with a white clasp and a keepar close up to the chin, but easily for heat to undoo when he list : seemly begyrt in a red caddiz gyrdle ; from that, a payr of capped Sheffeld knivez hanging a to side : out of his bozom draune foorth a lappet of his napkin, edged with a blu lace, and marked with a truloove, a hart, and A.D. for *Damian,* for he was but a bachelar yet.

" His gooun had syde sleevez dooun to midlegge, slit from the shoolder too the hand, and lined with white cotton. His dooblet sleevez of blak woorsted : upon them a payr of poynets of tawny chamblets, laced along the wreast wyth blu threeden points : a wealt toward the hand of fustian anapes : a payr of red neather stocks : a payr of pumps on hiz feet, with a cross cut at the toze for cornz ; not nu indeede, yet cleanly blakt, with soot and shining az a shoing horn. About his neck a red rebond sutable to his girdl : his harp in good grace dependaunt before him ; his wreast tyed to a green lace and hanging by : Under the gorget of his goound a fayr flagon cheyn of pewter (for sylver ;) as a *squire minstrel* of *Middlesex,* that travaild the cuntree thys soomer season unto fayrz, and woorshipful menz houzez. From his cheyn hoong schoochiar with metall and cooler resplendant upon hiz breast of the auncient armes of Islington . . . ." (Then follows an absurd and affected description of these arms, evidently the sole manufacture of master Langham, or some other coxcomb of the same turn . . . . This being ridiculed by "a good fello of the company") "every man

laught a good, saue the minstrell : that thoogh THE FOOL wear
made privy all was but for sport, yet to see himself thus crost with
a contrary kue that he lookt not for, woold straight have ge'en over
all, waxt very wayward, eager and soour ; hoowbeit at laste, by sum
entreaty, and many fair woordz, with sak and suger, we sweetned
him againe : and after he became az mery as a py. Appeerez then
afresh in hiz ful formalitie with a louely loock. After three lowlie
cooursiez, cleered his vois with a hem and reach, and spat oout
withal ; wiped hiz lips with the hollo of his hand for syling his
napkin, temperd a string or too with his wreast, and after a little
warbling on hiz harp for a prelude, came foorth with a sollem song,
warraunted for story oout of *King Arthurs* acts ; the first booke
and 26 chapter ; whearof i gate a copy : and that iz this, *viz.* :

' So it befell upon a Pentecost day,' etc.

At this the minstrel made a pauz and a curtezy, for primus pastus
(*passus*). More of the song iz thear, but i gat it not. Az for the
matter, had it cum to the sheaw, i think the fello would have handled
it well ynoough."

The poor fellow thus brought forward to represent, and even to
ridicule, the respectable character of an ancient minstrel, may be
readily admitted to have been himself a humble retainer to that once
illustrious profession. This appears by his being able to accompany
his song with the melody of the harp. He was, therefore, it is likely,
one of those "*cantabanqui* upon benches and barrels' heads, where
they had no other audiences then boys or countrey-fellows," as
already described by Puttenham ; or else one of his "taverne-
minstrels that (used to) give a fit of mirth for a groat." Our critic,
however, finds no fault with his performance, and even pays him a
sort of parting compliment. It is sufficiently manifest, at the same
time, from this identical narrative, that there was, at the above
period, no minstrel performer distinguished by his dress or manners,
as the real or accurate representative of a minstrel of the three pre-
ceeding centuries, who would, in the puritanical times of that bigoted
and bloody tigress, have been treated with merited respect.

By an act of the 39th of Queen Elizabeth (1597), chap. iv., intitled
"An act for punishment of rogues, vagabonds, and sturdy beggars,"
"All bearwards, common players of enterluds, and MINSTRELS,
wandering abroad ; all juglers, tinkers, pedlers, &c. shall be
adjudged and deemed rogues, vagabonds, and sturdy beggers,"
subject, however, to a proviso or exception in favour of John Dutton,
of Dutton, in the county of Chester, esquire, "for any liberty,
preheminence, authority, jurisdiction," which he then lawfully used,
"by reason of any ancient charters or of any prescription, usage or
title whatsoever." *

---

* This clause continued to be inserted in all vagrant acts down to the present
reign, in which it has been omitted.

This statute is concluded to have nearly put an end to the pro-fession of minstrel, base and beggarly as it had become, an ordinance during the usurpation in 1656 being the last public notice that is taken of it, whereby it is enacted that if any of the "persons com-monly called FIDLERS or MINSTRELS shall be taken playing, fidling, and making music in any inn, ale-house, or tavern, or proffering themselves, or desiring, or intreating, any to hear them play or make music," they are to be "adjudged and declared to be rogues, vagabonds and sturdy beggars."

> "Then, for the truth's sake, come along, come along!
> Leave this place of superstition,
> Were it not for me, that the brethren be,
> You would sink into perdition." *

Shakespeare calls these persons "feast-finding minstrels" in his *Rape of Lucrece*; and Ben Jonson, in his *Tale of a Tub*, introduces "Old Father *Rosin*, chief *minstrel* of Highgate, and his two boys." They are *fiddlers*, and play the tunes called for by the company, as *Tom Tiler, The Jolly Joiner*, and *The Jovial Tinker*. The same dramatist, in his *Masque of the Metamorphosed Gypsies*, calls a *bagpiper*, or *taborer*, "the miracle of *minstrels*," and, in another part, makes one of the characters say, "The king has his noise of gypsies, as well as of *bearwards*, and OTHER MINSTRELS." So that, of whatever consequence they might have been in ancient periods, they ended their career as vagabonds and fiddlers. Doctor Bull, who wrote satirical verses against them (which, though extant in one of the Harleian manuscripts, cannot be recovered), pays them the following parting compliment :—

> "When Jesus went to Jairus house,
> (Whose daughter was about to dye,)
> He turned the minstrels out of doors,
> Among the rascal company :
> BEGGERS THEY ARE WITH ONE CONSENT,
> AND ROGUES, BY ACT OF PARLIAMENT."

---

* *Loyal Songs,* i., 5.

METRICAL ROMANCES.

YWAINE AND GAWIN.

THE original of this romance is that of "*Le chevalier au lion*," by Crestien, or Christian, de Troyes, an eminent French poet, who died in 1191. That original, which is still extant, though not in this country, consists of 7784 verses. See the *Bibliotheque universelle des romans, Avril*, 1772, *premier volume*, p. 95. It is presumed to be the same with that which Du Fresnoy calls "*Le roman d'Yvain*, in folio, *manuscrit*."

This *Ywaine, Ewen*, or *Owen*, was the son of Urian, the brother of Augusel, king of Albania, now Scotland, and of Lot, the consul of Loudonesia, being himself honoured by king Arthur with the sceptre of Murray, according to that veracious historian, Geoffrey of Monmouth, who calls him *Eventus :* Augusel, king of Albania, he says, who fell in the battle of Camblan [*anno* 542], was succeeded in his kingdom by *Eventus*, his brother Urian's son, who afterward performed many famous exploits in these wars." (B. 11, C. 1). In *Mort d'Arthur* he is called Ewen *as blanches mains.*

The Welsh have the story of *Ouen ab Yrien*, in their own language ; but whether an original, or a translation from the French or English, cannot be ascertained. See Lloyd's *MSS. Britan. Cata.* (Archæologia Britan. P. 265.) He is mentioned, however, by Taliesfin and Llywarch Hen, two celebrated British bards, of the sixth century ; both of them his contemporaries, and the latter, his relation. (*Ibi.* P. 259, 264 ; Lewis's *History of Great Britain*, P. 201, &c. ; and "Heroic Elegies &c. of Llywarch Hen," P. 29, &c.) Urien, the father of Owen, petty king or prince of Reged in Cumbria, a little kingdom, part of England and the south-west of modern Scotland, was treacherously slain about the year 567. He was one of the greatest encouragers of the bards of his age. Owen, his son, is celebrated in the ancient Welsh *Triades*, a composition, it is pretended, of the seventh century, as one of "The three blessed princes of the isle of Britain," and one of "The three blessed burdens of the womb of the isle of Britain." The name of his bard was *Dygynelw*, one of the three "who tinged spears with blood" (Lly. Hen, P. xix.) In a curious fragment of the life of St. Kentegern, written by an unnamed author, at the instance of Herbert bishop of Glasgow (1147 to 1164), the lover of that saint's mother is pointed out in these words: "*Erat namque procus ejus juvenis quidam elegantissimus*, Ewen *videlicet*, filius Erwegende, *nobilissima Britonum prosapia ortus* .... In gestis hystrionum vocatur Ewen filius Ulien [r. Urien]." (*Vitæ SS. qui habitaverunt in Scotia*, p. 203.) Kentegern, who was born about 516, is, in the Welsh pedigrees, made the son of this Ewen or Owain, the son of Urien: so that he would seem to have come into the world before his father, no unusual anticipation in Welsh pedigrees. (See Owen's account of Llywarch Hen, &c.) Carte, speaking of Ida, king of Northumberland, says, "He was slain in battle by Owen, son of Urian Rheged, as Taliessin says in an elegy which he composed upon the death of this gallant Britain, to whose bravery, vigilance, and conduct, his country had been chiefly indebted for its defence and security." (History of England, I, 209.)[1] The actual existence, therefore, of these two persons seems unquestionable. *Urien* [*Urbgen*] is mentioned by Nennius, or his interpolator, C. 64: and this misnomer seems to have given birth to the "*Urbgennius Badonensis*" of Geoffrey of Monmouth.

King *Urience*, in the old romance of *Mort d'Arthur*, is the husband of *Morgan le fay* (half-sister to king Arthur), who unnaturally attempts to kill him sleeping; but is prevented by their son *sir Ewaine*.[2] Now, it seems, the death of Urien was actually procured by the instigation of *Morgant Mwynvaur*, another of the four princes of *Cumbria*. Urien's wife, however, was not the sister of Arthur, but *Modron*, daughter of *Avallach*. Owain himself was twice married, first to *Penarwen*, daughter of *Cul Vanawyd Prydain*, and, secondly, to *Denyw*, daughter of *Llewddyn Luyddawg* of Edinburgh: according to what the literary Welsh idiots publish, in the eighteenth century, as authentic history; and which Geoffrey of Monmouth, lyar as he was, would have disdained to retail in the twelfth. See the Life of Llywarch Hen, prefixed to his "Heroic elegies, &c." P. vii.

Gawain, called, by Geoffrey of Monmouth, *Walganus*, was another nephew of Arthur, being the son of Lot of *Loudonesia*, the

---

[1] The death of Ida is placed by the Saxon chronicle in 560; but it does not appear, from that authority, to have happened in battle. The pretended antiquities of the Welsh abound with imaginary victories.

[2] The old romance of *Merlin*, (vo. I, fo. 116.) calls *Yvain* a bastard, son, it adds, to king Urien, whom he begot on the wife of his seneschal, who was of such great beauty that for the love of her he forgot his wife, and left her for more than five years, and held her in his castle in spite of his steward so long that he begot this child: but all this is scandal.

nephew and successor of *Sichelin*, king of the Norwegians, who had married Anne his sister. According, however, to *Mort d'Arthur*, when Uther-Pendragon married the lady Igrayne (or *Igerna*), the widow of Gorlois, "king Lot of Lowthan and of Orkeny then wedded *Margawse* [one of her three daughters by Gorlois], that was Gawayns mother." (Part 1, C. 3.) This Gawain, or *Walwenus*, as we learn from William of Malmesbury, reigned in that part of Britain which is called *Walwertha*, and his burying-place was found in the time of king William I. in the province of Ros, in Wales, upon the margin of the sea, being fourteen feet long;[1] he having, as was asserted by some, been wounded by enemies, and cast up by ship-wreck; or, by others, been killed, by the citizens, at a public feast. (*De gestis regum*, L. 1.) He appears to have been highly cele-brated. His death, of course, is otherwise represented by the old romancers, who were not particularly conversant with William of Malmesbury.

Sir Ewaine and sir Gawain were sincere friends; and, when the latter knew that sir Ewaine was banished from court by king Arthur, on suspicion that he was of council with his mother Morgan, who was constantly practising treason against that monarch, he accom-panied him into banishment. See *Mort d'Arthur*, P. 1, C. 75.

The only ancient copy of the present poem is contained in the Cotton MS. Galba E. IX. which seems to have been written in the time of Richard II., or toward the close of the fourteenth century; and not, as appeared to Warton, who knew nothing of the age of MSS. and probably never saw this, "in the reign of king Henry the sixth" (III, P. 108). The language of all the poems in this MS. is a strong northern dialect, from which it may be reasonably inferred that they are the composition of persons, most likely monks, resident in that part of England, where, in former times, were several flourishing monasteries. One singularity of this MS. is that the *y* is generally used at the commencement of a syllable for *th*, instead of the Saxon þ [properly þ], (as *Yai, yat, ye*, &c. for *thai, that, the*, &c.) which sometimes, though rarely, occurs: a singularity which is still in use for the abbreviations y^t, y^y, y^m, &c. The letter *z* also is frequently used for *y* consonant at the beginning of a syllable.[1] These, however, have not been retained, though the ancient orthography is carefully preserved in every other respect.

---

[1] This seems the established size of an ancient hero. "In Murray-land," accord-ing to that most veracious historian maister Hector Bois, "is the kirke of Pette, quhare the banis of LYTILL JOHNE remanis in gret admiratioun of pepill. He hes bene fourtene fut of hycht, with square membris effering theirto." (*Historie of Scotland, translatit be maister Johne Bellenden*, Edin. fo. b. l.)

[2] It may be proper to observe here, once for all, that in the MSS. made use of in this collection, and most others in English of the same age, this letter or character *z*, beside its usual pronunciation, as in *grantz*, is used with the powers of *y* con-sonant, and *gh*, as in *ze, zing, rizt, knyzth*, &c. and, to avoid a false or equivocal

The present, or some other, romance on the story of Sir Ywain, may possibly have been printed, though no copy of it is known to be preserved. In Wedderburn's *Complainte of Scotlande*, St. Andrews, 1549, among the " storeis " or " flet taylis," rehearsed by the shepherds, whereof " sum vas in prose and sum vas in verse," we meet with " The tail of syr Euan, Arthours knycht." See also the adventures of sir Percival in *Mort d'Arthur*.

A romance of " Syr Gawayne," mentioned in Laneham's *Letter from Killingworth*, 1575, was "Imprynted at London in Paules churcheyarde at the sygne of the Maydens heed by Thomas Petyt " (4to. b. l.) It was in six-line stanzas, but no more than the last leaf is known to be preserved. "A jeste of syr Gawayne," probably the same book, was licensed to John Kynge, in 1557-8. Two other romances on the same subject, but in a dialect and metre peculiar to Scotland, are printed in Pinkerton's *Scotish poems* ; the one from an edition at Edinburgh in 1508 ; the other from a MS, the property of the present editor, which the said Pinkerton came by very dishonestly.

The history of Ywaine seems to have been popular in the north. In the library of Stockholm is a MS. intitled " *Sagan af Ivent Eingland kappe : Historia de Ivento regis Arturi in Anglia pugile inter magnates carissimo : continens ejus cum gigantibus atque Blamannis plurima atque periculosa certamina. Cap. 12.*" (*Hickesii Thesaurus*, III, 315). Two modern copies of the same, or a similar article ("*Artur kongs og Iventi saga,*" and " *Ivents saga* "), expressly from the French (" *Von Franseysen i Nor- rænu* "), are in the B. Museum (Sloane's MSS. 4857, 4859). The *sig*, or tale, of *herr Ywan und herr Gawan*, was extant in German in the year 1450. (*Symbolæ ad literaturam Teuto. Hauniæ*, 1787 4to, P. xxxvi.)

YWAINE AND GAWIN.[1]

Almyghti god that made mankyn,
He schilde his servandes out of syn,
And mayntene tham, with might and mayne,
That herkens Ywayne and Gawayne :

[1] The MS. reads " Here begyns Ywaine and Gawin."

Thai war knightes of the tabyl rownde,
Tharfore listens a lytel stownde.
Arthur, the kyng of Yyngland,[1]
That wan al Wales with his hand,

---

[1] This monarch was the son of Uther-Pendragon, king of Britain, by Igerna, the beautiful wife of Gorlois, duke of Cornwall, into whose semblance (like another Jupiter) he was metamorphosed, by a miracle of the enchanter Merlin. Gorlois being slain in battle by the king's troops, while the monarch himself was passing his time with Igerna, they were shortly afterwards united in the bands of holy wedlock. Arthur, having succeeded his father, conquers the Saxons, Picts and Scots ; adds to his government Ireland, Iceland, Gothland, and the Orkneys ; subdues Norway, Dacia, Aquitain, and Gaul ; and even the Romans.* But, hearing, upon his march to Rome, that his nephew Modred, or Mordred, whom he had left vicegerent, had, by tyrannical and treasonable practices, set the crown upon his own head, and that his queen *Guanhumara*, or Guenever, was wickedly married to this undutiful relation, he returned with speed to Britain ; and, after a dreadful engagement, in which Modred was slain, being himself mortally wounded, and carried to the isle of Avalon (now Glastonbury) to be cured of his hurts, he resigned the crown in favour of his kinsman Constantine, the son of Cador, duke of Cornwall, in the year 542. Such, at least, is the account given by Geoffrey of Monmouth, in the *British history*, which he professes to have translated from a very ancient book in that tongue, brought out of Armorica, and presented to him for the purpose by Walter [*Calenius*] archdeacon of Oxford, in or about the year 1138. It is unquestionably fabulous and romantic ; but that "Arthur was merely a name given by the Welsh to Aurelius Ambrosius," or that "the Arthur of Welsh history is a nonexistence," as asserted by the author of "An enquiry into the history of Scotland" (I, 76), is a much more impudent and unqualified falsehood than any in that book. That he was a brave warrior, and, in all probability, a petty king, is manifest from authentic history, which this mendacious impostor pretends to have consulted. See Nennius, C. 61 ; William of Malmesbury, *De gestis regum Anglorum*, L. 1 ; Henry of Huntingdon, *Historiæ*, L. 2 ; *Vita S. Gildæ, per Caradocum Llancarvanensem*, among the king's MSS. 13 B VII ; and Carte's history of England, I, 202. Of these authors Nennius was dead three hundred years, at least, before the publication of *The British history*,* which the monk of Malmesbury never saw, nor the archdeacon of Huntingdon till after he had published his own. Carádoc, also, a contemporary writer, certainly borrows nothing from Geoffrey ; and Carte, though a modern, seems to have made use of good materials. His sepulchre, if we may believe Girald Barry, surnamed *Cambrensis*, who professes to have seen the cross and bones found therein, was discovered at Glastonbury in the reign of king Henry II. —after that monarch's death. He has been the subject of innumerable romances, as well French as Welsh and English ; and old songs, in the time of Malmesbury, fabled that he was yet to come.‡

That there were stories, and perhaps romances and ballads, upon the subject of

---

* The French, or English, romance supposes him to come to Rome, and be there "crowned emperor by the pope's own hands." *Mort d'Arthur*, P. 1, C. 99.

† The writer already mentioned has the impudence to assert "that the chapter on Arthur is not of Nennius, but an addition taken from Geoffrey's romance ;" the falsehood of which latter assertion will be manifest to every one who consults the two books ; and, it is universally admitted, that Samuel, the interpolator of Nennius, was nearly of the same age.

‡ An interpolator of the *Scotichronicon* observes that " because in the monasterial church of *Glasinberi* he is say'd to be bury'd with this sort of epitaph,

Hic jacet Arthurus, rex quondam atque futurus,

it is believe'd by the vulgar that he still lives, and, as is sung in comedys, is hereafter to come

And al Scotland, als sayes the buke,[1]
And mani mo, if men will luke,   10
Of al knightes he bare the pryse,
In werld was non so war ne wise ;
Trew he was in alkyn thing,
Als it byfel to swilk a kyng.
He made a feste, the soth to say,
Opon the Witsononday,[2]
At Kerdyf, that es in Wales,[3]
And, efter mete, thar in the hales,
Ful grete and gay was the assemblè,
Of lordes and ladies of that cuntrè,   20

Arthur, in the Welsh language, anterior to the publication of Geoffrey's British
history, is manifest, not only from that very work, where he says "*cum et gesta
eorum* [Arthurii, scilicet, &c.] *à multis populis quasi inscripta mentibus et jucunde
et memoriter predicantur;*" but also from William of Malmesbury : "*Hic est
Arthurus de quo Brittonum nugæ hodieque delirant.*" *Maistre Wace*, likewise, a
writer of the same age or century, says,

> "*Fist Artur la ronde table,*
> *Dunt Breton dient meinte fable.*"

Even William of Newbrough allows that the fables of Arthur in Geoffrey's history
were partly taken "*ex priscis Britonum figmentis.*" Nothing of this kind, how-
ever, appears to be now extant.

  [1] The book alluded to is probably Geoffrey of Monmouth's *British history*, which
gave rise, within a very short period, to a multitude of voluminous romances on the
subject of Arthur. The phrase, however, is common in the old French histories of
the round table, &c. in which a chapter is frequently introduced with "*Or dict le
compte*, &c." So, likewise, in *La mort d'Arthur :* " And as the boke telleth, &c."
or, sometimes, "As the French booke saith."

  [2] It was the custom of the ancient monarchs of France and England, to hold
what was then called a *cour pleniere*, or plenary court, at the three principal feasts
of Easter, Whitsuntide, and Christmas ; at which they were attended by the earls
and barons of the kingdom, their ladies, and children ; who dined at the royal
table with great pomp and eclat ; minstrels flocking thither from all parts ; justs
and tournaments being performed, and various other kinds of divertisement, which
lasted several days. A very elaborate description of the coronation of king Arthur,
at the feast of Pentecost, is given by Geoffrey of Monmouth (B. ix, C. xii); which
has served as a model to his successors ; and the ceremony is frequently noticed
by our early historians, as Roger Hoveden, Matthew Paris, &c. &c. It is, of
course, still more common in the old romances.

  [3] Now Cardiff, in Glamorganshire.

---

to restore the dispersed and exiled Britons to their own." (Hearne's edition, P. 218.) This
tradition is mentioned by Girald and other old writers ; but the epitaph found at Glastonbury
is very different, and the cross delineated by Camden, if not the whole transaction, a palpable
forgery. Cervantes, upon whatever authority, makes don Quixote report, as an ancient and
common tradition in the whole kingdom of Great-Britain, that king Arthur did not die, but,
by art of enchantment, was converted into a crow ; and that, in process of time, he is to return
again to reign, and recover his kingdom and sceptre ; for which reason, he adds, it cannot be
proved that since that time any Englishman hath ever killed a crow." (Part 1, chap. 13.)
The French have an old MS. intitled " *Roman d'Artur le Rethoré* " (i.e. *le restauré :* Arthur
restored, or revived).

And als of knyghtes war and wyse,
And damisels of mykel pryse ;
Ilkane with other made grete gamin,
And grete solace, als thai war famin ;
Fast thai carped and curtaysly,
Of dedes of armes and of veneri,
And of gude knightes that lyfed then,
And how men might tham kyndeli ken,
By doghtines of thaire gude dede,
On ilka syde wharesum thai yede :   30
For thai war stif in ilka stowre,
And tharfore gat thai grete honowre.
Thai tald of more trewth tham bitwene,[1]
Than now omang men here es sene ;
For trowth and luf es al bylaft,
Men uses now another craft ;
With worde men makes it trew and stabil,
Bot in thair faith es noght bot fabil ;
With the mowth men makes it hale,
Bot trew trowth es nane in the tale.   40
Tharfore her-of now wil i blyn,
Of the kyng Arthur i wil bygin,
And of his curtayse cumpany,
That[2] was the flowr of chevallry ;
Swilk lose thai wan with speres horde,
Over al the werld went the worde.
   After mete went the kyng
Into chamber to slepeing,
And also went with him the quene,[3]
That byheld thai al-bydene,   50

---

[1] In the MS. this word reads "*bitwne.*"
[2] In the MS. this word reads "*thar.*"
[3] Guenever, in the old French romances, is the daughter of king Leodegrance of the land of Cameliard. Geoffrey of Monmouth calls her *Guanhumara,* * and says she was descended from a noble family of Romans ; had been educated under duke Cador ; and in beauty surpassed all the women in the island (B. 9, C. 9). According to this author, during Arthur's absence in Gaul or Italy, she married his nephew Mordred (whom the romance also makes his son †) ; they having been left joint-regents of the kingdom by Arthur ; upon whose return she fled from York to Chester, where she resolved to lead a chaste life, among the nuns, in the church of Julius the martyr, and enter herself one of their order. The romance, however, supposes her to have taken refuge in the tower of London, which was besieged by Mordred ; and to have, afterward, become a nun of Ambresbury,‡ where she died,

---

* *Guenureui,* Winifred. *Lloyd,* P. 255.
† By his sister *Margause,* the wife of king Lot, whom he did not, however, at the time know to be so. *L. du lac,* tome 3, fo. 16, b.
‡ The French romance of *Launcelot* does not name the nunnery to which the queen retired, and only says it was near London.

For thai saw tham never so
On high dayes to chamber go ;
Bot sone when thai war went to *slepe*,[1]
Knyghtes sat the dor to kepe,
Sir Dedyne, and sir Segramore,[2]
Sir Gawayn, and sir Kay, sat thore,[3]
And also sat thar sir Ywaine,
And Colgrevance of mekyl mayn.[4]
This knight that hight Colgrevance
Tald his felows of a chance,   60
And of a stowr he had in bene,
And al his tale herd the quene ;
The chamber-dore sho has unshet,
And down omang tham scho hir set ;
Sodainli sho sat down right,
Or ani of tham of hir had sight ;
Bot Colgrevance rase up in hy,
And thar-of had syr Kay envy,
For he was of his tong a skalde,
And forto boste was he ful balde.   70

and whence she was brought, by sir Lancelot, her former paramour, then a priest,
and his eight fellows, to Glastonbury, to be there interred in one and the same
tomb with the king her husband. It appears from the inscription on the cross
mentioned by Girald Barry, as found with her and her husband's remains, to
have been Arthur's second wife : and the Welsh antiquaries, never deficient in absurdity,
assert him to have had three wives, all of the name of *Guenever*.* We know, at
the same time, from better authority, that she was actually violated and ravished
by Melvas, king of *Estiva*, or Somersetshire, and taken to Glastonbury, as a place
of security, which Arthur besieged for a twelvemonth, till, by the mediation of
the abbot, and Gildas, surnamed *sapiens*, she was peaceably restored. See the life
of St. Gildas, by Carádoc of Lancarvan (*MSS. regia*, 13 B VII). He calls her
Guennimar. This *Melvas*, in all likelihood, is the *Meleagant* of the old French
romance, who achieves the queen in single combat with sir Kay, and carries them
both off to his father's castle. In *La mort d'Arthur*, where the story is differently
related, he is called *Meliagrance*. He was, afterward, slain by sir Lancelot.

   [1] This word is illegible in the MS.

   [2] *Sir Dedyne* is probably the same with *Dynadam* or *Dinadan*, surnamed *de
Estranger*, one of the knights of the round table.
   Sagremors le desree, or Segramour *le desirous*, was also a knight of the round
table, and is to be met with in *Lancelot du lac*, *Mort d'Arthur*, &c.

   [3] This sir Kay, the *Caius seneschallus* of Geoffrey of Monmouth, or *sire Keux
le seneschall* of the old French romances, was the son of sir *Ector*, or *Authon*, young
Arthur's tutor, and was, of course, that king's foster-brother. He has the same
character in *Mort d'Arthur* (P. 1, C. 120, &c.) and is elsewhere called to his face
" the shamefullest knight of his tongue " that was then living in the world.

   [4] So, in *Mort d'Arthur*, where he is said to be a knight of the round table. In
the French romance of *Lancelot du lac*, he is called *Gallogrenant*. In the former
book (P. 3, C. 80), he is slain by sir Lionell ; the sir Colgrevance of Gore, slain by
sir Lancelot, in C. 145, being, apparently, a different person.

   * See *Prisci Historiæ Brit. defensio*, P. 134, and Lewis's History of Britain, P. 185.

Ow, Colgrevance, said sir Kay,
Ful light of lepes has thou bene ay,
Thou wenes now that the sal fall,
For to be hendest of us all ;
And the quene sal understand,
That her es none so unkunand ;
Al if thou rase, and we sat styll,
We ne dyd it for none yll,
Ne for no maner of fayntise,
Ne for us donyd noght forto rise,   80
That we ne had resen had we hyr sene.
Sir Kay, i wote wele, sayd the quene,
And it war gude thou left swilk sawes,
And noght despise so thi felawes.
    Madame, he said, by goddes dome,[1]
We ne wist no thing of thi come ;
And if we did noght curtaysly,
Takes to no velany ;
Bot pray ye now this gentil man,
To tel the tale that he bygan.   90
Colgrevance said to sir Kay,
Bi grete god, that aw this day,
Na mar moves me thi flyt
Than it war a flies byt ;
Ful oft wele better men than i
Has thou desspised desspytusely ;
It es ful semeli, als me think,
A brok omang men forto stynk ;
So it fars by the, syr Kay,
Of weked wordes has thou bene ay,   100
And sen thi wordes er wikked and fell,
This time tharto na mor i tell,
Bot of the thing that i bygan.
And sone sir Kay him answerd than,

---

[1] Oaths are frequent throughout these poems, and in most kinds of ancient poetry ; being, manifestly, in common use amongst our ancestors, and even with young ladies, and princesses of the blood-royal ; by all of whom, it is presumed, they were regarded as perfectly innocent. Our ancient monarchs had their peculiar oaths : William the conqueror usually swore, By the resurrection of God ; William the red, By God's face, By the holy face of saint Luke ; John, by the feet of the Lord ; Henry the third, By God's head ; Edward the first, By the blood of God As the Lord liveth ; Edward the third, By God's soul ; Edward the fourth, By God's blessed lady ; Richard the third, By saint Paul ; Henry the eighth was by no means sparing ; and his daughter Elizabeth had *By God* in her mouth as frequently as a fishwoman. Chaucer's fellow-pilgrims have their several oaths, which are accurately enumerated by the historian of English poetry : see volume II, Sig. f 3. Oaths and curses, in fact, are, at this day, common to most nations in the world, as they were, formerly, to the Greeks and Romans.

And said ful tite unto thc quene,
Madame, if ye had noght her bene,
Wc sold have herd a selly case,
Now let yc us of our solace ;
Tharfor, madame, we wald yow pray,
That ye cumand him to say,   110
And tel forth als hc had tyght.
Than answerd that hendc knight,
Mi lady es so avysè,
That scho wil noght cumand me,
To tel that towches me to ill,
Scho es noght of so weked will.
Sir Kai said than, ful smertli,
Madame, al halc this cumpani
Praies yow hertly, now omell,
That he his tale forth might tell ;   120
If ye wil noght for our praying,
For faith ye aw unto the kyng,
Cumandes him his tale to tell,
That wc mai her how it byfell.
    Than said the quene, Sir Colgrevance,
I prai thc tak to no grevance,
This kene karping of syr Kay,
Of weked wordes has he bene ay,
So that none may him chastise,
Tharfor i prai thee, on al wise,   130
That thou let noght for his sawes,
At tel to me and thi felawes,
Al thi tale how it bytid,
For my luf i the pray and byd.
Sertes, madame, that es me lath,
Bot for i wil noght mak yow wrath,
Yowr cumandment i sal fulfill,
If ye will listen me untill ;
With hertes and eres understandes,
And i sal tel yow swilk tithandes,   140
That ye herd never none slike
Reherced in no kynges ryke ;
Bot word fares als dose the wind,
Bot if men it in hert bynd ;
And wordes woso trewly tase
By the eres into the hert it gase ;
And in thc hert thar es the horde,
And knawing of ilk mans worde.
    Herkens, hendc, unto my spell,
Trosels sal i yow nane tell,   150
Nc lesinges forto ger yow lagh,
Bot i sal say right als i sagh.

Now, als this time sex yer,
I rade allane, als ye sal her,
Obout, forto seke aventurs,
Wele armid in gude armurs,
In a frith i fand a strete,
Ful thik and hard, i yow bihete,
With thornes, breres, and moni a quyn,
Ner hand al day i rade thare-yn,   160
And thurgh i past, with mekyl payn,
Than come i sone into a playn,
Whar i gan se a bretise brade,
And thederward ful fast i rade ;
I saw the walles and the dyke,
And hertly wele it gan me lyke ;
And on the draw-brig saw i stand,
A knight with fawkon on his hand ;
This ilk knight, that be ye balde,
Was lord and keper of that halde.   170
I hailsed him kindly, als i kowth,
He answerd me mildeli with mowth ;
Mi sterap toke that hende knight,
And kindly cumanded[1] me to lyght,
His cumandment i did onane,
And into hall sone war we tane.
He thanked god, that gude man,
Sevyn sithes or ever he blan,
And the way that me theder broght,
And als the aventurs that i soght.   180
Thus went we in, god do him mede !
And in his hand he led my stede.
When we war in that fayre palays,
It was ful worthly wroght always,
I saw no man of moder born,
Bot a burde hang us biforn,
Was nowther of yren, ne of tre,
Ne i ne wist whar-of it might be ;
And by that bord hang a mall,
The knyght smate on thar-with-all   190
Thrise, and by then might men se,
Bifore ham come a fair menyè
Curtayse men in worde and dede,
To stabil sone thai led mi stede,
A damisel come unto me,
The semeliest that ever i se,
Lufsumer lifed never in land,
Hendly scho toke me by the hand,

---

[1] Conjectural emendation : *cumand,* as in verse 110.

And sone that gentyl creature
Al unlaced myne armure ;   200
Into a chamber sho me led,
And with a mantil scho me cled ;
It was of purpur, fair and fine,
And the pane of riche ermyne ;
Al the folk war went us fra,
And thare was none than bot we twa ;
Scho served me¹ hendely to hend,
Hir maners might no man amend ;
Of tong sho was trew and renable,
And of hir semblant soft and stabile ;   210
Ful fain i wald, if that i might,
Have woned with that swete wight :
And when we sold go to sopere,
That lady, with a lufsom chere,
Led me down into the hall,
Thar war we served wele at all.
It nedes noght to tel the mese,
For wonder wele war we at esse.²
Byfor me sat the lady bright,
Curtaisly my mete to dyght ;   220
Us wanted nowther baken³ ne roste,
And, efter soper, sayd myne oste,
That he cowth noght tel the day
That ani knight are with him lay,
Or that ani aventures soght,
Tharfor he prayed me, if i moght,
On al wise when i come ogayne,
That i sold cum to him sertayne.
I said, Sir, gladly, yf i may,
I had bene shame have said him nay.   230
That night had i ful gude rest,
And mi stede esed of the best.
Alsone als it was dayes lyght,
Forth to far sone was i dyght ;
Mi leve of mine ost toke i thare,
And went my way with-owten mare,
Aventures for to layt in land.
    A fair forest sone i fand,
Me thoght mi hap thare fel ful hard,
For thar was mani a wilde lebard,   240
Lions, beres, bath bul and bare,
That rewfully gan rope and rare ;

---

¹ The MS. reads "*le.*"
² Conjectural emendation : *ese* (as *esed*, v. 232).
³ Conjectural emendation : *bake.*

Oway i drogh me, and with that,
I saw sone whar a man sat,
On a lawnd, the fowlest wight
That ever yit man saw in syght ;
He was a lathly creatur,
For fowl he was out of mesur ;
A wonder mace in hand he hade,
And sone my way to him i made ;   250
His hevyd, me-thought, was als grete
Als of a rowncy or a nete.
Unto his belt hang his hare,
And efter that byheld i mare ;
To his forhede byheld i than,
Was bradder than twa large span ;
He had eres als ane olyfant,
And was wele more than geant ;
His face was ful brade and flat ;
His nese was cutted als a cat ;   260
His browes war like litel buskes ;
And his tethe like bare tuskes ;
A ful grete bulge opon his bak ;
Thar was noght made with-owten lac ;
His chin was fast until his brest ;
On his mace he gan him rest.
Also it was a wonder wede
That the cherle yn yede ;
Nowther of wol, ne of line,
Was the wede that he went yn.   270
When he me sagh, he stode up-right,
I frayned him if he wolde fight,
For tharto was i in gude will,
Bot als a beste than stode he still ;
I hopid that he no wittes kowth,
No reson forto speke with mowth.
To him i spak ful hardily,
And said, What ertow, belamy ?
He said, ogain, I am a man.
I said, Swilk saw i never nane ;   280
What ertow ? al sone said he.
I said, Swilk als thou her may se.
I said, What dose thou here allane ?
He said, I kepe thir bestes ilkane.
I said, That es mervaile think me,
For i herd never of man bot the,
In wildernes, ne in forestes,
That keping had of wilde bestes,
Bot thai war bunden fast in halde.
He sayd, Of thir es none so balde,   209

Nowther by day ne bi night,
Anes to pas out of mi sight.
I sayd, How so ? tel me thi scill.
Perfay, he said, gladly i will.
He said, In al this fair foreste
Es thar none so wilde beste,
That renin dar bot stil stand,
When i am to him cumand ;
And ay, when that i wil him fang,
With mi fingers, that er strang,   300
I ger him cri, on swilk manere,
That al the bestes when thai him here,
Obout me than cum thai all,
And to mi fete fast thai fall,
On thair maner merci to cry ;
Bot understand now, redyli,
Olyve es thar lifand no ma,
Bot i, that durst omang tham ga,
That he ne sold sone be al to-rent,
Bot thai er at my comandment ;   310
To me thai cum, when i tham call,
And i am maister of tham all.
Than he asked, onone right,
What man i was. I said, A knyght,
That soght aventurs in that land,
My body to asai and fande :
And i the pray of thi knownsayle,
Thou teche me to sum mervayle.
He sayd, I can no wonders tell,
Bot her-bisyde es a well,   320
Wend theder, and do als i say,
Thou passes noght al quite oway.
Folow forth this ilk strete,
And sone sum mervayles sal thou mete,
The well es under fairest tre,
That ever was in this cuntrè ;
By that well hinges a bacyne,
That es of gold gude and fyne,
With a cheyne, trewly to tell,
That wil reche into the well.   330
Thare es a chapel ner thar-by,
That nobil es, and ful lufely,
By the well standes a stane,
Tak the bacyn sone onane,
And cast on water with thi hand,
And sone thou sal se new tithand.
A storme sal rise, and a tempest,
Al obout by est and west ;

Thou sal here mani thonor blast,
Al obout the blawand fast;   340
And there sal cum slik slete and rayne,
That unnese sal thou stand ogayne;
Of lightnes sal thou se a lowe,
Unnethes thou sal thi-selven knowe;
And if thou pas with-owten grevance,
Than has thou the fairest chance
That ever yit had any knyght
That theder come to kyth his myght.
    Than toke i leve, and went my way,
And rade unto the midday;   350
By than i come whare i sold be,
I saw the chapel and the tre;
Thare i fand the fayrest thorne,[1]
That ever groued sen god was born;
So thik it was with leves grene,
Might no rayn cum thar-bytwene,
And that grenes lastes ay,
For no winter dere yt may.
I fand the bacyn, als he talde,
And the wel with water kalde,   360
An amerawd was the stane,
Richer saw i never nane,
On fowr rubyes on heght standand,
Thair light lasted over al the land;
And when i saw that semely syght,
It made me bath joyful and lyght;
I toke the bacyn sone onane,[2]
And helt water opon the stane:
The weder wex than wonder blak,
And the thoner fast gan crak.   370
Thar come slike stormes of hayl and rayn,
Unnethes i might stand thare ogayn:
The store windes blew ful lowd,
So kene come never are of clowd;
I was drevyn with snaw and slete,
Unnethes i might stand on my fete;
In my face the levening smate,
I wend have brent, so was it hate.

---

[1] The MS. has "*tlorne.*"

[2] This incident is introduced into "The noble hystory of kyng Ponthus of Galyce," 1511, 4to. b. 1. (a translation from the French): "The knyght toke a cuppe of golde, and put it in the well, and wette the stone withall; and the water sprang abrode; and it began to thunder and to hayle, and to be a stronge tempest; but it dured not long; and moche mervaylled the straungers of that well, for alway he spryncled it tofore that he went to fyghte."

That weder made me so will of rede,
I hopid sone to have my dede ; 380
And, sertes, if it lang had last,
I hope i had never thethin past ;
Bot, thorgh his might that tholed wownd,
The storme sesed within a stownde ;
Than wex the weder fayr ogayne,
And tharof was i wonder fayne ;
For best comforth of al thing
Es solace efter myslikeing.
    Than saw i sone a mery syght,
Of al the fowles that er in flyght 390
Lighted so thik opon that tre,
That bogh ne lefe none might i se ;
So merily than gon thai sing.
That al the wode began to ring ;
Ful mery was the melody,
Of thaire sang and of thaire cry ;
Thar herd never man none swilk,
Bot if ani had herd that ilk ;
And when that mery dyn was done
Another noyse than herd i sone, 400
Als it war of horsmen,
Mo than owther nyen or ten.
    Sone than saw i cum a knyght,
In riche armurs was he dight,
And sone when i gan on him loke,
Mi shelde and sper to me i toke ;
That knight to me hied ful fast,
And kene wordes out gan he cast ;
He bad that i sold tel him tite
Whi i did him swilk despite, 410
With weders wakend him of rest,
And done him wrang in his forest ;
Tharfore, he said, thou sal aby,
And with that come he egerly,
And said, i had, ogayne resowne,
Done him grete destrucciowne,
And might it nevermore amend,
Tharfor he bad i sold me fend ;
And sone i smate him on the shelde,
Mi schaft brac out in the felde, 420
And then he bar me sone bi strenkith
Out of my sadel my speres lenkith.
I wate that he was largely
By the shuldres mare that i,
And, bi the ded that i sal thole,
Mi stede by his was but a fole ;

For mate i lay down on the grownde,
So was i stonayd in that stownde.
A worde to me wald he noght say,
Bot toke my stede, and went his way.　　430
Ful farily than thare i sat
For wa i wist noght what was what.
With my stede he went in hy,
The same way that he come by,
And i durst folow him no ferr,
For dout me solde bite werr,
And also yit, by goddes dome,
I ne wist whar he bycome.
　　Than i thoght how i had hight
Unto myne oste, the hende knyght,　　440
And also til his lady bryght,
To com ogayn, if that i myght ;
Mine armurs left i thare ilkane,
For els myght i noght have gane ;
Unto myne in i come by day ;
The hende knight, and the fayre may,
Of my come war thai ful glade,
And nobil semblant thai me made,
In al thinges thai have tham born,
Als thai did the night biforn.　　450
Sone thai wist whare i had bene,
And said, that thai had never sene
Knyght, that ever theder come,
Take the way ogayn home.
On this wise that tyme i wroght,
I fand the folies that i soght.
　　Now, sekerly, said sir Ywayne,
Thou ert my cosyn jermayne,
Trew luf suld be us bytwene,
Als sold bytwyx brether bene,　　460
Thou ert a fole, at thou ne had are
Tald me of this ferly fare,
For, sertes, i sold onone ryght
Have venged the of that ilk knyght ;
So sal i yit, if that i may.
And than als smertly sayd syr Kay :
He karpet to tham wordes grete :
It es sene now es efter mete,
Mare boste es in a pot of wyne,
Than in a karcas of saynt Martyne ;　　470
Arme the smertly,[1] syr Ywayne,
And sone that thou war cumen ogayne,

---

[1] The MS. reads "*smestly*."

Luke thou fil wele thi pancle,
And in thi sadel set the wele ;
And when thou wendes, i the pray,
Thi baner welc that thou desplay;
And rede i, or thou wende,
Thou tak thi leve at ilka frende ;
And if it so bytide this nyght,
That the in slepe dreche ani wight,   480
Or any dremis mak the rad,
Turn ogayn, and say i bad.
   The quene answerd, with milde mode,
And said, Sir Kay, ertow wode ?
What the devyl es the withyn,
At thi tong may never blyn
Thi felows so fowly to shende ?
Sertes, sir Kay, thou ert unhende.
By him that for us sufferd pine,
Syr, and thi tong war myne,   490
I sold bical it tyte of treson,
And so might thou do by gude reson ;
Thi tong dose the grete dishonowre,
And tharefore is it thi traytowre.
And than alsone syr Ywayne
Ful hendly answerd ogayne ;
Al if men sayd hym velany,
He karped ay ful curtaysly :
Madame, he said unto the quene,
Thare sold na stryf be us bytwene,   500
Unkowth men wele may he shende,
That to his felows es so unhende ;
And als, madame, men says sertayne,
That woso slites, or turnes ogayne,
He bygins al the mellè,
So wil i noght it far by me ;
Lates him say halely his thoght,
His wordes greves me right noght.
   Als thai war in this spekeing,
Out of the chamber come the kyng,   510
The barons that war there sertayn,
Smertly rase thai him ogayne.
He bad tham sit down albydene,
And down he set him by the quene ;
The quene talde him, fayr and wele,
Als sho kowth, everilka dele,
Ful apertly, al the chance,
Als it byfel syr Colgrevance.
When sho had talde him how it ferd,
And the king hyr tale had herd,   520

He swar by his owyn crowne,
And his fadersowl, Uter-Pendragowne,
That he sold se that ilk syght,
By that day thethin a fowretenight,
On saint John's evyn the baptist,
That best barn was under Crist:
Swith, he sayd, wendes with me,
Whoso wil that wonder se.
The kynges word might noght be hid,
Over al the cowrt sone was it kyd,   530
And thar was none so litel page
That he ne was fayn of that vayage,
And knyghtes and swiers war ful fayne,
Mysliked none bot syr Ywayne;
To himself he made grete mane,
For he wald have went allane;
In hert he had grete myslykyng
For the wending of the kyng,
Al for he hopid, withowten fayle,
That sir Kay sold ask the batayle,   540
Or els sir Gawayn, knyght vailant,
And owther wald the king grant,
Whoso it wald first crave,
Of tham two, sone might it have.
The kynges wil wald he noght bide,
Worth of him what may bityde,
By him allane he thoght to wende,
And tak the grace that god wald send.
He thoght to be wele on hys way,
Or it war passed the thryd day,   550
And to asay if he myght mete
With that ilk narow strete.
With thornes and with breres set,
That mens way might lightli let;
And also forto fynd the halde
That sir Colgrevance of talde,
The knyght and the mayden meke.
The forest fast than wald he seke,
And als the karl of Kaymes kyn,
And the wilde bestes with him;   560
The tre with briddes thare-opon;
The chapel, the bacyn, and the stone.
His thoght wald he tel to no frende,
Until he wyst how it wald ende.
    Than went Ywaine to his yn,
His men he fand redy tharyn,
Unto a swier gan he saye,
Go swith, and sadel my palfray,

And so thou do my strang stede,
And tak with the my best wede,   570
At yone yate i wil out-ryde,
Withowten town i sal the bide,
And hy the smertly unto me,
For i most make a jornè.
Ogain sal thou bring¹ my palfra,
And forbede the oght to say,
If thou wil any more me se,
Lat none wit of my prevetè ;
And if ani man the oght frayn,
Luke now lely that thou layn.   580
Sir, he said, with ful gude will,
Als ye byd, i sal fulfyll ;
At yowr awyn wil may ye ride,
For me ye sal noght be ascryed.
    Forth than went sir Ywayne,
He thinkes, or he cum ogayne,
To wreke his kosyn at his myght ;
The squier has his hernays dyght,
He did right als his mayster red,
His stede, his armurs, he him led.   590
When Ywayn was withowten town,   .
Of his palfray lighted he down,
And dight him right wele in his wede,
And lepe up on his gude stede.
Furth he rade onone right,
Until it neghed nere the nyght,
He passed many high mowntayne,
In wildernes, and mony a playne,
Til he come to that lethir sty,
That him byhoved pass by ;   600
Than was he seker forto se
The wel, and the fayre tre ;
The chapel saw he at the last,
And theder hyed he ful fast ; ²
More curtaysi and mor honowr
Fand he with tham in that tour,
And mar conforth, by mony falde,
Than Colgrevance had him of talde :

---

¹ The MS. reads "*brring*."

² The poet, in this place, has either forgot himself, or mistaken his original. Sir Ywain, according to sir Colgrevances relation, as well as to the story, neither could, nor did, see these wonders till afterward. See V. 352. He means to say that sir Ywain came in sight of the palace or castle, where Sir Colgrevance had been so kindly entertained, and where he himself finds so much courtesy and honour. The mistake may be, in part, corrected by reading *castle* for *chapel.*

That night was he herberd thar,
So wele was he never are. 610
   At morn he went forth by the strete,
And with the cherel sone gan he mete,
That sold tel to him the way,
He sayned him, the soth to say,
Twenty sith, or ever he blan,
Swilk mervayle had he of that man ;
For he had wonder that nature
Myght mak so fowl a creature.
Than to the well he rade gude pase,
And doun he lighted in that place, 620
And sone the bacyn has he tane,
And kest water upon the stane,
And sone thar wex, withowten fayle,
Wind, and thonor, and rayn, and haile.
When it was sesed, than saw he
The fowles light opon the tre,
Thai sang ful fayre opon that thorn,
Right als thai had done byforn ;
And sone he saw cumand a knight,
Als fast so the fowl in flyght, 630
With rude sembland, and sterne cher,
And hastily he neghed nere ;
To speke of lufe na time was thar,
For aither hated uther ful sar ;
Togeder smertly gan thai drive,
Thair sheldes sone bigan to ryve,
Thair shaftes cheverd to thair hand,
Bot thai war bath ful wele syttand.
Out thai drogh thair swerdes kene,
And delt strakes them bytwene ; 640
Al to peces thai hewed thair sheldes,[1]
The culpons flegh out in the feldes ;
On helmes strake thay so with yre
At ilka strake out-brast the fyr ;
Aither of tham gude buffettes bede ;
And nowther wald styr of the stede ;
Ful kenely thai kyd thair myght,
And feyned tham noght forto fight ;
Thair hauberkes, that men myght ken,
The blode out of thair bodyes ren. 650
Aither on other laid so fast.
The batayl might noght lang last ;
Hauberkes er broken, and helmes reven,
Stif strakes war thar gyfen ;

---

[1] The MS. has "*sleldes.*"

Thai faght on hors stifly always,
The batel was wele inor to prays :
Bot, at the last, syr Ywayne
On his felow kyd his mayne,
So egerly he smate him than,
He clefe the helme and the hern-pan.   660
The knyght wist he was nere ded,
To fle than was his best rede,
And fast he fled, with al his mayne,
And fast folow syr Ywayne,
Bot he ne might him overtake,
Tharfore grete murning gan he make ;
He folowd him ful stowtlyk,
And wald have tane him ded or quik ;
He folowd him to the cetè,
Na man lyfand met he.   670
When thai come to the kastel-yate,
In he folowd fast tharate,
At aither entre was, i wys,
Straytly wroght, a port-culis,
Shod wele with yren and stele,
And also grunden wonder wele.
Under that than was a swyke,
That made syr Ywain to myslike ;
His hors fote toched thareon,
Than fel the port-culis onone,   680
Bytwyx him and his hinder arsown,
Thorgh sadel and stede, it smate al down ;
His spores of his heles it schare,
Than had Ywaine murnyng mare,
Bot so he wend have passed quite,
That fel the tother bifore als tyte.
A faire grace yit fel him swa,
Al if it smate his hors in twa,
And his spors of aither hele,
That himself passed so wele.   690
Bytwene tha yates now es he tane,
Tharfor he mase ful mykel mane,
And mikel murnyng gan he ma,
For the knyght was went him fra.
Als he was stoken in that stall,
He herd byhind him, in a wall,
A dor opend fair and wele,
And tharout come a damysel,
Efter hir the dore sho stak,
Ful hinde wordes to him sho spak.   700
Syr, sho said, by saint Myghell,
Her thou has a febil ostell ;

Thou mon be ded, es noght at laine,
For my lord that thou has slayne;
Seker it es that thou him slogh,
My lady makes sorrow ynogh,
And al his menye everilkane
Her has thou famen manyane,
To be thi bane er thai ful balde,
Thou brekes noght out of this halde,   710
And, for thai wate thai may noght fayl,
Thai¹ wil the sla in playn batayl.
He sayd, Thai ne sal, so god me rede,
For al thair might, do me to dede,
Ne no handes opon me lay.
Sho said, Na, sertes, if that i may,
Al if thou be here straytly stad,
Methink thou ert noght ful adrad :
And sir, sho said, on al wise,
I aw the honor and servyse ;   720
I was in message at the king,
Bifor this time, whils i was ying,
I was noght than so avesè,²
Als a damysel aght to be,
Fro the tyme that i was lyght
In cowrt was none so hend knyght
That unto me than walde take hede
Bot thou allane, god do the mede !
Grete honor thou did to me,
And that sal i now quite the.   730
I wate, if thou be seldom sene,
Thou art the kyng son Uriene,
And thi name es sir Ywayne,
Of me may thou be sertayne,
If thou wil my kownfail leve,
Thou sal find na man the to greve ;
I sal lene the her mi ring,
Bot yelde it me at myne askyng,
When thou ert broght of al thi payn,
Yelde it than to me ogayne ;   740
Als the bark hilles the tre,
Right so sal my ring do the ;
When thou in hand has the stane,
Der sal thai do the nane,
For the stane es of swilk myght,
Of the sal men have na syght,
  Wit ye wele that sir Ywayne
Of thir wordes was ful fayne.

---

¹ The MS. has " *Ye.*"   ² The MS. has "*savese.*"

In at the dore sho him led,
And did him sit opon hir bed,   750
A quylt ful nobil lay tharon,
Richer saw he never none.
Sho said, if he wald any thing,
He sold be served at his liking.
He said, that ete wald he fayn.
Sho went, and come ful sone ogain ;
A capon rosted broght sho sone,
A clene klath, and brede tharone,
And a pot with riche wine,
And a pece to fil it yne.   760
He ete and drank, with ful gude cher,
For tharof had he grete myster.
When he had eten and dronken wele,
Grete noyse he herd in the kastele,
Thai soght over al him to have slayn,
To venge thair lorde war thai ful bayn,
Or that the cors in erth was layd.
The damysel sone to him sayd,
Now seke thai the fast forto sla,
Bot whoso ever com or ga,   770
Be thou never the mor adred,
Ne styr thou noght out of this stede :
In this here secke thai wyll,
Bot on this bed luke thou be styll ;
Of tham al mak thou na force,
Bot when that thai sal ber the cors
Unto the kyrk forto bery,
Than sal thou here a sary cry ;
So sal thai mak a doleful dyn,
Than wil thay seke the eft herin ;   780
Bot loke thou be of hert lyght,
For of the sal thai have no syght ;
Her sal thou be mawgre thair berd,
And tharfor be thou noght aferd ;
Thi famen sal be als the blynd,
Both byfor the and byhind ;
On ilka side sal thou be soght ;
Now most i ga, bot drede the noght,
For i sal do that the es lefe,
If al it turn me to mischefe.   790
When sho come unto the yate,
Ful many men fand sho tharate,
Wele armed, and wald ful fayn
Have taken and slane sir Ywaine,
Half his stede thar fand thai,
That within the yates lay,

Bot the knight thar fand thai noght,
Than was thar mekil sorow unsoght,
Dore ne window was thar nanc
Whar he myght oway gane.   800
Thai said he sold thare be laft,
Or els he cowth of wechecraft,
Or he cowth of nygromancy,
Or he had wenges for to fly.
Hastily than went thai all,
And soght him in the maydens hall,
In chambers high, es noght at hide,
And in solers on ilka side.
Sir Ywaine saw ful welc al that,
And still opon the bed he sat ;   810
Thar was nane that anes mynt
Unto the bed at smyte a dynt,
Al obout thai smate so fast
That mani of thair wapins brast.
Mekyl sorow thai made ilkane,
For thai ne myght wreke thair lord bane.
Thai went oway, with dreri chere,
And sone tharefter come the ber,
A lady folowd, white so mylk,
In al that land was none swilk :   820
Sho wrang her fingers, out-brast the blode,
For mekyl wa sho was nere wode,
Hir fayr har scho al to-drogh,
And ful oft fel sho down in swogh ;
Sho wepe, with a ful dreri voice.
The hali water, and the croyce,
Was born bifor the procession,
Thar folowd mani a moder son.
Bifore the cors rade a knyght,
On his stede that was ful wight,   830
In his armurs welc arayd,
With sper and target gudely grayd.
Than sir Ywayn herd the cry,
And the dole of that fayr lady,
For mor sorow myght nane have
Than sho had when he went to grave.
Prestes and monkes, on thaire wyse,
Ful solempnly did the servyse.
Als Lunet thar stode in the thrang,[1]
Until sir Ywaine thoght hir lang,   840

---

[1] *Lynet* is the name of the damsel, in *Mort d'Arthur*, sister of dame Liones, who comes for a champion to the court of king Arthur, where she obtains sir Beaumains, and accompanies him back. See Part 1, C. 132.

Out of the thrang the wai sho tase,
Unto sir Ywaine fast sho gase ;
Sho said, Sir, how ertow stad ?
I hope ful wele thou has bene rad.
Sertes, he said, thou sais wele thar,
So abayst was i never are.
He said, Leman, i pray the,
If it any wise may be,
That i might luke a litel throw
Out at sum hole or sum window ;   850
For wonder fayn, he sayd, wald i
Have a sight of the lady.
The maiden than ful sone unshet
In a place a prevé weket,
Thar of the lady he had a syght,
Lowd sho cried to god almyght,
" Of his sins do him pardowne,
For sertanly in no regyowne
Was never knight of his bewtè,
Ne efter him sal never nane be ;   860
In al the werld, fro end to ende,
Es none so curtayse, ne so hende.
God grant the grace thou mai won
In hevyn with his owyn son !
For so large lifes none in lede,
Ne none so doghty of gude dede."
When sho had thus made hir spell,
In swownyng ful oft-sithes sho fell.
    Now lat we the lady be,
And of sir Ywaine speke we.   870
Luf that es so mekil of mayne,
Sar had wownded sir Ywayne,
That whareso he sal ride or ga
His hert sho has that es his fa,
His hert he has set albydene
Whar him self dar noght be sene ;
Bot thus in langing bides he,
And hopes that it sal better be.
Al that war at the enterement
Toke thair leve at the lady gent,   880
And hame¹ now er thai halely gane,
And the lady left allane,
Dweland with hir chamberer,
And other mo that war hir der.
Than bigan hir noyes al new,
For sorow failed hir hide and hew.

---

¹ The MS. has "*y anc*" on an erasure in a modern hand.

Unto his sawl was sho ful hulde,
Opon a sawter al of gulde,
To say the salmes fast sho bigan,
And toke no tent unto no man.   890
Than had sir Ywain mekyl drede,
For he hoped noght to spede,
He said, I am mekil to blame,
That i luf tham that wald me shame,
Bot yit i wite hir al with wogh,
Sen that i hir lord slogh,
I can noght se, by nakyn gyn,
How that i hir luf sold wyn.
That lady es ful gent and small,
Hir yghen cler als es cristall ;   900
Sertes thar es no man olive
That kowth hir bewtese wele descrive.
Thus was syr Ywayne sted that sesowne,
He wroght fu mekyl ogayns resowne,
To set his luf in swilk a stede,
Whare thai hated him to the dede :
He sayd he sold have hir to wive,
Or els he sold lose his lyve.
   Thus als he in stody sat,
The mayden come to him with that :   910
Sho sayd, How has to farn this day,
Sen that i went fro the oway ?
Sone sho saw him pale and wan,
Sho wist wele what him ayled than ;
Sho said, I wote thi hert es set,
And sertes i ne sal noght it let,
Bot i sal help the fra presowne,
And bring the to thi warisowne.
He said, Sertes, damysele,
Out of this place wil i noght stele,   920
Bot i wil wende by dayes lyght,
That men may of me have sight,
Opinly on ilka syde,
Worth of me what so bityde ;
Manly wil i hethin wende.
Than answerd the mayden hende :
Sir, thou sal wend with honowr,
For thou sal have ful gude socowr ;
Bot, sir, thou sal be her sertayne,
A while unto i cum ogayne :   930
Sho [kend] altrewly his entent,
And tharfor es sho wightly went
Unto the lady faire and bright,
For unto hir right wele sho myght

Say what-som hyr willes es,
For sho was al hir maystres,
Her keper, and hir cownsayler :
To hir sho said, als ye sal her,
Bytwix tham twa in gude cownsayl :
Madame, sho sayd, i have mervayl   940
That ye sorow thus ever onane ;
For goddes luf lat be yowr mane ;
Ye sold think over alkyn thyng,
Of the kinges Arthurgh cumyng.
Menes yow noght of the message
Of the damysel savage,
That in hir lettre to yow send ;
Allas, who sal yow now defend,
Yowr land, and al that es tharyn ?
Sen ye wil never of wepeing blyn.   950
A madame, takes tent to me,
Ye ne have na knyght in this cuntre,
That durst right now his body bede,
Forto do a doghty dede,
Ne forto bide the mekil boste
Of king Arthurgh and of his oste,
And if he find none hym ogayn,
Yowr landes er lorn, this es sertayn,
    The lady understode ful wele
How sho hyr cownsaild ilka dele,   960
Sho bad hyr go hir way smertly,
And that sho war na mor hardy
Swilk wordes to hyr at speke,
For wa hir hert wold al to-breke.
Sho bad go wightly hethin oway.
Than the maiden thus gan say :
Madame, it es oft wemens will
Tham forto blame that sais tham scill.
Sho went oway als sho noght roght,
And than the lady hyr bythoght   970
That the maiden said no wrang,
And so sho sat in stody lang.
    In stody thus allane sho sat,
The mayden come ogayn with that :
Madame, sho said, ye er a barn,
Thus may ye sone yowr self forfarn.
Sho sayd, chastise thy hert madame,
To swilk a lady it es grete shame
Thus to wepe, and make slike cry,
Think upon thi grete gentri.   980
Trowes thou the flowr of chevalry
Sold al with thi lord dy,

And with him be put in molde ?—
God forbede that it so solde !
Als gude als he, and better bene,
Thou lyes, sho said, by hevyn quene.
Lat se if thoue me tel kan,
Whar es any so doghty man
Als he was that wedded [1] me.
"Yis, and ye kun me na mawgrè,   990
And that ye mak me sekernes,
That ye sal luf me nevertheles."
Sho said, Thou may be ful sertayn,
That for na thing that thou mai sayn,
Wil i me wreth on nane maner.
Madame, sho said, than sal ye her :
I sal yow tel a prevetè,
An na ma sal wit bot [2] we.
Yf twa knyghtes be in the felde,
On twa stedes, with spere and shelde,   1000
And the tane the tother may sla,
Whether es the better of tha ?
Sho said, He that has the bataile.
Ya, said the mayden, sawnfayle,
The knyght that lifes es mar of maine,
Than yowr lord that was slayne;
Yowr lord fled out of the place,
And the tother gan hym chace
Heder into his awyn halde,
Thar may ye wit he was ful balde.   1010
The lady said, This es grete scorne,
That thou nevyns him me biforne,
Shou sais nowther soth, ne right,
Swith out of myne eghen syght !
The mayden said, So mot i the,
Thus ne hight ye noght me,
That ye sold so me myssay.
With that sho turned hir oway,
And hastily sho went ogayn,
Unto the chameber to sir Ywayne.   1020
  The lady thoght than, al the nyght,
How that sho had na knyght,
Forto seke hir land thorghout,
To kepe Arthurgh and hys rowt.
Than bigan hir forto shame,
And hir self fast forto blame ;

---

[1] Between *that* and *wedded* is a syllable of two letters, interlined, illegible, and unnecessary to the sense.
[2] The MS. reads " *bo*."

Unto hir self fast gan sho flyte,
And said With wrang now i hir wite ;
Now hopes sho i will never mar
Luf hir, als i have done ar ;   1030
I wil hir luf, with main and mode,
For that sho said was for my gode.
  On the morn the mayden rase,
And unto chamber sone sho gase ;
Thar sho fyndes the faire lady
Hingand hir hevyd ful drerily,
In the place whar sho hir left,
And ilka dele sho talde hir eft,
Als sho had said to hir bifor.
Than said the lady, Me rewes for,   1040
That i missayd the yisterday,
I wil amend if that i may ;
Of that knyght now wald i her,
What he war, and whether he wer ;
I wate that i have sayd omys,
Now wil i do als thou me wys :
Tel me baldely, or thou blin,
If he be cumen of gentil kyn.
Madame, sho said, i dar warand
A genteler lord es none lifand.   1050
The hendest man ye sal him fynde,
That ever come of Adams kynde.
" How hat he ? sai me for sertayne."
Madame, sho said, sir Ywayne,
So gentil knight have ye noght sene,
He es the kings¹ son Uryene.
Sho held hir paid of that tithyng,²
For that his fader was a kyng.
" Do me have him here in my sight,
Bitwene this and the thrid night,   1060
And ar if that it are myght be,
Me langes far him forto se ;
Bring him if thou mai this night."
Madame, sho sayd, that I ne might,
For his wonyng es hethin oway,
More than the jorné of a day ;
Bot i have a wele rinand page,
Wil stirt thider right in a stage,
And bring him by to morn at nyght.
The lady saide, Loke, yf he myght   1070
To-morn by evyn be here ogayn.
Sho said, Madame, With al his mayn.

---

¹ The MS. reads "*kius.*"   ² The MS. reads "*tiyng.*"

" Bid him hy, on alkyn wyse,
He sal be quit wele his servyse,
Avancement sal be hys bone,
If he wil do this erand sone."
Madame, sho said, i dar yow hight,
To have him her or the thrid nyght ;
Towhils efter yowr kownsayl send,
And ask tham wha sal yow defend,   1080
Yowr well, yowr land, kastel, and towr,
Ogayns the nobil king Arthur,
For thar es nane of tham ilkane
That dar the batel undertane.
Then sal ye say, nedes bus me take
A lorde to do that ye forsake :
Nedes bus yow have sum nobil knyght
That wil and may defend yowr right ;
And sais also to suffer ded
Ye wil noght do out of thair rede: 1090
Of that worde sal thai be blyth,
And thank yow ful many sithe.
The lady said, By god of myght,
I sal areson tham this night ;
Me think thou dwelles ful lang her,
Send forth swith thi messanger.
    Than was the lady blith and glad,
Sho did al als hir mayden bad,
Efter hir cownsail sho sent onane,
And bad thai sold cum sone ilkane.   1100
The maiden redies hyr ful rath,
Bilive sho gert syr Ywaine bath,
And cled him sethin in gude scarlet,
Forord wele and with gold fret,
A girdel ful riche for the nanes,
Of perry and of preciows stanes.
Sho talde him al how he sold do,
When that he come the lady to ;
And thus when he was al redy,
Sho went and talde to hyr lady,   1110
That cumen was hir messager.
Sho said smertly, Do lat me her,
Cumes he sone, als have thou wyn ?
Medame, sho said, i sal noght blin,
Or that he be byfor yow here.
Then said the lady, with light cher,
Go bring him heder prevely,
That none wit bot thou and i :
Then the maiden went ogayn,
Hastily to sir Ywayn :   1120

Sir, sho sayd, als have i wyn,
My lady wate thou ert hereyn ;
To cum bifor hir luke thou be balde,
And tak gode tent what i have talde.
By the hand sho toke the knyght,
And led him unto chamber right,
Byfor hir lady, es noght at layne,
And of that come was sho ful fayne ;
Bot yit sir Ywayne had grete drede,
When he unto chamber yede.   1130
The chamber flore, and als the bed,
With klothes of gold was al over spred,
Hir thoght he was withowten lac,
Bot no word to him sho spak,
And he for dred oway he drogh,
Than the mayden stode and logh :
Sho sayd, Mawgre have that knyght,
That haves of swilk a lady syght,
And can noght shew to hir his nede ;
Cum furth sir, the thar noght drede,   1140
That mi lady wil the smyte,
Sho loves the wele withowten lite,
Pray to hir of hir mercy,
And for thi sake right so sal i,
That sho forgif the, in this stede,
Of Salados the rouse ded,
That was hir lord that thou hast slayne.
On knese him set than syr Ywaine :
" Madame, i yelde me yow untill,
Ever to be at yowre wyll,   1150
Yf that i might i ne wald noght fle.
Sho said, Nay, whi sold so be ?
To ded yf i gert do the now,
To me it war ful litel prow,
Bot for i find the so bowsum,
That thou wald thus to me cum,
And for thou dose the in my grace,
I forgif the thi trispase.
Syt down, sho said, and lat me her,
Why thou ert thus deboner.   1160
Madame, he said, anis, with a luke,
Al my hert with the thou toke,
Sen i first of the had syght,
Have i the lufed with al my might,
To mo than the, mi lady hende,
Sal never mor my luf wende.
For thi luf ever i am redy
Lely forto lif or dy.

Sho said, Dar thou wele undertake
In my land pese forto make, 1170
And forto maintene al mi rightes,
Ogayns king Arthur and his knyghtes?
He said, That dar I undertane,
Ogaynes ilka lyfand man.
Swilk kownsail byfor had sho tane,
Sho said, Sir, than er we at ane.
　Hir barons hir ful rathly red
To tak a lord hir forto wed.
Than hastily she went to hall,
Thar abade hir barons all, 1180
Forto hald thair parlement,
And mari hir by thair asent.
Sho sayd, Sirs, with an acorde,
Sen me bus nedely have a lord,
My landes forto lede and yeme,
Sais me sone howe ye wil deme.
Madame, thai said, how so ye will,
Al we sal assent thartyll.
　Than the lady went ogayne,
Unto chameber to sir Ywaine: 1190
Sir, sho said, so god me save,
Other lorde wil i nane have,
If i the left i did noght right,
A kingson and a noble knyght.
　Now has the maiden done hir thoght,
Sir Ywayne out of anger broght,
The lady led him unto hall,
Ogains him rase the barons all,
And al thai said, Ful sekerly,
This knight sal wed the lady; 1200
And ilkane said, tham-self bitwene,
So fair a man had thai noght sene,
For his bewtè in hal and bowr,
Him semes to be an emperowr;
We wald that thai war trowth-plight,
And weded sone this ilk nyght.
The lady set hir on the dese,
And cumand al to hald thaire pese;
And bad hir steward sumwhat say,
Or men went fra cowrt oway: 1210
The steward said, Sirs, understandes,
Wer es waxen in thir landes,
The king Arthur es redy dight
To be her byn this fowretenyght,
He and his menye ha thoght
To win this land if thai moght;

Thai wate ful wele that he es ded
That was lord her in this stede,
None es so wight wapins to welde,
Ne that so boldly mai us belde,   1220
And wemen may maintene no stowr,
Thai most nedes have a governowre,
Tharfor mi lady most nede
Be weded hastily for drede,
And to na lord wil sho tak tent
Bot if it be by yowr assent.
Than the lordes, al on raw,
Held tham wele payd of this saw,
Al assented hyr untill
To tak a lord at hyr owyn wyll.   1230
Than said the lady, onone right,
How hald ye yow paid of this knight ?
He profers hym, on al wyse,
To myne honor and my servyse ;
And sertes, sirs, the soth to say,
I saw him never or this day ;
Bot talde unto me has it bene
He es the kyngson Uriene,
He es cumen of hegh parage,
And wonder doghty of vaselage,   1240
War and wise and ful curtayse,
He yernes me to wife alwayse,
And ner the lese i wate he might
Have wele better, and so war right.
With a voice halely thai sayd,
Madame, ful wele we hald us payd ;
Bot hastes fast, al that ye may,
That ye war wedded this ilk day :
And grete prayer gan thai make,
On al wise that sho suld hym take.   1250
     Sone unto the kirk thai went,
And war wedded in thair present ;
Thar wedded Ywaine in plevyne
The riche lady Alundyne,
The dukes doghter of Landuit ;
Els had hyr lande bene destruyt.
Thus thai made the maryage,
Omang al the riche barnage,
Thai made ful mekyl mirth that day,
Ful grete festes on gude aray.   1260
Grete mirthes made thai in that stede,
And al forgetyn es now the ded
Of him that was thair lord fre,
Thai say that this es worth swilk thre,

And, that thai lufed him mekil mor,
Than him that lord was thare byfor.
  The bridal sat, for soth to tell,
Til kyng Arthur come to the well,
With al his knyghtes everilkane,
Byhind leved thar noght ane.   1270
Than sayd sir Kay, Now whar es he
That made slike bost her forto be,
Forto venge his cosyn-germayne?
I wist his wordes war al in vayne;
He made grete boste bifor the quene,
And her now dar he noght be sene;
His prowd wordes er now al purst,
For, in fayth, ful ill he durst
Anes luke opon that knyght,
That he made bost with to fyght.   1280
Than sayd Gawayn hastily,
Syr, for goddes luf, mercy,
For i dar hete the for sertayne
That we sal here of sir Ywayne,
This ilk day, that be thou balde,
Bot he be ded or done in halde:
And never in no cumpany
Herd i him speke the velany.
Than sayd sir Kay, Lo, at thi will,
Fra this time forth i sal be still.   1290
  The king kest water on the stane,
The storme rase ful sone onane
With wikked weders kene and calde,
Als it was byfore-hand talde;
The king and his men ilkane
Wend tharwith to have bene slane;
So blew it stor with slete and rayn:
And hastily than syr Ywayne
Dight him graythly in his ger,
With nobil shelde and strong sper.   1300
When he was dight in seker wede,
Than he umstrade a nobil stede,
Him thoght that he was als lyght,
Als a fowl es to the flyght,
Unto the well fast wendes he,
And sone when thai myght him se,
Syr Kay, for he wald noght fayle,
Smertly askes the batayl;
And alsone than said the kyng,
Sir Kay, i grante the thine askyng.   1310
Than sir Ywayn neghed tham ner,
Thair cowntenance to se and her;

Sir Kay than on his stede gan spring.
Ber the wele now, sayd the kyng,
Ful glad and blith was syr Ywayne,
When sir Kay come him ogayn ;
Bot Kay wist noght wha it was,
He findes his fer now or he pas ;
Syr Ywaine thinkes now to be wroken,
On the grete wordes that Kay has spoken.   1320
   Thai rade togeder with speres kene,
Thar was no reverence tham bitwene ;
Sir Ywayn gan sir Kay bere,
Out of his sadel lenkith of his sper,
His helm unto the erth smate,
A fote depe tharin yt bate ;
He wald do him na mor despite,
Bot down he lighted als tyte,
Sir Kay stede he toke in hy,
And presand the king ful curtaysly.   1330
Wonder glad than war thai all,
That Kay so fowl a shame gan fall,
And ilkone sayd til other then,
This es he that scornes al men.
Of his wa war thai wele paid.
Syr Ywain than to the kyng said,
Sir kyng, i gif to the this stede,
For he may help the in thi nede,
And to me war it grete trispas
Forto withhald that yowres was.   1340
What man ertow ? quod the kyng,
Of the have i na knawyng,
Bot if thou unarmed were,
Or els thi name that i might her.
Lord, he sayd, i am Ywayne.
Than was the king ferly fayne.
A sari man than was sir Kay,
That said that he was stollen oway,
Al descumfite he lay on grownde,
To him that was a sary stownde.   1350
The king and his men war ful glad,
That thai so syr Ywayne had,
And ful glad was sir Gawayne,
Of the welefar of sir Ywayne,
For nane was to him half so der
Of all that in the court were.
   The king sir Ywayn sone bisoght,
To tel him al how he had wroght,
And sone sir Ywaine gan him tell
Of al his far how it byfell,   1360

With the knight how that he sped,
And how he had the lady wed,
And how the mayden hym helpid wele :
Thus tald he to him ilka dele.
   Sir kyng, he sayd, i yow byseke,
And al yowr menye milde and meke,
That ye wald grante to me that grace
And wend with me to my purchace,
And se my kastel and my towre,
Than myght ye do me grete honowr.   1370
The kyng granted him ful right
To dwel with him a fowretenyght.
Sir Ywayne thanked him oft sith,
The knyghtes war al glad and blyth
With sir Ywaine forto wend,
And sone a squier has he send :
Unto the kastel the way he nome,
And warned the lady of thair come,
And that his lord come with the kyng ;
And, when the lady herd this thing,   1380
It es no lifand man with mowth
That half hir cumforth tel kowth.
   Hastily that lady hende
Cumand al hir men to wende,
And dight tham in thair best aray,
To kepe the king that ilk day.
Thai keped him in riche wede,
Rydeand on many a nobil stede,
Thai hailsed him ful curtaysly,
And also al his cumpany.   1390
Thai said he was worthy to dowt,
That so fele folk led obowt.
Thar was grete joy, i yow bihete,
With clothes spred [1] in ilka strete,
And damysels danceand ful wele,
With trompes, pipes, and with fristele :
The castel and ceté rang
With mynstralsi and nobil sang ;
Thai ordand tham ilkane in fer,
To kepe the king on fair maner.   1400
The lady went withowten towne,
And with hir many bald barowne,
Cled in purpur and ermyne,
With girdels al of gold ful fyne.
The lady made ful meri chere,
Sho was al dight with drewries der ;

---

[1] The MS. reads "*spered*," the *d* above being in a modern hand.

Abowt hir was ful mekyl thrang.
The puple cried, and sayd omang,
Welkum ertou, kyng Arthoure,
Of al this werld thou beres the flowr,   1410
Lord kyng of all kynges,
And blessed be he that the brynges.
   When the lady the kyng saw,
Unto him fast gan sho draw,
To hald his sterap whils he lyght,
Bot sone when he of hir had syght,
With mekyl myrth thai samen met,
With hende wordes sho him gret.
A thowsand sithes, Welkum, sho says,
And so es sir Gawayne the curtayse.   1420
The king said, Lady, white so flowr,
God gif the joy and mekil honowr,
For thou ert fayr with body gent ;
With that he hir in armes hent,
And ful fair he gan hir falde,
Thar was many to bihalde.
It es no man with tong may tell
The mirth that was tham omell ;
Of maidens was thar so gude wane,
That ilka knight myght tak ane.   1430
Ful mekil joy syr Ywayn made,
That he the king til his hows hade,
The lady omang tham al samen
Made ful mekyl joy and gamen.
   In the kastel thus thai dwell,
Ful mekyl myrth wase tham omell.
The king was thare with his knyghtes
Aght dayes and aght nyghtes,
And Ywayn tham ful mery made,
With alkyn gamyn tham for to glade ;   1440
He prayed the kyng to thank the may
That hym had helpid in his jornay,
And ilk day had thai solace ser
Of huntyng and als of revere,
For thar was a ful fayre cuntrè,
With wodes and parkes grete plentè,
And castels wroght with lyme and stane,
That Ywayne with his wife had tane.
   Now wil the king no langer lende,
Bot til his cuntre wil he wende.   1450
Ay whils thai war thar, for sertayne,
Syr Gawayn did al his mayne
To pray sir Ywaine, on al maner,
For to wende with tham in fere ;

He said, Sir, if thou ly at hame,
Wonderly men wil the blame ;
That knyght es nothing to set by
That leves al his chevalry,
And ligges bekeand in his bed,
When he haves a lady wed.   1460
For when that he has grete endose
Than war tyme to win his lose ;
For, when a knyght es chevalrouse,
His lady es the more jelows ;
Also sho lufes him wele the bet :
Tharfore, sir, thou sal noght let
To haunt armes in ilk cuntrè,
Than wil men wele mor prayse the ;
Thou hase inogh to thi despens,
Now may thow wele hante turnamentes ;   1470
Thou and i sal wende in fer,
And i wil be at thi banere.
I dar noght say, so god me glad,
If i so fayr a leman had ;
That i ne most leve al chevalry,
At hame ydel with hir to ly,
Bot yit a fole, that litel kan,
May wele cownsail another man.
So lang sir Gawayn prayed so,
Sir Ywayne grantes him forto go   1480
Unto the lady, and tak his leve ;
Loth him was hir forto greve.
Til hyr onane the way he nome,
Bot sho ne wist noght whi he come ;
In his arms he gan hir mete,
And thus he said, My leman swete,
My life, my hele, and al my hert,
My joy, my comforth, and my quert,
A thing prai i the unto,
For thine honor and myne also.   1490
The lady said, Sir, verrayment,
I wil do al yowr cumandment.
Dame, he said, i wil the pray,
That i might the king cumvay,
And also with my feres founde,
Armes forto haunte a stownde,
For in bourding men wald me blame,
If i sold now dwel at hame.
The lady was loth him to greve ;
Sir, sho said, i gif yow leve,   1500
Until a terme that i sal sayn,
Bot that ye cum than ogayn.

Al this yer hale i yow grante
Dedes of armes for to hante,
Bot, syr, als ye luf me dere,
On al wise that ye be her
This day twelmoth, how som it be,
For the luf ye aw to me ;
And, if ye com noght by that day,
My luf sal ye lose for ay :   1510
Avise yow wele now or ye gone,
This day is the evyn ef saint Jon,
That warn i yow now or ye wende,
Luke ye cum by the twelmoth ende.
Dame, he said, i sal noght let,
To hald the day that thou has set,
And, if i might be at my wyll,
Ful oft ar sold i cum ye till ;
Bot, madame, this understandes,
A man that passes divers landes   1520
May sumtyme cume in grete destres,
In preson, or els in sekenes,
Tharfore i pray yow or i ga,
That ye wil out-tak thir twa.
The lady sayd, This grant i wele,
Als ye ask, everilka dele,
And i sal lene to yow my ring,
That es to me a ful der thing,
In nane anger[1] sal ye be,
Whils ye it have and thinkes on me   1530
I sal tel to yow onane
The vertu that es in the stane :
It es, na preson yow sal halde,
Al if yowr fase be many falde ;
With sekenes sal ye noght be tane ;
Ne of yowr blode ye sal lese nane ;
In batel tane sal ye noght be,
Whils ye it have and thinkes on me ;
And ay, whils ye er trew of love,
Over al sal ye be above ;   1540
I wald never for nakyn wight,
Lene it ar unto na knyght,
For grete luf i it yow take,
Yemes it wele now for my sake.
Sir Ywayne said, Dame, gramercy.
Than he gert ordain in hy
Armurs, and al other gere,
Stalworth stedes, both sheld and sper,

---

[1] Query, *danger*.

And also squyer, knave, and swayne :
Ful glad and blith was sir Gawayne.
   No lenger wald syr Ywayne byde,
On his stede sone gan he stride ;
And thus he has his leve tane,
For him murned many ane.
The lady toke leve of the kyng,
And of his menyé ald and ying ;
Hir lord sir Ywayne sho bisekes,
With teris trikland on hir chekes,
On al wise that he noght let
To halde the day that he had set.
The knightes thus thair ways er went,
To justing and to turnament ;
Ful dughtily did sir Ywayne,
And also did sir Gawayne ;
Thai war ful doghty both in fer,
Thai wan the prise both fer and ner.
   The kyng that time at Cester lay,
The knightes went tham for to play,
Ful really thai rade obout,
Al that twelmoth out and out,
To justing and to turnament,
Thai wan grete wirships als thai went.
Sir Ywayne oft had al the lose,
Of him the word ful wide gose ;
Of thair dedes was grete renown
To and fra in towre and towne.
   On this wise in this life thai last
Unto saint Johns day was past ;
Than hastily thai hied home,
And sone unto the kyng thai come ;
And thar thai held grete mangeri,
The kyng with al his cumpany.
Sir Ywayne umbithought him than
He had forgeten his leman ;
Broken i have hir cumandment
Sertes, he said, now be i shent ;
The terme es past that sho me set,
How ever sal this bale be bet ?
Unnethes he might him hald fra wepe,
And right in this than toke he kepe.
   Into court come a damysele,
On a palfray ambland wele,
And egerly down gan sho lyght,
Withouten help of knave or knyght,
And sone sho lete hyr mantel fall,
And hasted hir fast into hall ;

1550

1560

1570

1580

1590

Sir kyng, sho sayd, god mot the se,
My lady gretes the wele by me,
And also, sir, gude Gawayne,
And al thi knyghtes, bot sir Ywayne,   1600
He es ateyned for traytur,
And fals and lither losenjoure :
He has bytrayed my lady,
Bot sho es war with his gilry ;
Sho hopid noght, the soth to say,
That he wald so have stollen oway ;
He made to hir ful mekyl boste,
And said of al he lufed hir moste ;
Al was treson and trechery,
And that he sal ful der haby.   1610
It es ful mekyl ogains the right
To cal so fals a man a knight.
My lady wend he had hir hert,
Ay forto kepe and hald in quert ;
Bot now with grefe he has hir gret,
And broken the term that sho him set,
That was the evyn of saynt John,
Now es that tyme for ever gone ;
So lang gaf sho him respite,
And thus he haves hir led with lite ;   1620
Sertainly so fals a fode,
Was never cumen of kynges blode,
That so sone forgat his wyfe,
That lofed him better than hyr life.
Til Ywayn sais sho, Thus thou es
Traytur untrew, and trowthles,
And also an unkind cumlyng ;
Deliver me my lady ring.
Sho stirt to him, with sterne loke,
The ring fro his finger sho toke,   1630
And, alsone als sho had the ring,
Hir leve toke sho of the king,
And stirted up on hir palfray,
With-owten more sho went hir way ;
With hir was nowther knave ne grome,
Ne no man wist wher sho bycome.
     Sir Ywayn, when he this gan her,
Murned, and made simpil cher,
In sorow than so was he stad,
That nere for murnyng wex he mad,   1640
It was no mirth that him myght mend,
At worth to noght ful wele he wend,
For wa he es ful wil of wane :
" Allas ! i am myne owen bane."

Allas, he sayd, that i was born!
Have i my leman thus forlorn ?
And al es for myne owen foly,
Allas! this dole wil mak me dy.
An evyl toke him als he stode,
Far wa he wex al wilde and wode ;   1650
Unto the wod the way he nome,[1]
No man wist whor he bycome.
Obout he welk in the forest,
Als it wore a wilde beste,
His men on ilka syde has soght,
Fer and ner, and findes him noght.
    On a day, als Ywayne ran
In the wod, he met a man,
Arowes brade and bow had he,
And when sir Ywaine gan him se,   1660
To him he stirt, with birful grim,
His bow and arwes reft he him,
Ilka day than at the leste,
Shot he him a wilde beste ;
Fless he wan him, ful gude wane,
And of his arows lost he nane.
Thare he lifed a grete sesowne,
With rotes, and raw venysowne,
He drank of the warm blode,
And that did him mekil gode.   1670
Als he went in that boskage,   ˙
He fand a letil ermytage ;
The ermyte saw, and sone was war
A naked man a bow bar,
He hoped he was wode that tide,
Tharfor no lenger durst he bide ;
He sperd his yate, and in he ran,
For fered of that wode man ;
And, for him thoght it charite,
Out of his window set he   1680
Brede and water for the wode man,
And tharto ful sone he ran.
Swilk als he him swilk he him gaf,
Barly brede with al the chaf ;
Tharof ete he ful gude wane,
And are swilk ete he never nane.

---

[1] A similar adventure is related in *Mort d'Arthur*, from the old French romance of sir Tristram (P. 2, C. 59, &c.) ; and of sir Lancelot du Lac (P. 3, C. 9, &c.) ; and to one or other of these stories was Ariosto indebted for the idea of Orlando's madness.

Of the water he drank thar-with,
Than ran he forth into the frith.
For, if a man be never so wode,
He wil kum whare man dose him gode ;   1690
And sertanly so did Ywayne,
Everilka day he come ogayne,
And with him broght he redy boun
Ilka day new venisowne,
He laid it at the ermite yate,
And ete, and drank, and went his gate.
Ever, al sone als he was gane,
The ermyt toke the flesh onane,
He flogh it, and seth it fayr and wele,
Than had Ywayne, at ilka mele,   1700
Brede and sothen venysowne.
Than went the ermyte to the towne,
And salde the skinnes that he broght,
And better brede tharwith he boght.
Than fand sir Ywayne in that stede
Venyson and better brede.
This life led he ful fele yer,
And sethen he wroght als ye sal her.
    Als Ywaine sleped under a tre
By him come thar rideand thre,   1710
A lady, twa bour-wemen alswa,
Than spak ane of the maidens twa,
A naked [man] me think i se,
Wit i wil what it may be.
Sho lighted doun, and to him yede,
And unto him sho toke gude hede ;
Hir thoght wele sho had him sene
In many stedes whar sho had bene ;
Sho was astonayd in that stownde,
For in hys face sho saw a wonde,   1720
Bot it was heled and hale of hew,
Tharby hir thoght that sho him knew.
Sho sayd, By god, that me has made ;
Swilk a wound sir Ywayne hade,
Sertaynly this ilk es he :
Allas, sho sayd, how may this be ?
Allas, that him es thus bityd !
So nobil a knyght als he was kyd !
It es grete sorow that he sold be
So ugly now opon to se.   1730
So tenderly for him sho gret,
That hir teres al hir chekes wet.
Madame, sho said, for sertayn,
Her have we funden sir Ywayne,

The best knyght that on grund mai ga,
Allas, him es bytid so wa !
In sum sorow was he stad,
And tharfore es he waxen mad ;
Sorow wil meng a mans blode,
And make him forto wax wode.   1740
Madame, and he war now in quert,
And al hale of will and hert,
Ogayns yowr fa he wald yow wer,
That has yow done so mekyl der ;
And he war hale, so god me mend,
Yowr sorow war sone broght to end.
The lady said, And this ilk be he,
And than ¹ he wil noght hethin fle,
Thorgh goddes help, than hope i yit
We sal him win ynto his wyt ;   1750
Swith at hame i wald we wer,
For thar i have an unement der,
Morgan the wise gaf it to me,²
And said, als i sal tel to the ;
He sayd, This unement es so gode,
That, if a man be brayn-wode,
And he war anes anoynt with yt,
Smertly sold he have his wit.
Fro hame thai wer bot half a myle,
Theder come thai in a whyle ;   1760
The lady sone the boyst has soght,
And the unement has sho broght.
Have, sho said, this unement her,
Unto me it es ful dere ;
And smertly that thou wend ogayne,
Bot luke thou spend it noght in vaine ;
And, fra the knyght anoynted be,
That thou leves bring it to me.
Hastily that maiden meke
Tok hose, and shose, and serk, and breke ;   1770

---

¹ Query. *that.*

² By Morgan the wise she probably means *Pelagius*, the heretic, abbot of Bangor, and a man of great learning for his age, whose proper name was *Morgan (Marigena)*, which, indeed, is, merely, latinised in *Pelagius*, implying, in the British tongue, one born from, or upon, the sea, or, perhaps, by the sea-side.* He is said to have flourished in 418, and, consequently, must have been well striken in years when acquainted with this good lady.

---

* From *mor*, the sea, and *gana*, Armorican, to beget, procreate or bring forth. Thus *Glamorganshire* (anciently *Morganwg*) is so called from its being upon the sea-coast ; and, in *Basse-Bretagne*, a mermaid is called *Marie-Morgan.* See Usher's *Antiquitates* (folio), p. 112).

A richc robe als gan sho ta,
And a saint of silk alswa,
And also a gude palfray,
And smertly come sho whar he lay.
On slepe fast yit sho him fande,
Hir hors until a tre sho band,
And hastily to him sho yede,
And that was a ful hardy dede ;
Sho enoynt his heved wele,
And his body ilka dele.   1780
Sho despended al ye unement,
Over hir ladies cumandment ;
For hir lady wald sho noght let,
Hir thoght that it was ful wele set.
Al his atyre sho left hym by,
At his rising to be redy,
That he might him cleth and dyght,
Or he sold of hyr have syght.
     Than he wakend of his slepe,
The maiden to him toke gude kepe,   1790
He luked up ful farily,
And said, Lady, saynt Mary.
What hard grace to me es maked,
That i am her now thus naked ?
Allas, wher any have her bene,
I trow sum has my sorow sene.
Lang he sat so in a thoght
How that ger was theder broght.
Than had he noght so mekyl myght
On his fete to stand up-right,   1800
Him failed might of fote and hand
That he myght nowther ga ne stand ;
Bot yit his clathes on he wan ;
Tharfor ful wery was he than ;
Than had he mister forto mete
Sum man that myght his bales bete.
Than lepe the maiden on hir palfray,
And nere byside him made hir way ;
Sho lete als sho him noght had sene,
Ne wetyn that he thar had bene.   1810
Sone, when he of hir had syght,
He cried unto hyr, on hight.
Than wald sho no ferrer ride
Bot fast sho luked on ilka syde ;
And waited obout fer and ner,
He cried, and sayd, I am her.
Than sone sho rade him till,
And sayd, Sir, what es thi will.

" Lady, thi help war mc ful lefe,
For i am her in grete meschefe ;   1820
I ne wate never by what chance,
That i have al this grevance,
Pur charite, i wald ye pray
For to lene me that palfray,
That in thi hand es redy bowne.
And wis me sone unto som towne.
I wate noght how i had this wa,
Ne how that i sal hethin ga."
Sho answerd him, with wordes hende,
Syr, if thou wil with me wende,   1830
Ful gladly wil i ese the
Until that thou amended be.
Sho helped him opon his hors ryg,
And sone thai come until a bryg,
Into the water the boist sho cast,
And sethin hame sho hied fast.
    When thai come to the castel yate,
Thai lighted and went in tharate.
The maiden to the chameber went,
The lady asked the unement.   1840
Madame, sho said, the boyst es lorn,
And so was i nerehand tharforn.
How so, sho said, for goddes tre ?
Madame, sho said, i sal tel the
Al the soth how that it was :
Als i over the brig sold pas,
Evyn in myddes, the soth to say,
Thar stombild my palfray ;
On the brig he fell al flat,
And the boyst, right with that,   1850
Fel fra me in the water down,
And had i noght bene titter boun
To tak my palfray bi the mane,
The water sone had bene my bane.
The lady said, Now am i shent,
That i have lorn my gude unement,
It was to me, so god me glade,
The best tresur that ever i hade ;
To me it es ful mekil skath,
Bot better es lose it than yow bath.   1860
Wend, sho said, unto the knight,
And luke thou ese him at thi myght.
Lady, sho said, els war me lathe.
Than sho gert him washe and bathe,
And gaf him mete and drink of main,
Til he had geten his might ogayn.

Thai ordand armurs ful wele dight,
And so thai did stedes ful wight.
  So it fell sone on a day,
Whils he in the castel lay,   1870
The ryche eryl, syr Alers,
With knightes, serjantes, and swiers,
And with swith grete vetale,
Come that kastel to asayle.
Sir Ywain than his armurs tase,
With other socure that he hase,
The erel he kepes in the felde,
And sone he hit ane on the shelde,
That the knyght, and als the stede,
Stark ded to the erth thai yede,   1880
Sone another, the thrid, the ferth,
Feld he doun ded on the erth.
He stird him so omang tham than,
At ilka dint he slogh a man,
Sum he losed of hys men,
Bot the eril lost swilk ten ;
Al thai fled fast fra that syde
Whar thai saw sir Ywayn ride,
He herted so his cumpany,
The moste coward was ful hardy,   1890
To fel al that thai fand in in felde.
The lady lay ever and bihelde :
Sho sais, Yon es a noble knyght,
Ful eger and of ful grete myght ;
He es welc worthy forto prayse
That es so doghty and curtayse.
The mayden said, with owten let,
Yowr oynement mai ye think welc set ;
Se, se,[1] madame, how he prikes !
And se, se, also, how fele he strikes![2] 1900
Lo, how he fars omang his fase !
Al that he hittes sone he slase ;
War thar swilk other twa als he,
Than hope i sone thair fase sold fle ;
Sertes, than sold we se ful tyte,
The eril sold be discumfite.
Madame, god gif his wil wer
To wed yow and be loverd here.
    The erils folk went fast to ded,
To fle than was his best rede ;   1910
The eril sone bigan to fle,
And than might men bourd se,

[1] The MS. has "*ye.*"   [2] The MS. has "*stikes.*"

How sir Ywayne and his feres
Folowd tham on fel maners,
And fast thai slogh the erils men,
Olive thai left noght over ten ;
The eril fled ful fast for drede,
And than sir Ywaine strake his stede,
And over-toke him in that tide,
At a kastel thar bysyde ;   1920
Sir Ywayne sone with-set the yate,
That the eril myght noght in tharate.
The eril saw al might noght gain,
He yalde him sone to sir Ywayn,
And sone he has his trowth plyght
To wend with him that ilk night
Unto the lady of grete renowne,
And profer him to hir presowne,
And to do him in hir grace,
And also to mend his trispase.   1930
The eril than unarmed his hevid,
And none armur on him he levid,
Helm, shelde, and als his brand,
That he bar naked in his hand,
Al he gaf to sir Ywayne,
And hame with him he went ogaine.
In the kastel made thai joy ilkane,
When thai wist the eril was tane,
And whan thai saw tham cumand ner,
Ogayns him went thai al in fere,   1940
And when the lady gan tham mete,
Sir Ywaine gudely gan hir grete :
He said, Madame, have thi presoun,
And hald him her in thi baundoun,
Bot he gert hir grante him grace
To mak amendes yn that space.
On a buke the erl swar
Forto restor bath les and mar,
And big ogayn bath tour and toune,
That by him war casten doune,   1950
And evermar to be hir frende,
Umage made he to that hende ;
To this forward he borows fand,
The best lordes of al that land.
   Sir Ywaine wald no lenger lend,
Bot redies him fast forto wend,
At the lady his leve he takes,
Grete murnyng tharfore sho makes :
Sho said, Sir, if it be yowre will,
I pray yow for to dwel her still,   1960

And i wil yelde into yowr handes
Myne awyn body, and al my landes,
Herof fast sho hym bysoght,
Bot al hir speche avayles noght.
He said, I wil no thing to mede,
Bot myne armurs, and my stede.
Sho said, Bath stedes and other thing
Es yowres at yowr owyn likyng ;
And if ye wald her with us dwell
Mekyl mirth war us omell.   1970
It was na bote to bid him bide,
He toke his stede, and on gan stride,
The lady and hyr maydens gent
Wepid far when that he went.
     Now rides Ywayn, als ye sal her,
With hevy he*rte* and dreri cher,
Thurgh a forest, by a sty,
And thar he herd a hydose cry,
The gaynest way ful sone he tase,
Til he come whare the noys was,   1980
Than was he war of a dragoun,
Had asayled a wilde lyown,
With his tayl he drogh him fast,
And fir ever on him he cast,
The lyoun had over litel myght
Ogaynes the dragon forto tyght ;
Than sir Ywayn made him bown
For to sucor the lyown,
His shelde bifor his face he fest,
For the fyr that the dragon kest,   1990
He strake the dragon in at the chavyl,
That it come out at the navyl ;
Sunder strake he the throte boll,
That fra the body went the choll ;
By the lioun tail the hevid hang yit,
For tharby had he tane his bit ;
The tail sir Ywayne strake in twa,
The dragon hevid than fel thar-fra.
He thoght, if the lyoun me asayle,
Redy sal he have batayle ;   2000
Bot the lyoun wald noght fyght,
Grete fawnyng made he to the knyght,
Down on the grund he set him oft,
His forther fete he held oloft,
And thanked the knyght als he kowth,
Al if he myght noght speke with mowth :
So wele the lyon of him lete,
Ful law he lay and likked his fete.

When syr Ywayne that sight gan se,
Of the beste him thoght petè ;   2010
And on his wai forth gan he ride,
The lyown folowd by hys syde ;
In the forest al that day,
The lyoun mekely foloud ay,
And never, for wele ne for wa,
Wald he part sir Ywayn fra,
Thus in the forest als thai war,
The lyoun hungerd swith sar,
Of a beste savore he hade,
Until hys lord sembland he made,   2020
That he wald go to get his pray,
His kind it wald, the soth to say ;
For his lorde sold him noght greve,
He wald noght go withowten leve.
Fra his lord the way he laght,
The mountance of ane arow draght,
Sone he met a barayn da,
And ful sone he gan hir sla,
Hir throte in twa ful sone he bate,
And drank the blode whils it was hate,   2030
That da he kest than in his nek,
Als it war a mele-sek,
Unto his lorde than he it bar,
And sir Ywayn persayved thar
That it was so ner the nyght
That no ferrer ride he might ;
A loge of bowes sone he made,
And flynt and fir-yren bath he hade,
And fir ful sone thar he slogh,
Of dry mos and many a bogh [1]   2040
The lioun has the da undone ;
Sir Ywayne made a spit ful sone,
And rosted sum to thaire soper :
The lyon lay, als ye sal here ;
Unto na mete he him drogh,
Until his maister had eten ynogh.
Him failed thare bath salt and brede,
And so him did whyte wine and rede,
Bot of swilk thing als thai had
He and his lyon made tham glad.   2050
The lyon hungerd for the nanes,
Ful fast he ete raw fless and banes.
Sir Ywayn, in that ilk telde,
Laid his hevid opon his shelde.

---

[1] The MS. has "*boght.*"

Alnyght the lyon obout yede,
To kepe his mayster and his stede :
Thus the lyon and the knyght
Lended thar a fourtenyght.
  On a day, so it byfell,
Syr Ywayne come unto the well,   2060
He saw the chapel and the thorne,
And said allas that he was born ;
And when he loked on the stane
He fel in swowing sone onane,
Als he fel his swerde out-shoke,
The pomel into the erth toke,
The poynt toke until his throte,
Wel ner he made a sari note,
Thorgh his armurs sone it smate,
And litel intil hys hals it bate :   2070
And wen the lyon saw his blude,
He brayded als he had bene wode,
Than kest he up so lathly rerde,
Ful mani folk myht he have ferde ;
He wend wele, so god me rede,
That his mayster had bene ded.
It was ful grete peté to her
What sorow he made on his maner.
He stirt ful hertly, i yow hete,
And toke the swerde bytwix his fete,   2080
Up he set it by a stane,
And thar he wald himself have slane,
And so he had sone, for sertayne,
Bot right in that rase syr Ywayne,
And alsone als he saw him stand
For fayn he liked fote and hand.
Sir Ywayn said oft-sithes, Allas !
Of alkins men hard es my grace,
Mi leman set me sertayn day
And i it brak, so wayloway !   2090
Allas for dole ! how may i dwell
To se this chapel and this well !
Hir fair thorn, hir riche stane !
My gude dayes er now al gane,
My joy es done now al bidene,
I am noght worthi to be sene ;
I saw this wild beste was ful bayn
For my luf himselfe have slayne,
Than sold i sertes, by mor right
Sla my self for swilk a wyght   2100
That i have for my foly lorn ;
Allas the while that i was born !

Als sir Ywayn made his mane,
In the chapel ay was ane,
And herd his murning haly al
Thorgh a crevice of the wall,
And sone it said, with simepel cher,
What ertou, that murnes her ?
A man, he said, sum tyme i was ;
What ertow ? tel me or i pas. 2110
I am, it said, the sariest wight
That ever lifed by day or nyght.
Nay, he said, by saynt Martyne,
Thar es na sorow mete to myne,
Ne no wight so wil of wane,
I was a man now am i nane.
Whilom i was a nobil knyght,
And a man of mekyl myght,
I had knyghtes of my menyè,
And of reches grete plentè, 2120
I had a ful fayre seignory,
And al i lost for my foly ;
Mi maste sorow als sal thou her,
I lost a lady that was me der.
The tother sayd, Allas ! allas !
Myne es a wele sarier case ;
To-morn i mun ber jewyse,
Als my famen wil devise.
Allas ! he said, what es the skill ?
" That sal thou her, sir, if thou will ; 2130
I was a mayden, mekil of pride,
With a lady her ner biside,
Men me bikalles of tresown,
And has me put her in presown,
I have no man to defend me,
Tharfore to morn brent mun i be."
He sayd, What if thou get a knyght,
That for the with thi fase wil fight ?
Syr, sho sayd, als mot i ga,
In this land er bot knyghtes twa, 2140
That me wald help to cover of car,
The tane es went i wate noght whar,
The tother es dweland with the king,
And wate noght of my myslykyng.
The tane of tham hat syr Gawayn,
And the tother hat syr Ywayn,
For hym sal i be done to dede,
To-morn right in this same stede,
He es the kinges son Uriene.
Perfay, he sayd, i have him sene ; 2150

I am he, and for my gilt
Sal thou never more be spilt ;
Thou ert Lunet, if i can rede,
That helpyd me yn mekyl drede ;
I had bene ded had thou noght bene,
Tharfor tel me us bytwene
How bical thai the of treson,
Thus forto sla, and for what reson.
" Sir, thai say, that my lady
Lufed me moste specially,   2160
And wroght al efter my rede,
Tharfor thai hate me to the ded.
The steward says, that done have i
Grete tresone unto my lady,
His twa brether sayd it als,
And i wist that thai said fals,
And sone i answerd, als a sot,
(For fole bolt es sone shot)
I said, that i sold find a knyght
That sold me mayntene in my right,   2170
And fegth with tham al thre,
Thus the batayl wajed we.
Than thai granted me als tyte
Fourty dayes unto respite,
And at the kynges court i was,
I fand na cumfort, ne na solase,
Nowther of knyght, knave, ne swayn."
Than, said he, Whar was syr Gawayn ?
He has bene ever trew and lele,
He fayled never no damysele.   2180
Scho said, In court [he] was noght sene,
For a knyght led oway the quene,
The kyng tharfor es swith grym,
Sir Gawayn folowd efter him ;
He coms noght hame for sertayne
Until he bryng the quene ogayne.
Now has thou herd, so god me rede,
Why i sal be done to ded.
He said, Als i am a trew knyght,
I sal be redy forto fyght   2190
To-morn with tham al thre,
Leman, for the luf of the.
At my might i sal noght fayl,

---

¹ Queen Guinever, having ridden a-maying, along with certain knights of the round-table, clothed all in green, was, after a sharp conflict, taken prisoner by sir Meliagrance, and led away to his castle. See *Mort d'Arthur*, Part 3, chap. 129, &c.

Bot how so bese of the batayle,
If ani man my name the frayne,
On al maner luke thou yt layne,
Unto na man my name thou say.
Syr, sho sayd, for soth nay,
I prai to grete god alweldand,
That thai have noght the hegher hand,   2200
Sen that ye wil my murnyng mend,
I tak the grace that god wil send.
Syr Ywayn sayd, I sal the hyght
To mend thi murnyng at my myght,
Thorgh grace of god in trenyte,
I sal the wreke of tham al thre :
Than rade he forth into frith,
And hys lyoun went hym with.
Had he redyn bot a stownde
A ful fayr castell he fownde,   2210
And syr Ywaine, the soth to say,
Unto the castel toke the way ;
When he come at the castel-yate,
Four porters he fand tharate,
The draw-bryg sone lete thai doun,
Bot al thai fled for the lyown :
Thai said, Syr, wythowten dowt,
That beste byhoves the leve tharout.
He sayd, Sirs, so have i wyn,
Mi lyoun and i sal noght twyn ;   2220
I luf him als welc, i yow hete,
Als my self at ane mete,
Owther sal we samyn lende,
Or els wil we hethin wende.
Bot right with that the lord he met,
And ful gladly he him gret,
With knyghtes and swiers grete plentè,
And fair ladies and maydens fre ;
Ful mekyl joy of him thai made,
Bot sorow in thair hertes thai hade ;   2230
Unto a chameber was he led,
And unarmed,[1] and sethin cled
In clothes that war gay and der ;
Bot oft-tymes changed thair cher,
Sum tyme he saw thai weped all,
Als thai wald to water fall ;
Thai made slike murnyng[2] and slik mane,
That gretter saw he never nane.

---

[1] The MS. has "*unharmed*" with a dot over the *h*, as if intended to be erased.
[2] The MS. reads "*murnyg.*"

Thai feynyd tham oft for hys sake
Fayre semblant forto make.   2240
Ful grete wonder sir Ywayn hade,
For thai swilk joy and sorow made.
Sir, he said, if yowr wil war,
I wald wyt why ye mak slike kar.
This joy, he said, that we mak now,
Sir, es al for we have yow,
And, sir, also we mak this sorow
For dedys that sal be done to-morow.
A geant wons her ner bysyde,
That es a devil of mekil pryde,   2250
His name hat Harpyns of mowntain,
For him we lyf in mekil payn,
My landes haves he robbed and reft,
Noght bot this kastel es me left,
And, by god that in hevyn wons,
Syr, i had sex knyghtes to sons,
I saw my self the twa slogh he,
To-morn the four als slane mun be.
He has al in hys presowne,
And, sir, for nane other enchesowne,   2260
Bot for i warned hym to wyve
My doghter, fayrest fode olyve,
Tharfor es he wonder wrath,
In depely has he sworn hys ath,
With maystry that he sal hir wyn,
And that the laddes of his kychyn,
And also that his werst fote-knave,
His wil of that woman sal have,
Bot i to-morn might find a knight,
That durst with hymselven fyght,   2270
And i have none to him at ga,
What wonder es if me be wa?
Syr Ywayn lystend him ful wele,
And, when he had talde ilka dele,
Syr, he sayd, methink mervayl
That ye soght never so kounsayl,
At the kynges hous her bysyde;
For, sertes, in al this werld so wyde
Es no man of so mekil myght
Geant, champioun, ne knight,   2280
That he ne has knyghtes of his menyè,
That ful glad and blyth wald be
For to mete with swilk a man,
That thai myght kith thair myghtes on.
He said, Syr, so god me mend,
Unto the kynges kourt i send,

To seke my mayster syr Gawayn,
For he wald socor me ful fain,
He wald noght leve for luf ne drede,
Had he wist now of my nede,   2290
For his sister es my wyfe,
And he lufes hyr als his lyfe.
Bot a knyght this other day,
Thai talde, has led the quene oway,
Forto seke hyr went sir Gawayn,
And yit ne come he noght ogayn.
Than syr Ywayne sighed sar,
And said unto the knyght right thar,
Syr, he sayd, for Gawayn sake,
This batayl wil i undertake,   2300
Forto fyght with the geant,
And that opon swilk a covenant,
Yif he cum at swilk a time,
So that we may fight by prime ;
No langer may i tent tharto,
For other thing i have to do,
I have a dede that most be done
To morn nedes byfor the none.
The knyght, far sighand, sayd him till,
Sir, god yelde the thi gode wyll ;   2310
And al that war thar in the hall,
On knese byfor hym gan thai fall ;
Forth thar come a byrd ful bryght,
The fairest man might se in sight,
Hir moder come with hir in fer,
And both thai morned and made yll cher ;
The knight said, Lo, verraiment,
God has us gude socur sent ;
This knight, that of his grace wil grant
Forto fyght with the geant.   2320
On knese thai fel doun to his fete,
And thanked him with wordes swete.
A, god forbede, said sir Ywain,
That the sister of sir Gawayn,
Or any other of his blode born,
Sold on this wise knel me byforn.
He toke tham up tyte both in fer,
And prayd tham to amend thair cher :
"And praies fast to god alswa,
That i may venge yow or yowr fa,   2330
And that he cum swilk tyme of day,
That i by tyme may wend my way,
For to do another dede,
For sertes theder most i nede ;

Sertes i wald noght tham byswike,
Forto win this kinges rike."
His thoght was on that damysel
That he left in the chapel.
Thai said, he es of grete renowne,
For with him dwels the lyoun;   2340
Ful wele confort war thai all,
Bath in bour and als in hall;
Ful glad war thai of thair gest,
And when tyme was at go to rest,
The lady broght him to his bed,
And for the lyoun sho was adred,
Na man durst neght ¹ his chamber ner,
Fro thai war broght thar-yn in fer.
Sone at morn, when it was day,
The lady and the fayr may   2350
Til Ywayn chamber went thai sone,
And the dor thai have undone.
    Sir Ywayn to the kyrk yede,
Or he did any other dede;
He herd the servise of the day,
And sethin to the knyght gan say:
Sir, he said, now most i wend,
Lenger her dar i noght lende,
Til other place byhoves me tar.
Than had the knyght ful mekel car.   2360
He said, Syr, dwells a litel thraw,
For luf of Gawayn that ye knaw,
Socor us now or ye wende,
I sal yow gif, with-owten ende,
Half my land, with toun and tour,
And ye wil help us in this stour.
Sir Ywayn said, Nai, god forbede,
That i sold take any mede.
Than was grete dole, so god me glade,
To se the sorow that thai made,   2370
Of tham sir Ywayn had grete petè,
Him thoght his hert myght breke in thre;
For in grete dede ay gan he dwell,
For the mayden in the chapell,
For sertes if sho war done to ded,
Of him war than none other rede,
Bot oither he sold hym-selven sla,
Or wode ogain to the wod ga.

---

¹ Conjectural emendation : *negh.*

Ryght with that thar come a grome,
And said tham that geant come ;　　　　2380
Yowr sons bringes he him byforn,
Wel ner naked als thai war born.
With wreched ragges war thai kled,
And fast bunden thus er thai led.
The geant was bath large and lang,
And bar a levor of yren ful strang,
Tharwith he pet tham bitterly,
Grete rewth it was to her tham cry,
Thai had no thing tham forto hyde.
A dwergh yode on the tother syde ;　　　2390
He bar a scowrge with cordes ten,
Thar-with he bet tha gentil men,
Ever onane, als he war wode,
Efter ilka band brast out the blode ;
And, when thai at the walles were,
He cried loud that men might her :
If thou wil have thi sons in hele,
Deliver me that damysele,
I sal hir gif to warisowne
Ane of the foulest quisteroun　　　　2400
That ever yit ete any brede,
He sal have hir mayden-hede,
Thar sal none other lig hir by
Bot naked herlotes and lowsy.
When the lord thir words herd,
Als he war wode for wa he ferd.
Sir Ywayn than, that was curtays,
Unto the knyght ful sone he sais,
This geant es ful fers and fell,
And of his wordes ful kruell,　　　　2410
I sal deliver hir of his aw,
Or els be ded within a thraw ;
For sertes it war a misaventur
That so gentil a creature
Sold ever so foul hap byfall,
To be defouled with a thrall.
Sone was he armed, sir Ywayn,
Tharfor the ladies war ful fayn ;
Thai helped to lace him in his wede,[1]

---

[1] This is an ordinary incident in old romances ; in allusion to which don Quixote was disarmed by the ladies of the castle. See B. 1, C. 2.

> " *Nunca fuera caballero*
> *De damas tan bien servido,*
> *Como fuera* don Quixote,
> *Quando de su aldea vino*

And sone he lepe up on his stede ;   2420
Thai prai to god that grace him grant,
For to sla that foul geant ;
The draw-brigges war laten doun,
And forth he rides with his lioun.
Ful mani sari murnand man
Left he in the kastel than,
That, on thair knese, to god of might,
Praied ful hertly for the knyght.[1]
   Syr Ywan rade into the playne,
And the geant come hym ogayne.   2430
His levore was ful grete and lang,
And himself ful mekyl and strang.
He said, What devil made the so balde
Forto cum heder out of thi halde ?
Who so ever the heder send
Lufed the litel, so god me mend,
Of the he wald be wroken fayn.
Do forth thi best, said sir Ywan.
Al the armure he was yn
Was noght bot of a bul-skyn.   2440
Sir Ywayn was to him ful prest,
He strake to him in middes the brest,
The sper was both stif and gode,
Whar It toke bit out-brast the blode ;
So fast sir Ywayn on yt soght
The bul-scyn availed noght.
The geant stombild with the dynt,
And unto sir Ywayn he mynt,
And on the shelde he hit ful fast,
It was a mervayl that it myght last ;   2450
The levor bended thar-with-all,
With grete force he let it fall.
The geant was so strong and wight
That never for no dint of knyght,
Ne for batayl that he sold make,
Wald he none other wapyn take.

Doncellas curaban del,
  Princesas de su rocino."

...... —   -Never was there cavalero
    So well served by a dame,
  As the famous knight, don Quixote,
   When he from his village came :
  Care of him took damsels dainty,
    Princesses of Rozinante.

[1] Between this and the next line the MS. reads—
    " *Here es the myddes of this boke.*"

Sir Ywain left his sper of hand,
And strake obout him with his brand,
And the geant, mekil of mayn,
Strake ful fast to him ogayn,　　　　　　　2460
Til at the last within a throw
He rest him on his sadel-bow,
And that percayved his lioun,
That his hevid so hanged doun,
He hopid that hys lord was hyrt,
And to the geant sone he styrt,
The scyn and fless bath rafe he down,
Fro his hals to hys cropoun ;
His ribbes myght men so onane,
For al was bar unto bane.　　　　　　　　2470
At the lyown oft he mynt,
Bot ever he lepis fro his dynt,
So that no strake on him lyght.
By than was Ywain cumen to myght.
Than wil he wreke him if he may :
The geant gaf he ful gude pay,
He smate oway al his left cheke,
His sholder als of gan he kleke,
That both his levor and his hand
Fel doun law open the land,　　　　　　　　2480
Sethin with a stoke to him he stert,
And smate the geant unto the hert ;
Than was nane other tale to tell,
Bot fast unto the erth he fell,
Als it had bene a hevy tre.
Than myght men in the kastel se
Ful mekil mirth on ilka side,
The yates kest thai opyn wyde ;
The lord unto syr Ywaine ran,
Him foloud many a joyful man,　　　　　　　2490
Also the lady ran ful fast,
And hir doghter was noght the last.
I may noght tel the joy thai had,
And the four brether war ful glad,
For thai war out of bales broght.
The lord wist it helpid noght
At pray sir Ywayn forto dwell,
For tales that he byfor gan tell,
Bot hertly, with his myght and mayn,
He praied him forto cum ogayn,　　　　　　2500
And dwel with him a litel stage,
When he had done hys vassage.
He said, Sir, that may i noght do,
Bileves wele, for me bus go.

Tham was ful wo he wald noght dwell,
Bot fain thai war that it so fell.
The neghest way than gan he wele,
Until he come to the chapele,
Thar he fand a mekil fir,
And the mayden with lely lire,   2510
In hyr smok was bunden fast,
Into the fir forto be kast.
Unto himself he said in hy,
And prayed to god al-myghty,
That he sold, for his mekil myght,
Save fro shame that swete wight :
" Yf thai be many, and mekil of pryse,
I sal let for no kouwardise,
For with me es bath god and right,
And thai sal help me forto fight,   2520
And my lyon sal help me,
Than er we four ogayns tham thre."
    Sir Ywayn rides, and cries then,
Habides, i bid yow, fals men !
It semes wele that ye er wode,
That wil spill this sakles blode,
Ye sal noght so yf that i may :
His lyown made hym redy way.
Naked he saw the mayden stand,
Behind hir bunden aither hand,   2530
Than sighed Ywain wonder oft,
Unnethes might he syt oloft,
Thar was no sembland tham bitwene,
That ever owther had other sene.
Al obout hyr myght men se
Ful mykel sorow and grete petè,
Of other ladies that thar were,
Wepeand with ful sory cher.
Lord, thai sayd, what es our gylt ?
Our joy, our confort, sal be spilt ;   2540
Who sal now our erandes say ?
Allas, who sal now for us pray ?
Whils thai thus karped was Lunet
On knese byfor the prest set,
Of hir syns hir forto schrive,
And unto hir he went bylive,
Hir hand he toke and up sho rase :
Leman, he sayd, whor er thi fase ?
" Sir, lo tham yonder, in yone stede,
Bideand until i be ded ;   2550
Thai have demed me with wrang,
Wel ner had ye dwelt over lang

I pray to god he do yow mede,
That ye wald help me in this nede.''
Thir wordes herd than the steward,
He hies him unto hir ful hard,
He said, Thou lies, fals woman,
For thi treson ertow tane :—
Sho has bitraied hir lady,
And, sir, so wil sho the in hy ;   2560
And, tharfor, syr, by goddes dome,
I rede thou wend right als thou com ;
Thou takes a febil rede
If thou for hir wil suffer ded.
Unto the steward than said he,
Whoso es ferd i rede he fle ;
And, certes, I have bene this day
Whar i had ful large pay ;
And yit, he sayd, i sal noght fail :
To tham he waged the batayl.   2570
Do away thi lioun, said the steward,
For that es noght our forward ;
Allane sal thou fight with us thre.
And unto him thus answerd he :
Of my lioun no help i crave,
I ne have none other fote-knave,
If he wil do yow any dere
I rede wele that ye yow wer.
The steward said, On alkins wise,
Thi lyoun, sir, thou most chastise,   2580
That he do her no harm this day,
Or els wend forth on thi way ;
For his warand mai thou noght be,   .
Bot thou allane fight with us thre.
Al thir men wote, and so wote i,
That sho bitrayed hir lady,
Als trayturés sal sho have hyr,
Sho be brent her in this fir.
Sir Ywayn sa[i]d, Nai god forbede !
(He wist wele how the soth yede)   2590
I trow to wreke hir with the best.
He bad his lyoun go to rest,
And he laid him sone onane
Doun byfor tham everilk ane,
Bitwene his legges he layd his tail,
And so biheld to the batayl.
Al thre thai ride to sir Ywayn,
And smertly rides he tham ogayn,
In that time nothing tint he,
For his an strake was worth thaires thre ;   2600

He strake the steward on the shelde,
That he fel doun flat in the felde,
Bot op he rase yit at the last,
And to sir Ywayn strake ful fast ;
Tharat the lyoun greved sare,
No lenger wald he than lig thar,
To help his mayster he went onane ;
And the ladies everilk ane,
That war thar forto se that fight,
Praied ful fast ay for the knight.   2610
      The lyoun hasted him ful hard,
And sone he come to the steward,
A ful fel mynt to him he made,
He bigan at the shulder-blade,
And with his pawm al rafe he downe,
Bath hauberk and his actoune,
And al the fless doun til his kne,
So that men myght his guttes se ;
To ground he fell, so al to-rent,
Was thar no man that him ment.   2620
Thus the lioun gan hym sla :
Than war thai bot twa and twa ;
And, sertanly, thare sir Ywayn
Als with wordes did his main
For to chastis hys lyowne,
Bot he ne wald na mor lig doun ;
The liown thoght how so he sayd,
That with his help he was wele payd.
Thai smate the lyown on ilka syd,
And gaf him many woundes wide.   2630
When that he saw hys lyoun blede
He ferd for wa als wald wede,
And fast he strake than in that stour,
Might thare none his dintes dour ;
So grevosly than he bygan,
That doun he bar bath hors and man ;
Thai yald tham sone to sir Ywayn,
And tharof war the folk ful fayne ;
And sone quit to tham thaire hir,
For both he kest tham in the fir,   2640
And said, Wha juges men with wrang,
The same jugement sal thai fang.
Thus he helpid the maiden ying,
And sethin he made the saghtelyng
Bitwene hyr and the riche lady ;
Than al the folk, ful hastily,
Proferd tham to his servise,
To wirship him ever on al wise ;

Nane of tham al wist, bot Lunet,
That thai with thair lord war met.   2650
The lady prayed him als the hend,
That he hame with tham wald wende,
Forto sojorn thar a stownd,
Til he wer warist of his wound.
By his sar set he noght a stra,
Bot for his lioun was him wa.
Madame, he said, sertes, nay,
I mai noght dwel, the soth to say.
Sho said, Sir, sen thou wyl wend,
Sai us thi name, so god the mend.   2660
Madame, he said, bi saint Symoun,
I hat the knight with the lyoun.
Sho said, We saw yow never or now,
Ne never herd we speke of yow.
Tharby, he sayd, ye understand
I am noght knawen wide in land.
Sho said, I prai the forto dwell,
If that thou may, her us omell.
If sho had wist wele wha it was,
Sho wald wele lever have laten him pas ;   2670
And tharfor wald he noght be knawen,
Both for hir ese and for his awyn.
He said, No lenger dwel i ne may,
Beleves wele, and haves goday.
I prai to crist, hevyn kyng,
Lady, len yow gude lifing,
And len grace that al yowr anoy
May turn yow unto mykel joy.
Sho said, God grant that it so be !
Unto himself than thus said he,   2680
Thou ert the lok and kay also
Of al my wele, and al my wo,
Now wendes he forth, and morning mase,
And nane of tham wist what he was,
Bot Lunet, that he bad sold layn,
And so sho did with al hir mayne.
Sho canvayd him forth on his way ;
He said, Gude leman, i the pray,
That thou tel to no moder son
Who has bene thi champion ;   2690
And als i pray the, swete wight,
Late and arly thou do the might,
With speche unto my lady fre,
Forto make hir frende with me ;
Sen ye er now togeder glade,
Help you that we war frendes made :

Sertes, sir, sho sayd, ful fayn,
Thar-obout wil i be bayn ;
And that ye have done me this day
God do yow mede, als he wele may.   2700
Of Lunet thus his leve he tase,
Bot in hert grete sorow he hase. .
His lioun feled so mekill wa
That he ne myght no ferrer ga ;
Sir Ywayn puld gres in the felde,
And made a kouche opon his shelde,
Tharon his lyoun laid he thar,
And forth he rides, and sighes sar :
On his shelde so he him led,
Than was he ful evyl sted.   2710
Forth he rides, by frith and fell,
Til he come to a fayr castell,
Thar he cald and swith sone
The porter has the yates undone,
And to him made he ful gude cher ;
He said, Sir, ye er welcum here
Syr Ywayn said, God do the mede,
For tharof have i mekil nede.
Yn he rode right at the yate,
Fair folk kepid him tharate ;   2720
Thai toke his shelde and his lyoun,
And ful softly thai laid it doun ;
Sum to stabil led his stede,
And sum also unlaced his wede :
Thai told the lorde than of that knyght
And sone he and his lady bryght
And thair sons and doghters all,
Come ful fair him forto kall ;
Thai war ful fayn he thor was sted,
To chaumber sone thai have him led ;   2730
His bed was ordand richely,
And his lioun thai laid him by.
Him was no mister forto crave,
Redy he had what he wald have.
Twa maydens with him thai laft,
That wele war lered of leche-craft.[1]

---

[1] A knowledge of medicine seems to have been part of the education of the fair sex in ancient times. See *Memoires sur l'ancienne chevalerie*, I, 14. In *Mort d'Arthur*, sir Tristram is put in the ward and keeping of *La beale Isoud*, king Anguishe's daughter, "because she was a noble surgion." Her namesake, *Iseult aux blanches mains*, was equally expert and successful. See, likewise, the *Histoire de Gerard comte de Nevers & de Euriant de Savoye sa mye*, T. 1, C. 19, 20.

The lordes doghters both thai wore,
That war left to kepe hym thore ;
Thai heled hym everilka wound,
And hys lyoun sone made thai sownd. 2740
I can noght tel how lang he lay,
When he was helyd he went his way.
  But whils he sojorned in that place,
In that land byfel this case :
A litil thethin in a stede
A grete lord of the land was ded,
Lifand he had none other ayr
Bot two doghters that war ful fayr ;
Als sone as he was laid in molde,
The elder sister sayd sho wolde 2750
Wend to court sone als sho myght,
Forto get hir som doghty knyght
Forto win hir al the land,
And hald it halely in hir hand.
The yonger sister saw sho ne myght
Have that fell until hir right,
Bot if that it war by batail,
To court sho wil at ask cownsayl.
The elder sister sone was yar,
Unto the court fast gan sho far, 2760
To sir Gawayn sho made hir mane,
And he has granted hyr onane :
" Bot yt bus be so prevely
That nane wit bot thou and i ;
If thou of me makes any yelp,
Lorn has thou al my help."
Then efter, on the tother day,
Unto kourt come the tother may,
And to sir Gawayn sone sho went,
And talde unto him hir entent ; 2770
Of his help sho him bysoght.
Sertes, he sayd, that may i noght.
Than sho wepe and wrang hir handes,
And right with that come new tithandes,
How a knyght with a lyoun
Had slane a geant ful feloun.
The same knight thar talde this tale
That syr Ywayn broght fra bale,
That had wedded Gawayn sister der,
Sho and hir sons war thar in fer ; 2780
Thai broght the dwergh, that be ye balde,
And to sir Gawayn have thai talde,
How the knyght with the lyowne
Delivred tham out of presowne,

And how he, for sir Gawayn sake,
Gan that batayl undertake ;
And als how nobilly that he wroght.
Sir Gawayn said, I knaw him n[o]ght.
The yonger mayden than alsone
Of the king askes this bone :   2790
To have respite of fourti dais,
Als it fel to landes lays.
Sho wist thar was no man of main
That wald fyght with sir Gawayn,
She thoght to seke, by frith and fell,
The knyght that sho herd tham of tell.
Respite was granted of this thing,
The mayden toke leve at [the] king,
And sethen at al the baronage,
And forth sho went on hir vayage.   2800
Day ne nyght wald sho noght spar,
Thurgh all the land fast gan sho far,
Thurgh castel, and thurgh ilka toun,
To seke the knight with the lyown ;
" He helpes al in word and dede,
That unto him has any nede."
Sho soght him thurgh al that land,
Bot of hym herd sho na tythand.
Na man kouth tel hir whar he was,
Ful grete sorow in hert sho has,   2810
So mikel murning gan sho make,
That a grete sekenes gan sho take ;
Bot in hir way right wele sho sped,
At that kastell was sho sted
Whar sir Ywayn ar had bene
Helid of his sekenes clene.
Thar sho was ful wele knawen,
And als welcum als til hyr awyn ,
With alkyn gamyn thai gan hir glade,
And mikel joy of hir thai made.   2820
Unto the lord sho tald hyr case,
And helping hastily sho hase ;
Stil in lecheing thar sho lay,
A maiden for hir toke the way,
Forto seke, yf that sho myght
In any land her of that knyght ;
And that same kastel come sho by.
Whar Ywayn wedded the lavedy,
And saft sho spird, in ylk sesown,
Efter the knight with the lioun.   2830
Thai tald hir how he went tham fra,
And also how they saw him sla

Thre nobil knyghtes, for the nanes,
That faght with him al at anes.
Sho said, Pur charite, i yow pray,
If that ye wate, wil ye me say,
Whederward that he es went?
Thai said forsoth thai toke na tent :
" Ne her es nane that the can tell,
Bot if it be a damysell,   2840
For whas sake he heder come,
And for hir the batyl he nome ;
We trow wele that sho can the wis,
Yonder in yone kyrk sho ys ;
Tharfor we rede to hyr thou ga :"
And hastily than did sho swa.
Aither other ful gudeli gret,
And sone sho frayned at Lunet,
If sho kouth ani sertan sayne ;
And hendly answerd sho ogayne :   2850
I sal sadel my palfray,
And wend with the forth on thi way,
And wis the als wele als i can.
Ful oft-sithes thanked sho hir than.
Lunet was ful smertly yar,
And with the mayden forth gan sho far,
Als thai went al sho hyr talde,
How sho was taken and done in halde,
How wikkedly that sho was wreghed,
And how that traytyrs on hir leghed,   2860
And how that sho sold have bene brent,
Had not god hir socor sent
Or that knight with the lyoun :
" He lesed me out of presoun."
Sho broght hir sone into a playn,
Whar sho parted fra sir Ywayn ;
Sho said, Na mare can i tel the,
Bot her parted he fra me ;
How that he went wate i no mar,
Bot wounded was he wonder sar.   2870
God, that for us sufferd wounde,
Len us to se him hale and sownde !
No lenger with the may i dwell,
Bot cumly Crist, that heried hell,
Len the grace, that thou may spede
Of thine erand, als thou has nede.
Lunet hastily hies hir home,
And the mayden sone to the kastel come,
Whar he was helid byfor-hand,
The lord sone at the yate sho fand,   2880

With knyghtes and ladies grete cumpani,
Sho haylsed tham al ful hendely,
And ful fayr praied sho to tham then,
If thai couth, thai sold hyr ken,
Whar sho myght fynd, in tour or toun,
A kumly knyght with a lyoun.
Than said the lord, By swete Jhesus,
Right now parted he fra us ;
Lo her the steppes of his stede,
Evyn unto him thai wil the lede.   2890
Than toke sho leve, and went hir way,
With sporrs sho sparid noght hir palfray ;
Fast sho hyed with al hyr myght,
Until sho of him had a syght,
And of his lyoun that by him ran,
Wonder joyful was sho than ;
And with hir force sho hasted so fast
That sho overtoke him at the last.
Sho hailsed him with hert ful fayn,
And he hir hailsed fayre ogayn.   2900
Sho said, Sir, wide have i yow soght,
And for myself ne es it noght,
Bot for a damysel of pryse,
That halden es both war and wise ;
Men dose to hir ful grete outrage,
Thai wald hir reve hyr heritage,
And in this land now lifes none
That sho traystes hyr opone,
Bot anly opon god and the,
For thou ert of so grete bountè ;   2910
Thorgh help of the sho hopes wele
To win hyr right everilka dele.
Scho sais, no knyght that lifes now
Mai help hir half so wele als thou :
Gret word sal gang of thi vassage,
If that thou win hir heritage ;
For thoght sho toke slike sekenes sar,
So that sho might travail no mar,
I have yow soght on sydes ser,
Tharfor yowr answer wald i her,   2920
Whether ye wil with me wend,
Or els whar yow likes to lend.
He said, That knyght that idil lies
Oft-sithes winnes ful litel pries,
For-thi mi rede sal sone be tane,
Gladly with the wil 1 gane,
Wheder so thou wil me lede,
And hertly help the in thi nede ;

Sen thou haves me so wide soght,
Sertes fail the sal i noght.   2930
   Thus thair wai forth gan thai hald,
Until a kastel, that was cald
The castel of the hevy sorow,
Thar wald he bide until the morow,
Thar to habide him thoght it best,
For the son drogh fast to rest ;
Bot al the men that thai with met,
Grete wonder sone on tham thai set ;
And [seyde], Thou wreche unsely man,
Whi wil thou her thi herber tane ?   2940
Thou passes noght without despite.
Sir Ywain answerd tham als tyte,
And said, Forsoth, ye er unhende,
An unkouth man so forto shende ;
Ye sold noght say hym velany,
Bot if ye wist encheson why.
Thai answerd than, and said ful sone,
Thou sal wit or tomorn at none.
Syr Ywaine said, For al yowr saw,
Unto yon castel wil i draw.   2950
He, and his lyoun, and the may,
Unto the castel toke the way.
When the porter of tham had sight,
Sone he said unto the knight,
Cumes forth, he said, ye altogeder,
Ful ille hail er ye cumen heder.
Thus war thai welkumd at the yate,
And yit thai went al in tharate,
Unto the porter no word thai said,
A hal thai fand ful gudeli graid ;   2960
And, als sir Ywaine made entrè,
Fast bisyde him than saw he
A proper place, and fair, i wis,
Enclosed obout with a palis.
He loked in bitwix the trese,
And many maidens thar he sese,
Wirkand silk and gold wir,
Bot thai war al in pover atir,
Thair clothes war reven on evil arai,
Ful tenderly al weped thai ;   2970
Thair face war lene and als unclene,
And blak smokkes had thai on bidene ;
Thai had mischefs ful manifalde,
Of hunger, of threst, and of calde ;
And ever onane thai weped all,
Als thai wald to water fall.

When Ywaine al this understode,
Ogayn unto the yates he yode,
Bot thai war sperred ferli fast,
With lokkes that ful wele wald last ;   2980
The porter kepid tham with his main,
And said, Sir, thou most wend ogain ;
I wate thou wald out at the yate,
Bot thou mai noght, by na gate ;
Thi herber es tane til to-morow,
And tharfor getes thou mekill sorow ;
Omang thi fase her sted ertow.
He said, So have i bene or now,
And past ful wele, so sal i her ;
Bot, leve frend, wiltou me ler   2990
Of thise maidens what thai ar,
That wirkes al this riche ware ?
He said, If thou wil wit trewly,
Forthermar thou most aspy.
Tharfore, he said, i sall n[o]ght lett.
He soght and fand a dern weket,
He opind it, and in he yede :
Maidens, he said, god mot yow spede !
And, als he sufferd woundes sar,
He send yow covering of yowr car,   3000
So that ye might mak merler chere.
Sir, thai said, god gif so wer !
Yowr sorow, he said, unto me say,
And i sal mend it yf i may.
Ane of tham answerd ogayne,
And said, The soth we sal noght layne,
We sal yow tel or ye ga ferr,
Why we er here, and what we err.
Sir, ye sal understand,
That we er al of Mayden-land,   3010
Our kyng, opon his jolitè,
Passed thurgh many cuntrè,
Aventures to spir and spy,
Forto asay his owen body,
His herber her anes gan he ta,
That was biginyng of our wa,
For heryn er twa champions,
Men sais thai er the devil sons,
Geten of a woman with a ram,
Ful many man have thai done gram ;   3020
What knight so herbers her anyght
With both at ones bihoves him fight,
So bus the do, by bel and boke :
Alas, that thou thine yns her toke !

Our king was wight himself to welde,
And of fourtene yeres of elde,
When he was tane with tham to fyght,
Bot unto tham had he no myght,
And when he saw him bud be ded,
Than he kouth no better rede,   3030
Bot did him haly in thair grace,
And made tham sureté in that place,
Forto yeld tham ilka yer,
So that he sold be hale and fer,
Threty maidens to trowage,
And al sold be of hegh parage,
And the fairest of his land ;
Herto held he up his hand.
This ilk rent byhoves hym gyf,
Als lang als the fendes lyf,   3040
Or til thai be in batayl tane,
Or els unto thai be al slane,
Then sal we pas al hethin quite,
That her suffers al this despite ;
Bot herof es noght for speke,
Es none in werld that us mai wreke.
We wirk her silver, silk and golde,
Es none richer on this molde,
And never the better er we kled,
And in grete hunger er we sted ;   3050
For al that we wirk in this stede,
We have noght half our fil of brede,
For the best that sewes her any styk,
Takes bot four penys in a wik,
And that es litel, wha-som tase hede,
Any of us to kleth and fede.
Ilkone of us, withouten lesyng,
Might win ilk wike fourty shilling,
And yit bot if we travail mar,
Oft thai bete us wonder sar :   3060
It helpes noght to tel this tale,
For thar bese never bote of our bale.
Our maste sorow, sen we bigan,
That es, that we se mani a man,
Doghty dukes, yrels, and barouns,
Oft-sithes slane with thir champiowns,
With tham to-morn bihoves the fight.
Sir Ywayn said, God, maste of myght,
Sal strenkith me in ilka dede,
Ogains tha devils and al thair drede :   3070
That lord deliver yow of yowr fase.
Thus takes he leve and forth he gase,

He passed forth into the hall,
Thar fand he no man him to call,
No bewtese wald thai to him bede,
Bot hastily thai toke his stede,
And also the maydens palfray,
War served wele with corn and hay :
For wele thai hoped that sir Ywayn
Sold never have had his stede ogayn.   3080
Thurgh the hal Sir Ywain gase,
Intil ane orcherd playn pase,
His maiden with him ledes he,
He fand a knyght under a tre,
Opon a clath of gold he lay,
Byfor him sat a ful fayr may ;
A lady sat with tham in fere,
The mayden red at thai myght her
A real romance in that place,
Bot i ne wote of wham it was.   3090
Sho was bot fiftene yeres alde,
The knyght was lord of al that halde,
And that mayden was his ayre,
Sho was both gracious, gode, and far.
Sone when thai saw sir Ywaine,
Smertly raise thai hym ogayne,
And by tho hand the lord him tase,
And unto him grete myrth he mase.
He said, Sir, by swete Jhesus,
Thou ert ful welcum until us.   3100
The mayden was bowsom and bayne
Forto unarme syr Ywayne,
Serk and breke bath sho hym broght,
That ful craftily war wroght,
Of riche cloth soft als the sylk,
And tharto white als any mylk.
Sho broght hym ful riche wedes to wer,
Hose and shose and alkins ger,
Sho payned hir with al hir myght,
To serve him and his mayden bright.   3110
Sone thai went unto soper,
Ful really served thai wer,
With metes and drinkes of the best,
And sethin war thai broght to rest.
In his chaumber by hym lay
His owin lyoun and his may ;
At morn, when it was dayes lyght.
Up thai rase, and sone tham dyght ;
Sir Ywayn and hys damysele
Went ful sone til a chapele,   3120

And thar thai herd a mes in haste,[1]
That was sayd of the haly gaste ;
Efter mes ordand he has
Forth on his way fast forto pas ;
At the lord hys leve he tase,
And grete thanking to him he mase.
The lord said, Tak it to na greve,
To gang hethin yit getes thou na leve ;
Herein es ane unsely law,
That has bene used of ald daw,   3130
And bus be done for frend or fa ;
I sal do com byfor the twa
Grete serjantes of mekil myght,
And whether it be wrang or right,
Thou most tak the shelde and sper,
Ogaynes tham the forto were.
If thou overcum tham in this stour,
Than sal thou have al this honour,
And my doghter in mariage,
And also al myne heritage.   3140
Then said, sir Ywayn, Als mot i the,
Thi doghter sal thou have for me,
For a king or ane emperour
May hir wed with grete honour.
The lord said, Her sal cum na knyght,
That he ne sal with twa champions fight ;
So sal thou do on al wise,
For it es knawen custum assise.
Sir Ywaine said, Sen i sal so,
Than es the best that i may do   3150
To put me baldly in thair hend,
And tak the grace that god wil send.
The champions sone war forth broght,
Sir Ywain sais, By him me boght,
Ye seme wele the devils sons,
For i saw never swilk champions.
Aither broght unto the place
A mikel rownd talvace,
And a klub, ful grete and lang,
Thik fret with mani a thwang ;[2]   3160
On bodies armyd wele thai war,
Bot thar hedes bath war bar.

---

[1] This was usual :—"he had with him right good chere, and fared of the best, with passing good wine, and had merry rest that night ; and on the morrow *he heard a masse*, and after dined, &c." (*Mort d' Arthur*, P. 1, C. 56.) Again : " On the morrow the damosell and sir Beaumains *heard masse*, and brake their fast, and so tooke their leave." (P. 1, C. 132.)

[2] The original reads " thawang."

The lioun bremly on tham blist,
When he tham saw, ful wele he wist
That thai sold with his mayster fight,
He thoght to help him at his myght ;
With his tayl the erth he dang,
Forto fyght him thoght ful lang;
Of him aparty had thai drede.
Thai said, Syr knight, thou most nede   3170
Do thi lioun out of this place,
For to us makes he grete manace,
Or yelde the til us als creant.
He said, That war noght mine avenant.
Thai said, Than do thi beste oway,
And als sone sal we samyn play.
He said, Sirs, if ye be agast,
Takes the beste and bindes him fast.
Thai said, He sal be bun or slane,
For help of him sal thou have nane ;   3180
Thi self allane sal with us fight,
For that es custume, and the right.
Than said sir Ywain to tham sone,
Whar wil ye that the best be done ?
" In a chamber he sal be loken,
With gude lokkes ful stifly stoken."
Sir Ywain led than his lioun
Intil a chamber to presoun ;
Than war bath tha devils ful balde,
When the lioun was in halde.   3190
Sir Ywayn toke his nobil wede,
And dight him yn, for he had nede,
And on his nobil stede he strade,
And baldely to tham bath he rade.
His mayden was ful sar adred,
That he was so straitly sted,
And unto god fast gan sho pray,
Forto wyn him wele oway.
Than strake thai on him wonder sar,
With thair clubbes that full strang war,   3200
Opon his shelde so fast thai feld,
That never a pece with other held ;
Wonder it es that any man
Might ber the strakes that he toke than.
Mister haved he of socour,
For he come never in swilk a stour,
Bot manly evyr with al his mayn,
And graithly hit he tham ogayn,
And, als it telles in the boke,
He gaf the dubbil of that he toke.   3210

Ful grete sorow the lioun has,
In the chameber whar he was,
And ever he thoght opon that dede,
How he was helpid in his nede,
And he might now do na socowr
To him that helpid him in that stour ;
Might he out of the chamber breke,
Sone he walde his maister wreke.
He herd thair strakes, that war ful sterin,
And yern he waytes in ilka heryn,   3220
And al was made ful fast to hald ;
At the last he come to the thriswald,
The erth thar kest he up ful sone,
Als fast als four men sold have done,
If thai had broght bath bill and spade ;
A mekil hole ful sone he made.
Yn al this [tyme] was sir Ywayn
Ful straitly parred with mekil payn,
And drede he had, als him wele aght,
For nowther,[1] of tham na woundes laght ;   3230
Kepe tham cowth thai wonder wele,
That dintes derid tham never a dele,
It was na wapen that man might welde
Might get a shever out of thair shelde.
Tharof cowth Ywayn no rede,
Sar he douted to be ded,
And also his damysel
Ful mekil murnyng[2] made omell,
And wele sho wend he sold be slane,
And, sertes, than war hir socor gane ;   3240
Bot fast he stighteld in that stowr,
And hastily him come socowre.
   Now es the lioun out-broken,
His maister sal ful sone be wroken ;
He rynnes fast with full fell rese,
Than helpid it noght to prai for pese,
He stirt unto that a glotowne,
And to the erth he brayd him downe ;
Than was thar nane obout that place
That thai ne war fayn of that fair chace ;   3250
The maiden had grete joy in hert ;
Thai said, He sal never rise in quert.
His felow fraisted with al his mayn,
To raise him smertly up ogayn,
And, right so als he stowped doun,
Sir Ywain with his brand was boun,

---

[1] The original reads ''*Nowyr.*''
[2] The original reads ''*Murnyg.*''

And strake his nek-bane right in sonder,
Tharof the folk had mekil wonder,
His hevid trindeld on the sand,
Thus had Ywain the hegher hand.   3260
When he had feld that fowl feloun,
Of his stede he lighted down,
His lioun on that other lay,
Now wil he help him if he may,
The lioun saw his maister cum,
And to hys part he wald have som ;
The right sholder oway he rase,
Both arm and klob with him he tase ;
And so his maister gan he wreke :
And als he might, yit gan he speke,   3270
And said, Sir knight, for thi gentry,
I prai the have of me mercy,
And by scill sal he mercy have
What man so mekely wil it crave ;
And tharfore grantes mercy to me.
Sir Ywain said, I grant it the,
If that thou wil thi selven say
That thou ert overcumen this day.
He said, I grant withowten fail,
I am overcumen in this batail,   3280
For pur ataynt and recreant.
Sir Ywayn said, Now i the grant
For to do the na mar der,
And fro my liown i sal the wer,
I grant the pese at my powèr.
Than come the folk ful fair in fer,
The lord and the lady als,
Thai toke him fair obout the hals.
Thai saide, Sir, now saltou be
Lord and syre in this cuntrè,   3290
And wed our doghter for sertayn.
Sir Ywayn answerd than ogayn :
He said, Sen ye gif me hir now,
I gif hir evyn ogayn to yow.
Of me for ever i grant hir quite ;
Bot, sir, takes it til no despite,
For, sertes, whif may i none wed
Until my nedes be better sped ;
Bot this thing, sir, i ask of the,
That al thir prisons may pas fre :   3300
God has granted me this chance,
I have made their delyverance.
The lord answerd than ful tyte,
And said, I grant the tham al quite ;

My doghter als i rede thou take,
Sho es noght worthi to forsake.
Unto the knyght sir Ywain sais,
Sir, I sal noght hir mysprays,
For sho es so curtays and hende,
That, fra hethin to the werldes ende,   3310
Es no kyng ne emperour,
Ne no man of so grete honowr,
That he ne might wed that bird bright,
And so wald i if that i myght.
I wald hir wed with ful gude cher,
Bot lo i have a mayden her,
To folow hir now most i nede,
Wheder so sho wil me lede :
Tharfor at this time haves goday.
He said, thou passes noght so oway,   3320
Sen thou wil noght do als i tell,
In my prison sal thou dwell.
He said, If i lay thar al my live
I sal hir never wed to wive,
For with this maiden most i wend,
Until we cum whar sho wil lend.
The lord saw it was na bote
Obout that mater mor to mote,
He gaf him leve oway to far,
Bot he had lever he had bene thar.   3330
    Sir Ywayn takes than forth in fer
Al the prisons that thar wer,
Bifor hym sone thai come ilkane,
Nerhand naked and wobigane,
Stil he hoved at the yate,
Til thai war went al forth tharate,
Twa and twa ay went thai samyn,
And made omang tham mikel gamyn.
If god had cumen fra hevyn on hight,
And on this mold omang tham light.   3340
Thai had noght made mar joy sertain
Than thai made to syr Ywayne.
Folk of the toun com him biforn,
And blissed the time that he was born,
Of his prowes war thai wele payd,
In this werld es none slike, thai said ;
Thai cunvayd him out of the toun,
With ful fair processiowne.
The maidens than thair leve has tane,
Ful mekil myrth thai made ilkane ;   3350
At thair departing prayed thai thus :
Our lord god, mighty Jhesus,

He help yow, sir, to have yowr will,
And shilde yow ever fra alkyns ill.
Maidens, he said, god mot yow se,
And bring yow wele whar ye wald be.
Thus thair way forth er thai went,
Na mor unto tham wil we tent.
  Sir Ywayn and his fair may
Al the sevenight traveld thai,   3360
The maiden knew the way ful wele
Hame until that ilk castele,
Whar sho lef the seke may,
And theder hastily come thai.
When thai come to the castel yate,
Sho led sir Ywain yn tharate,
The mayden was yit seke lyand,
Bot when thai talde hir this tithand,
That cumen was hir messager,
And the knyght with hyr in fér,   3370
Swilk joy tharof sho had in hert,
Hir thoght that sho was al in quert.
Sho said, I wate my sister will
Gif me now that falles me till.
In hir hert sho was ful light,
Ful hendly hailsed sho the knight.
A, sir, sho said, god do the mede,
That thou wald cum in swilk a nede :
And al that in that kastel wer
Welkumd him with meri cher.   3380
I can noght say, so god me glade,
Half the myrth that thai him made.
That night he had ful nobil rest,
With alkins esment of the best.
Als sone als the day was sent,
Thai ordaind tham and forth thai went,
Until that town fast gan thai ride
Whar the kyng sojorned that tide,
And thar the elder sister lay,
Redy forto kepe hyr day.   3390
Sho traisted wele on sir Gawayn,
That no knyght sold cum him ogayn,
Sho hopid thar was no knyght lifand
In batail that might with him stand.
Al a sevenight dayes bidene
Wald noght sir Gawayn be sene ;
Bot in ane other toun he lay,
For he wald cum at the day.
Als aventerous into the place,
So that no man sold se his face.   3400

The armes he bar war noght his awyn,
For he wald noght in court be knawyn.
Syr Ywayn and his damysell
In the town toke thaire hostell.
And thar he held him prevely,
So that none sold him ascry ;
Had thai dwelt langer by a day,
Than had sho lorn hir land for ay.
Sir Ywain rested thar that nyght,
And on the morn he gan hym dyght,   3410
On slepe left thai his lyowne,
And wan tham wightly out of toun ;
It was hir wil, and als hys awyn,
At cum to court als knyght unknawyn.
Sone obout the prime of day,
Sir Gawayn, fra thethin thar he lay,
Hies him fast into the felde,
Wele armyd with sper and shelde.
No man knew him, les ne mor,
Bot sho that he sold fight sore.   3420
The elder sister to court come,
Unto the king at ask hir dome,
Sho said, I am cumen with my knyght,
Al redy to defend my right,
This day was us set sesowne,
And i am her al redy bowne,
And sen this es the last day,
Gifes dome and lates us wend our way.
My sister has al sydes soght,
Bot wele i wate her cums sho noght,   3430
For sertainly sho findes nane,
That dar the batail undertane,
This day for hir forto fyght,
Forto reve fra me my right,
Now have i wele wonnen my land,
Withowten dint of knightes hand ;
What so my sister ever has mynt,
Al hir part now tel i tynt,
Al es myne, to sell and gyf,
Als a wreche ay sal sho lyf :   3440
Tharfor, sir king, sen it es swa,
Gifes yowr dome, and lat us ga.
    The king said, Maiden, think noght lang,
(Wele he wist sho had the wrang)
Damysel, it es the assyse,
Whils sityng es of the justise,
The dome nedes you most habide,
For per aventur it may bityde,

Thi sister sal cum al bityme,
For it es litil passed prime.   3450
When the king had tald this scill,
Thai saw cum rideand over a hyll,
The yonger sister and hir knyght,
The way to town thai toke ful right,
On Ywains bed his liown lay,
And thai had stollen fra him oway.
The elder maiden made il cher,
When thai to court cumen wer.
The king withdrogh his jugement,
For wele he trowed in his entent   3460
That the yonger sister had the right,
And that sho sold cum with sum knyght.
Himself knew hyr wele inogh.
When he hir saw ful fast he logh,
Him liked it welc in his hert,
That he saw hir so in quert.
Into the court sho toke the way,
And to the king thus gan sho say,
God, that governs alkin thing,
The save and se, syr Arthur the kyng,   3470
And al the knyghtes that langes to the,
And also al thi mery menyè ;
Unto yowre court, sir, have i broght
An unkouth knyght that ye knaw noght ;
He sais that, sothly, for my sake,
This batayl wil he undertake,
And he haves yit in other land
Ful felle dedes underhand,
Bot al he leves, god do him mede !
Forto help me in my nede.   3480
Hir elder[1] sister stode hyr by,
And tyl hyr sayd sho hastily,
For hys luf that lens us life,
Gif me my right withouten strife,
And lat no man tharfor be slayn.
The elder sister sayd ogayn,

---

[1] So, doubtless, the MS. originally read ; the word *zonger* being written by a different, and, apparently, later, hand, upon an erasure.

Here is, likewise, another mistake, either of the author or of the translator. The younger sister, being in search of sir Ywain, falls sick, and comes to the same castle where he and his lion had been cured of the wounds they got in their engagement with the steward and his two brothers. Here she stays, to be healed of her malady ; and, in the mean time, the lord of the castle dispatches a damsel to proceed in the search. This damsel goes to the chapel, and meets with Lunet, who tells her of the combat, and sir Ywain's wounds ; and brings her to the place where she had parted with him. The damsel rides forward, and comes to *the*

Thi right es noght for al es myne,
And i wil have yt mawgre thine ;
Tharfore if thou preche alday,
Her sal thou nothing ber oway.   3490
The yonger mayden to hir says,
Sister, thou ert ful curtays,
And gret dole es it forto se
Slike two knightes al[s] thai be
For us sal put tham-self to spill,
Tharfor now, if it be thi will,
Of thi gude wil to me thou gif
Sum thing that i may on lif.
The elder said, So mot i the,
Who so es ferd i rede thai fle ;   3500
Thou getes right noght withowten fail,
Bot if thou win yt thurgh batail.
The yonger said, Sen thou wil swa,
To the grace of god her i me ta,
And, lord, als he es maste of myght,
He send his socor to that knyght,
That thus in dede of charitè
This day antres hys lif for me.
The twa knightes come bifor the king,
And that was sone ful grete gedering,   3510
For ilka man that walk might,
Hasted sone to se that syght ;
Of tham this was a selly case,
That nowther wist what other wase ;
Ful grete luf was bitwix tham twa,
And now er aither other fa ;
Ne the king kowth tham noght knaw,
For thai wald noght thair faces shew,
If owther of tham had other sene,
Grete luf had bene tham bitwene.   3520
Now was this a grete selly,
That trew luf and so grete envy
Als bitwix tham twa was than
Might bath at anes be in a man.
The knightes, for thase maidens love,
Aither til other kast a glove,
And wele armed with sper and shelde,
Thai riden both forth to the felde.

---

castle where he had been healed of his wounds; whence, she is informed, he
was *just departed.* This contradiction has, most likely, arisen from the
inaccuracy of the translator ; and, by the first castle, we should, no doub ,
understand that where Ywain fought and slew the giant, before he went to assist
Lunet.

14

Thai stroke their stedes that war kene,
Litel luf was tham bitwene ;　　　　　　　　3530
Ful grevosly bigan that gamyn,
With stalworth speres strake thai samen,
And thai had anes togeder spoken,
Had thar bene no speres broken,
Bot in that time bitid it swa,
That aither of tham wald other sla.
Thai drow swerdes, and swang obout,
To dele dyntes had thai no dout ;
Thair sheldes war shiferd, and helms rifen,
Ful stalworth strakes war thar gifen,　　　　　　　3540
Bath on bak and brestes thar,
War bath wounded wonder far,
In many stedes might men ken
The blode out of thair bodies ren.
On helmes thai gaf slike strakes kene,
That the riche stanes albidene,
And other ger that was ful gude,
Was over-covered al in blode.
Thar helmes war evel brusten bath,
And thai also war wonder wrath ;　　　　　　　3550
Thair hauberks als war alto torn,
Both behind and als byforn ;
Thair sheldes lay cheverd on the ground :
Thai rested than a litel stound,
Forto tak thair ande tham till,
And that was with thair bother will.
Bot ful lang rested thai noght,
Til aither of tham on other soght,
A stronge stowr was tham bitwene,
Harder than men never sene,　　　　　　　3560
The king and other that thar war,
Said that thai saw never ar
So nobil knightes in no place
So lang fight bot by goddes grace.
Barons, knightes, squiers, and knaves,
Said, It es no man that haves
So mekil tresor ne nobillay
That might tham quite thair dede this day.
Thir wordes herd the knyghtes twa,
It made tham forto be mor thra.　　　　　　　3570
　　Knightes went obout gude wane,
To mak the two sisters at ane,
Bot the elder was so unkinde,
In hir thai might no mercy finde,
And the right that the yonger hase
Puttes sho in the kinges grace.

The king himself and als the quene,
And other knightes albidene,
And al that saw that dede that day
Held al with the yonger may,   3580
And to the king al thai bisoght,
Whether the elder wald or noght,
That he sold evin the landes dele,
And gif the yonger damysele
The half, or els sum porciowne,
That sho mai have to warisowne,
And part the two knightes in twyn ;
For sertis, thai said, it war grete syn
That owther of tham sold other sla,
For in the world is noght swilk twa.   3590
When other knightes said thai sold sese,
Tham self wald noght assent to pese.
Al that ever saw that batayl
Of thair might had grete mervayl,
Thai saw never under the hevyn
Twa knightes that war copled so evyn.
Of al the folk was none so wise
That wist whether sold have the prise ;
For thai saw never so stalworth stour ;
Ful der boght thai that honowr.   3600
Grete wonder had sir Gawayn
What he was that faght him ogain,
And sir Ywain had grete ferly
Wha stode ogayns him so stifly.
On this wise lasted that fight
Fra midmorn unto mirk night,
And by that time, i trow thai twa
War ful weri and sare alswa ;
Thai had bled so mekil blode
It was grete ferly that thai stode,   3610
So far thai bet on bak and brest,
Until the sun was gon to rest,
For nowther of tham wald other spar,
For mirk night thai than namar,
Tharfor to rest thai both tham yelde,
Bot, or thai past out of the felde,
Bitwix tham two might men se
Both mekil joy and grete pete.
By speche might no man Gawain knaw,
So was he hase and spak ful law,   3620
And mekil was he out of maght,
For the strakes that he had laght,
And sir Ywain was ful wery,
Bot thus he spekes, and sais in hy :

He said, Syr, sen us failes light,
I hope it be no lifand wight
What wil us blame if that we twin,
For of al stedes i have bene yn
With no man yit never i met
That so wele kowth his strakes set,   3630
So nobil strakes has thou gifen
That my sheld es alto reven.
Sir Gawayn said, Sir, sertanly,
Thou ert noght so weri als i,
For if we langer fightand wer
I trow I might do the no dere,
Thou ert nothing in my det,
Of strakes that i on the set.
Sir Ywain said, in Cristes name,
Sai me what thou hat at hame.   3640
He said, Sen thou my name wil her,
And covaites to wit what it wer,
My name in this land mani wote,
I hat Gawayn the king son Lote.
Than was sir Ywayn for agast,
His swerde fra him he kast,
He ferd right als he wald wede,
And sone he stirt down of his stede,
He said, her es a fowl mischance,
For defaut of conisance ;   3650
A sir, he said, had i the sene,
Than had her no batel bene,
I had me yolden to the als tite
Als worthi war for discumfite.
What man ertou ? said sir Gawain.
Syr, he sayd, I hat Ywayne,
That lufes the more, by se and sand,
Than any man that es lifand,
For mani dedes that thou me did,
And curtaysi ye have me kyd :   3660
Tharfor, sir, now in this stour,
I sal do the this honowr
I grant that thou hast me overcumen,
And by strenkyth in batayl nomen.
Sir Gawayn answerd, als curtays,
Thou sal noght do, sir, als thou sais ;
This honowr sal noght be myne,
Bot sertes it aw wele at be thine ;
I gif it the her, withowten hone,
And grantes that i am undone.
Sone thai light, so sais the boke,
And aither other in armes toke,   3670

And kissed so, ful fele sithe,
Than war thai both glad and blithe ;
In armes so thai stode togeder,
Unto the king com ridand theder,
And fast he covait forto her
Of thir knightes what thai wer,
And whi thai made so mekil gamyn
Sen thai had so foghten samyn.

  Ful hendli then asked the king
Wha had so sone made saghteling   3680
Betwix tham thai had bene so wrath,
And aither haved done other scath ?
He said, I wend ye wald ful fain
Aither of yow have other slayn,
And now ye er so frendes der.
Sir king, said Gawain, ye sal her ;
For unknawing and hard grace,
Thus have we foghten in this place ;   3690
I am Gawayn, yowr awin nevow,
And sir Ywayn faght with me now ;
When we war ner weri, i wys,
Mi name he frayned and i his,
When we were knawin, sone gan we sese ;
Bot, sertes, sir, this es no lese,
Had we foghten forth a stownde,
I wote wele i had gone to grounde,
By his prowes and his mayne,
I wate for soth i had bene slayne.   3700
Thir wordes menged al the mode,
Of sir Ywain als he stode :
Sir, he said, so mot i go,
Ye kn[a]w yowr self it es noght so.
Sir king, he said, withowten fail,
I am overcumen in this batayl.
Nai, sertes, said Gawain, bot am i.
Thus nowther wald have the maistri.
Bifor the king gan aither grant
That himself was recreant ;   3710
Than the king, and hys menyè
Had bath joy and grete petè,
He was ful fayn thai frendes wer,
And that thai war so funden in fer.
The kyng said, Now es wele sene
That mekil luf was yow bitwene.
He said, sir Ywain, welkum home,
For it was lang sen he thar come.
He said, I rede ye both assent
To do yow in my jujement,   3720

And i sal mak so gude ane ende,
That ye sal both be halden hende.
Thai both assented sone thartill,
To do tham in the kynges will,
If the maydens wald do so.
Than the king bad knyghtes two
Wend efter the maydens bath,
And so thai did ful swith rath,
Bifor the kyng when thai war broght,
He tald unto tham als him thoght :
" Lystens me now, maydens hende,
Yowr grete debate es broght til ende,
So fer forth now es it dreven
That the dome most nedes be gifen,
And i sal deme yow als i can."
The elder sister answerd than,
Sen ye er king that us sold wer,
I pray yow do to me na der.
He said, I wil let for na saw,
For to do the landes law.
Thi yong sister sal have hir right,
For i se wele that thi knyght,
Es overcumen in this wer.
Thus said he anely hir to fer,
And for he wist hir wilful wele,
That sho wald part with never a dele.
Sir, sho said, sen thus es gan,
Now most i, whether i wil or nane,
Al yowr cumandment fulfill,
And tharfor dose right als ye will.
The king said, Thus sal it fall,
Al yowr landes depart i sall :
Thi wil es wrang, that have i knawin,
Now sal thou have noght bot thin awin,
That es the half of al-bydene,
Than answerd sho, ful tite in tene,
And said, Me think ful grete outrage
To gif hir half myne heritage.
The king said, For yowr bother esse,
In hir land i sal hir sese
And sho sal hald hir land of the,
And to the tharfor mak fewtè,
Sho sal the luf als hir lady,
And thou sal kith thi curtaysi,
Luf hir efter thine avenant,
And sho sal be to the tenant.
This land was first, i understand,
That ever was parted in Ingland.

3730

3740

3750

3760

Than said the king, Withowten fail,
For the luf of that batayl,   3770
Al sisters that sold efter bene
Sold part the landes tham bitwene.
   Than said the king to sir Gawain,
And als he prayed sir Ywain,
Forto uulace thair riche wede,
And tharto had thai bath grete nede.
Als thai thus-gate stod and spak,
The lyown out of the chamber brak,
Als thai thair armours sold unlace,
Come he rinand to that place,   3780
Bot he had, or he come thar,
Soght his mayster whide-war.
And ful mekil joy he made,
When he his mayster funden hade.
On ilka side than might men se
The folk fast to toun gan fle,
So war thai ferd for the liowne,
When thai saw him theder bown.
Syr Ywain bad tham cum ogayn,
And said, Lordinges, for sertayn,   3790
Fra this beste i sal yow wer,
So that he sal dy yow no der ;
And, sirs, ye sal wele trow mi sawes,
We er frendes and gude felaws ;
He es mine, and i am his,
For na tresor i wald him mys.
When thai saw this was sertain,
Than spak thai al of sir Ywaine :
This es the knight with the liown,
That es halden of so grete renown ;   3800
This ilk knight the geant slogh,
Of dedis he es doghty inogh.
Then said sir Gawayn sone in hi,
Me es bitid grete velani ;
I cri the mercy, sir Ywayne,
That i have trispast the ogayn ;
Thou helped mi sister in hir nede,
Evil have i quit the now thi mede ;
Thou anterd thi life for luf of me,
And als mi sister tald of the ;   3810
Thou said that we, ful fele dawes,
Had bene frendes, and gude felawes ;
Bot wha it was ne wist i noght,
Sethen have i had ful mekil thoght,
And yit for al that i do can
I cowth never her of na man

That me cowth tell, in tour ne toun,
Of the knight with the liown.
When thai had unlaced thair wede,
Al the folk toke ful gode hede 3820
How that beste, his bales to bete,
Likked his maister both hend and fete.
Al the men grete mervail hade
Of the mirth the lyown made.
When the knightes war broght to rest,
The king gert cum sone of the best
Surgiens that our war sene,
For to hele tham both bidene.
Sone so thai war hale and sownd,
Sir Ywain hies him fast to found. 3830
Luf was so in his hert fest,
Night ne day haved he no rest ;
Bot he get grace of his lady,
He most go wode, or for luf dy.
Eul preveli forth gan he wende
Out of the court fra ilka frende ;
He rides right unto the well,
And thar he thinkes forto dwell ;
His gode lyon went with him ay,
He wald noght part fro him oway, 3840
He kest water opon the stane,
The storm rase ful sone onane,
The thoner grisely gan out-brest,
Him thoght als al the grete forest,
And al that obout the well,
Sold have sonken into hell.
The lady was in mekil dout,
For al the kastel walles obout
Quoke so fast that men might think
That al into the erth sold synk ; 3850
Thai trembled fast both bour and hall,
Als thai unto the grund sold fall ;
Was never, in this mydle-erde,[1]
In no kastell folk so ferde.
Bot wha it was wele wist Lunet,
Sho said, Now er we hard byset ;
Madame, i ne wate what us es best,
For her now may we have no rest ;
Ful wele i wate ye have no knight
That dar wende to your wel, and fight. 3860
With him that cumes yow to assaile ;
And if he have her no batayle,

---

[1] The original reads "*mydlerde.*"

Ne findes none yow to defend,
Yowr lose ben lorn withouten end.
The lady said, sho wald be dede:
" Der Lunet, what es thi rede ?
Wirk i wil by thi kounsail,
For i ne wate noght what mai avail."
Madame, sho said, i wald ful fayn
Kownsail yow if it might gayn,   3870
Bot in this case it war mystere
To have a wiser kownsayler:
And by desait than gan sho say,
Madame, per chance, this ilk day,
Sum of yowr knightes mai cum hame,
And yow defend of al this shame.
A, sho said, Lunet, lat be!
Speke na mor of my menyè,
For wele i wate, so god me mend,
I have na knight me mai defend ;   3880
Tharfor my kownsail bus the be,
And i wil wirk al efter the ;
And tharfor help at al thi myght.
Madame, sho said, had we that knyght,
That es so curtais and avenant,
And has slane the grete geant,
And als that the thre knightes slogh,
Of him ye myght be trist inogh ;
Bot forthermar, madame, i wate
He and his lady er at debate,   3890
And has bene so ful many day,
And als i herd hym-selvyn say,
He wald bileve with no lady,
Bot on this kownand utterly,
That thai wald mak sertayn ath
To do thair might and kunyng bath,
Trewly both by day and naght,
To make him and hys lady saght,
The lady answered sone hir tyll,
That wil i do with ful gode will ;   3900
Unto the her mi trowth i plight,
That i sal tharto do mi might.
Sho said, Madame, be ye noght wrath,
I most nedes have of yow an ath,
So that i mai be sertayn.
The lady said, That will i fayn.
Lunet than riche relikes toke,
The chalis and the mes boke,
On knese the lady down hir set,
Wit ye wele than liked Lunet: 3910

15

Hir hand opon the boke sho laid,
And Lunet alkyns¹ to hir said :
Madame, sho said, thou salt swer her,
That thou sal do thi power,
Both dai and night, opon al wise,
Withouten alkyns² fayntise,
To saghtel the knyght with the liown
And his lady of grete renowne,
So that no faut be funden in the.
Sho said, I grant it sal so be.   3920
Than was Lunet wele paid of this,
The boke sho gert hir lady kys :
Sone a palfray sho bistrade,
And on hir way fast forth sho rade.
The next way ful sone sho nome,
Until sho to the well come.
Sir Ywain sat under the thorn,
And his lyown lay him byforn ;
Sho knew him wele by his lioun,
And hastily sho lighted downe ;   3930
And als sone als he Lunet sagh³
In his hert than list him lagh :
Mekil mirth was when thai met,
Aither other ful fair has gret.
Sho said, I love grete god in trone,
That i have yow fun so sone,
And tithandes tel i yow biforn,
Other sal my lady be manesworn,
On relikes, and bi bokes brade,
Or els ye twa er frendes made.   3940
Sir Ywain than was wonder glad,
For the tithandes that he had.
He thanked hir ful fele sith,
That sho wald him slike gudenes kith ;
And sho him thanked mekill mar,
For the dedes that war done ar :
So ather was in other det,
That both thair travail was wele set.
He sais, Talde thou hir oght my name ?
Sho said, Nay, than war i to blame ;   3950
Thi name sho sal noght wit for me,
Til ye have kyssed, and saghteld he.
    Than rade thai forth toward the town,
And with tham ran the gude lyoun.
When thai come to the castel-yate,
Al went thai in thareat ;

Thai spak na word to na man born,
Of al the folk thai fand byforn.
Als sone so the lady herd sayn,
Hir damisel was cumen ogayn,   3960
And als the liown and the knight,
Than in hert sho was ful lyght ;
Scho covait ever of al thing
Of him to have knawlageing.
Sir Ywain sone on knese him set,
When he with the lady met.
Lunet said to the lady sone,
Take up the knight, Madame, have done,
And, als covenand betwix us was,
Makes his pese fast or he pas.   3970
Than did the ladi him up-rise,
Sir, sho said, opon al wise
I wil me pain in al thing
Forto mak thi saghtelyng
Bitwix the and thi lady bryght.
Medame, said Lunet, that es right,
For nane bot ye has that powere,
Al the soth now sal ye her.
Madame, sho said, es noght at layn,
This es my lord, sir Ywaine ;   3980
Swilk luf god bitwix yow send,
That may last to yowr lives end.
Than went the lady fer obak,
And lang sho stode or that sho spak ;
Sho said, How es this, damysele ?
I wend thou sold be to me lele,
That makes me whether i wil or noght
Luf tham that me wa has wroght ;
So that me bus be forsworn,
Or luf tham that wald i was lorn ;   3990
Bot, whether it torn to wele or ill,
That i have said i sal fulfill.
Wit ye wele than, sir Ywaine
Of tha wordes was ful fayne.
Madame, he said, i have miswroght[1]
And that i have ful der boght ;
Grete foly i did, the soth to say,
When that i past my terme-day ;
And sertes wha so had so bityd,
Thai sold have done right als i dyd,   4000
Bot i sal never, thorgh goddes grace,
At mi might do mor trispase ;

---

[1] Original reads "*misworoght.*"

And what man so wil mercy crave,
By goddes law he sal it have.
Than sho asented saghteling to mak,
And sone in arms he gan hir tak,
And kissed hir ful oft sith,
Was he never ar so blith.
 Now has sir Ywain ending made
Of al the sorows that he hade ;   4010
Ful lely lufed he ever hys whyfe,
And sho him als hyr owin life ;
That lasted to thair lives ende ;
And trew Lunet, the maiden hende,
Was honord ever with ald and ying,
And lifed at hir owin likyng.
Of alkins thing sho has maystri,
Next the lord and the lady ;
Al honord hir in tour and toun.
Thus the knyght with the liown   4020
Es turned now to syr Ywayn,
And has his lordship al ogayn ;
And so sir Ywain and his wive
In joy and blis thai led thair live ;
So did Lunet, and the liown,
Until that ded haves dreven tham down :
Of tham na mar have i heid tell,
Nowther in rumance, ne in spell.
Bot Jhesu Criste, for his grete grace,
In hevyn blis grante us a place   4030
To bide in, if his wills be.
Amen, amen, *pur charité.*

www.ingramcontent.com/pod-product-compliance
Lightning Source LLC
Chambersburg PA
CBHW020613030726
47497CB00007B/2227